Winning CHESS TRAPS

300 WAYS TO WIN IN THE OPENING

by Irving Chernev

Published by CHESS REVIEW, 134 West 72nd Street, New York

Distributed by DAVID McKAY COMPANY, INC., New York, N.Y.

PUBLISHED BY CHESS REVIEW

REPRINTED JUNE 1967
REPRINTED AUGUST 1970
REPRINTED MAY 1972

Printed in the United States of America

Contents

THE AVERAGE PLAYER who wants to improve his game knows that he must "learn the openings." But this process is often unrewarding and sometimes meaningless. When he plays through the scores of master games, he is baffled: after the first dozen or so moves, nothing much has happened. Positions that seem to invite exciting complications fizzle out into peaceful equality. Opportunities to win Pawns, or even pieces, are disregarded—or are they overlooked? Instead of forcing the attack at once with whatever pieces are available, the players prefer to bring out more pieces.

One question arises over and over again. We know that in most games, the advantage of a Pawn is sufficient for victory. Yet well-worn opening analysis shies away repeatedly from the win of a Pawn; at times the gain of material is sanctioned by theory. Why the distinction? Why is it good policy to win a Pawn in one case and avoid it in another position? Sometimes these questions are answered. A player captures an "innocent" Pawn—and as a result, loses the game. A new trap has seen the light of day.

Who falls into these traps? Do they catch only the beginner, or the average player? Or do they also number the expert and even the master player among their victims? The answer is truly astonishing: Masters, Grandmasters and even World Champions are listed among the casualties. For example:

Former World Champion Capablanca fell into *trap 260* against Euwe.

Grandmaster Reuben Fine, outstanding authority on openings, succumbed to *trap 227* sprung by Yudovich, and was snared by *trap 145* in a game with Borochow.

Grandmaster Akiba Rubinstein was caught in the milder form of *trap 222* by Euwe in 1928; two years later he found himself in the very same trap against Alekhine!

Tartakover, another noted authority on opening play, was a victim of *trap 154* set by Reti. He also walked into *trap 170* against Kashdan, who, however, missed the crucial point!

Spielmann lost a twelve-mover via *trap 157* to Botvinnik.

Grandmaster Siegbert Tarrasch, a world-famous analyst for decades, was caught by *trap 267*, playing Bogolyubov.

Former World Champion Euwe lost twice to Reti through *trap 88* and *trap 291*.

Marshall's line in the Ruy Lopez (*see trap 18*) felled Lajos Steiner; Grunfeld, a walking encyclopedia of opening analysis, stumbled into *trap 217* devised by Bogolyubov.

While this is only a partial list, it proves the point: master players must necessarily consider a knowledge of opening traps —how to set them and how to avoid falling into them—a vital element of chess tactics. If a knowledge of traps is important for the master, how much more so is it for the average player?

The three hundred traps in this book are based on modern master play and modern opening analysis. The great majority occur in openings which enjoy the greatest popularity today. A few of the older traps have been included, as they bear on openings which disappear at times but never go completely out of fashion.

In these opening traps, brilliancy is blended harmoniously with material which is of the utmost practical value to every chessplayer. Hence we present these delightful traps to the reader in the confidence that he will learn a great deal about opening play, and that he will thoroughly enjoy himself as he learns.

Irving Chernev

New York, N. Y. May 25, 1946

White to Play. Black's opening play has been faulty, and now White can initiate an overwhelming attack, with a brilliant finish.

WHITE	BLACK	WHITE	BLACK
1 P–K4	P–K4	9 Q–Q4	NxN
2 N–KB3	N–QB3	10 PxN	B–R4?[2]
3 B–N5	P–QR3	11 B–R3	P–QN3[3]
4 B–R4	N–B3		SEE DIAGRAM
5 N–B3	B–B4[1]	12 P–K6[4]	Q–B3[5]
6 NxP	NxN	13 BxPch	K–Q1
7 P–Q4	B–N5	14 B–B6ch!	QxQ
8 PxN	NxP	15 P–K7	....

Black has been checkmated

[1] Better is 5 . . . P–Q3; 6 P–Q4, P–QN4; 7 PxP! etc.
[2] 10 . . . B–K2 and 11 . . . O–O is a much better continuation.
[3] Hoping to develop the Bishop. Not a good move, but there are no good moves left!
[4] Actually threatening to win the Queen with 13 P–K7!
[5] Or 12 , . . PxP; 13 QxKNP, and White wins.

Black to Play. White h a s captured a Pawn mechanically, and without thought. Black now wins a piece, with three forceful moves.

WHITE	BLACK	WHITE	BLACK
1 P–K4	P–K4	7 B–N3[2]	PxP
2 N–KB3	N–QB3	8 NxQP?[3]	....
3 B–N5	P–QR3		SEE DIAGRAM
4 B–R4	N–B3	8	NxN
5 N–B3[1]	P–Q3	9 QxN	P–B4
6 P–Q4	P–QN4	11 Q moves	P–B5[4]

Black wins the Bishop

[1] 5 O–O is best. Black then has choice of two good lines of play: 5 . . . NxP; 6 P–Q4, P–QN4; 7 B–N3, P–Q4; 8 PxP, B–K3; 9 P–B3, B–K2 etc., or 5 . . . B–K2; 6 R–K1, P–QN4; 7 B–N3, P–Q3; 8 P–B3, N–QR4; 9 B–B2, P–B4; 10 P–Q4, Q–B2.

[2] 7 PxP is preferable.

[3] White could still save himself with 8 B–Q5, NxB; 9 NxN, regaining the Pawn in due course.

[4] This is the famous "Noah's Ark" trap. Despite its venerable character, it still claims thousands of victims annually.

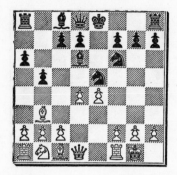

White to Play. *Inferior opening moves have exposed Black to a powerful Pawn assault. White can now force the win of a piece.*

WHITE	BLACK	WHITE	BLACK
1 P–K4	P–K4	8 P–Q4	B–Q3?[2]
2 N–KB3	N–QB3	SEE DIAGRAM	
3 B–N5	P–QR3	9 PxN	BxP
4 B–R4	N–B3	10 P–KB4	B–Q3
5 O–O	P–QN4	11 P–K5	B–B4ch[3]
6 B–N3	B–B4?[1]	12 K–R1	N–N1[4]
7 NxP!	NxN	13 Q–Q5[5]	....

White wins a Rook

[1] The combination of Black's last two moves is incorrect. The Bishop belongs at K2.

[2] Black would fare better with 8 . . . B–N2, but his game would still be difficult.

[3] This move which not only saves the Bishop from immediate capture, but also gains time for the flight of the Knight, is apparently the saving clause.

[4] There is no better alternative: if 12 . . . N–K5; 13 Q–Q5, N–B7ch; 14 RxN, BxR; 15 QxB mates Black.

[5] White's Queen threatens mate at B7, and attacks Rook and Bishop at the same time.

4 Ruy Lopez

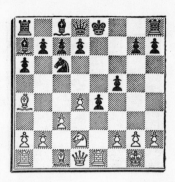

White to Play. *Black is a Pawn ahead, and seems to have the initiative. It is up to White to demonstrate that his optimistic opponent has gone too far.*

WHITE	BLACK	WHITE	BLACK
1 P–K4	P–K4	9 QN–Q2	NxN
2 N–KB3	N–QB3	10 NxN	P–K5?[2]
3 B–N5	P–QR3		SEE DIAGRAM
4 B–R4	N–B3	11 NxP!	O–O[3]
5 O–O	B–B4?[1]	12 B–KN5	N–K2[4]
6 P–B3	B–R2	13 N–N3	R–B2[5]
7 P–Q4	NxKP	14 Q–K2	K–B1
8 R–K1	P–B4	15 NxP[6]	....

White wins material

[1] Questionable, as the Bishop is exposed to attack here.

[2] More discreet was the return of the Pawn by 10 . . . O–O.

[3] The capture of the Knight results in mayhem: 11 . . . PxN; 12 RxPch, K–B1 (if 12 . . . N–K2; 13 B–KN5 wins); 13 Q–B3ch, K–N1 (13 . . . Q–B3 loses by 14 R–B4); 14 B–N3ch, P–Q4; 15 BxPch, QxB; 16 R–K8 mate.

[4] After 12 . . . Q–K1; 13 N–B6ch wins Black's Queen.

[5] The Knight needed protection.

[6] The pressure cannot be relieved. 15 . . . RxN; 16 BxNch is too costly—but there is no way to prevent a substantial loss in material.

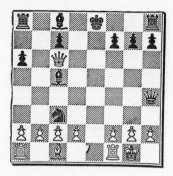

Black to Play. White's combination to win material has left his King inadequately defended. What is Black's sharpest reply to get out of check?

WHITE	BLACK	WHITE	BLACK
1 P–K4	P–K4	11 QxQBPch[2]	....
2 N–KB3	N–QB3	SEE DIAGRAM	
3 B–N5	P–QR3	11	B–Q2![3]
4 B–R4	N–B3	12 QxRch	K–K2
5 O–O	B–B4?	13 QxR	N–K7ch
6 NxP	NxP	14 K–R1	BxP[4]
7 NxN	QPxN	15 P–KR3	QxPch!
8 Q–B3[1]	Q–R5	16 PxQ	B–B3ch
9 N–B3	NxN!	17 K–R2	B–N6
10 BxPch	PxB!		

White has been checkmated

[1] 8 R–K1 would be a mistake because of 8 . . . BxPch. Best is 8 Q–K2, Q–K2; 9 R–K1!, N–B3 (if 9 . . . BxPch; 10 QxB!, NxQ; 11 RxQch, KxR; 12 KxN, and White wins), 10 Q–Q1, B–K3; 11 B–N3, and after exchange of Bishops, Black will be left with a weak King Pawn.

[2] All this looks formidable, but Black has calculated the consequences accurately.

[3] The brilliant first move of an exquisite mating combination.

[4] Now Black threatens N–N6 mate. After 15 RxB, QxR, mate at N8 cannot be stopped.

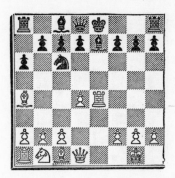

White to Play. There a r e
threats on the King file which
White can use to build up a terrific attack. Can you find the
strongest continuation?

WHITE	BLACK	WHITE	BLACK
1 P–K4	P–K4	SEE DIAGRAM	
2 N–KB3	N–QB3	10 P–Q5	N–R2
3 B–N5	P–QR3	11 Q–K2	P–QN4[2]
4 B–R4	N–B3	12 B–N5!	P–KB3[3]
5 O–O	B–B4	13 P–Q6!	PxP[4]
6 NxP	NxN	14 BxBP!	KNPxB
7 P–Q4	NxP	15 Q–R5ch	K–B1
8 R–K1	B–K2	16 B–N3	Q–K1[5]
9 RxN	N–B3?[1]	17 Q–R6	....

Black has been checkmated

[1] 9 . . . N–N3 was imperative to prevent the coming attack.
[2] Black is in difficulties because he cannot castle. 11 . . .
K–B1 would be somewhat better, but even then he would never
be able to obtain a normal development.
[3] On 12 . . . PxB; 13 BxB wins Black's Queen.
[4] Again, the capture of either Bishop would lose the Queen
after 14 PxB.
[5] Preventing 17 Q–B7 mate, but allowing a different mate.

White to Play. *A premature pin gets Black into difficulties, resulting in loss of material.*

WHITE	BLACK	WHITE	BLACK
1 P–K4	P–K4	7 B–N3	N–QR4
2 N–KB3	N–QB3	8 P–Q4	B–N5?[2]
3 B–N5	P–QR3	SEE DIAGRAM	
4 B–R4	N–B3	9 PxP	NxB[3]
5 O–O	P–Q3[1]	10 RPxN	PxP
6 Q–K2	P–QN4	11 RxP![4]	....

White has won a Pawn

[1] This is weak. Best is either 5 . . . B–K2, or 5 . . . NxP.

[2] Better is 8 . . . NxB; 9 RPxN, N–Q2; 10 R–Q1, P–KB3; 11 N–B3, B–N2.

[3] If 9 . . . PxP; 10 BxPch, KxB; 11 NxPch followed by 12 NxB.

[4] If 11 . . . RxR; 12 QxPch, followed by 13 QxR would cost Black another Pawn.

White to Play. *Once again the King file can be opened, with disastrous results for Black. How many moves can you foresee of the winning continuation?*

WHITE	BLACK	WHITE	BLACK
1 P–K4	P–K4	9 P–K5!	PxP
2 N–KB3	N–QB3	10 NxKP![3]	B–K3
3 B–N5	P–QR3	11 NxP!	KxN[4]
4 B–R4	N–B3	12 BxBch	K–N3[5]
5 0–0	P–Q3[1]	13 Q–Q3ch	N–K5[6]
6 R–K1	P–QN4	14 QxNch	K–B3
7 B–N3	N–QR4	15 Q–R4ch	K–N3
8 P–Q4	PxP?[2]	16 Q–N4ch	K–B3
SEE DIAGRAM		17 Q–N5	....

Black has been checkmated

[1] More usual is 5 . . . NxP, or 5 . . . B–K2—the latter leading to close positions.

[2] Carelessly permitting a strong attack. More prudent is 8 . . . NxB; 9 RPxN, N–Q2; 10 PxP, NxP!

[3] With the immediate threat of winning Black's Queen, by discovered check.

[4] Black must accept the Knight.

[5] If 12 . . . K–K1; 13 B–Q5ch wins at least the exchange.

[6] After 13 . . . K–R4, the win is forced by 14 Q–R3ch, and 15 Q–B5 mate.

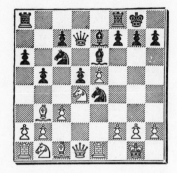

White to Play. *Black's last Queen move seems to consolidate his position. Appearances are deceptive, however, for White can now win a piece.*

WHITE	BLACK	WHITE	BLACK
1 P–K4	P–K4	8 PxP	B–K3
2 N–KB3	N–QB3	9 P–B3	B–K2
3 B–N5	P–QR3	10 R–K1	O–O
4 B–R4	N–B3	11 N–Q4	Q–Q2?[1]
5 O–O	NxP		SEE DIAGRAM
6 P–Q4	P–QN4	12 NxB	QxN[2]
7 B–N3	P–Q4	13 RxN[3]	....

White has won a piece

[1] One of those "obvious" moves which lose on the spot. Black should play 11 . . . NxKP with good attacking chances, as in the next trap.

[2] 12 . . . PxN is no better, for after 13 RxN, Black's Queen Pawn is still pinned, though in a different way!

[3] Black's Queen Pawn is pinned, and dares not capture. Simple as this trap may appear to be, it is worthy of note that Dr. Tarrasch sprung it successfully on such masters as Zukertort and Gunsberg.

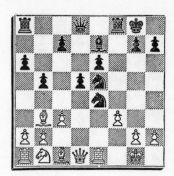

Black to Play. *It looks as though White will win one of the Knights. Fortunately for Black, there is a counter-thrust which turns the tables neatly.*

WHITE	BLACK	WHITE	BLACK
1 P–K4	P–K4	10 R–K1	O–O
2 N–KB3	N–QB3	11 N–Q4	NxKP
3 B–N5	P–QR3	12 NxB?[1]	PxN
4 B–R4	N–B3	13 P–B3?[2]	....
5 O–O	NxP		SEE DIAGRAM
6 P–Q4	P–QN4	13	B–B4ch
7 B–N3	P–Q4	14 B–K3[3]	Q–N4!
8 PxP	B–K3	15 BxB	NxPch
9 P–B3	B–K2	16 QxN[4]	RxQ

And Black wins

[1] The correct line is 12 P–B3, B–Q3; 13 PxN, B–KN5, which leads to a complicated game with Black having a strong attack for the sacrificed piece.

[2] White expects to win a piece, but he forgets the danger to his King.

[3] There is nothing better. On 14 K–B1 (14 K–R1 allows 14 ... N–B7ch), Q–R5; 15 Q (or R)–K2, N–N6ch; 16 PxN, Q–R8 is mate. Nor does 14 K–B1, Q–R5; 15 Q–B2, NxKBP; 16 PxN, RxPch, followed by 17 ... R–B7ch yield any better results, for White's game is torn to shreds.

[4] If 16 K–R1, N–N6ch; 17 PxN, Q–R4 mate.

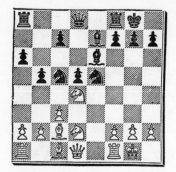

White to Play. After completing his development, Black saw no danger in capturing an unprotected Pawn. But White's King Bishop Pawn makes a spectacular advance and wins a piece.

WHITE	BLACK	WHITE	BLACK
1 P–K4	P–K4	11 B–B2	N–B4?[1]
2 N–KB3	N–QB3	12 N–Q4	NxP?
3 B–N5	P–QR3		SEE DIAGRAM
4 B–R4	N–B3	13 Q–R5	N–N3[2]
5 O–O	NxP	14 P–KB4[3]	B–Q2[4]
6 P–Q4	P–QN4	15 P–B5	N–R1
7 B–N3	P–Q4	16 P–B6[5]	P–N3
8 PxP	B–K3	17 PxB	PxQ
9 P–B3	B–K2	18 PxQ(Q)	....
10 QN–Q2	O–O		

White has won a piece

[1] The ensuing play shows how important it is to restrain the advance of White's King Bishop Pawn; 11 . . . P–B4 must be played.

[2] The only defense against the double threat of 14 QxP mate, and 14 QxN.

[3] Threatening the fork with 15 P–B5.

[4] If 14 . . . P–B4; 15 P–QN4, N–Q2; 16 NxB wins a piece.

[5] Again threatening mate at KR7.

White to Play. *Black has failed to provide against White's pinning and forking threats. His unprotected Knight at B3 makes a good target for White's minor pieces.*

WHITE	BLACK	WHITE	BLACK
1 P–K4	P–K4	8 P–QR4	P–N5[1]
2 N–KB3	N–QB3	9 P–R5	B–K2?[2]
3 B–N5	P–QR3		SEE DIAGRAM
4 B–R4	N–B3	10 PxP[3]	B–K3
5 O–O	NxP	11 B–R4[4]	B–Q2[5]
6 P–Q4	P–QN4	12 QxP[6]	....
7 B–N3	P–Q4		

White wins a Knight

[1] 8 . . . NxQP! gives Black a good game.

[2] This gets Black into difficulties. 9 . . . NxQP is absolutely essential.

[3] Threatens to win a piece by 11 BxP.

[4] A decisive pin; the Knight cannot be saved.

[5] If 11 . . . Q–Q2; 12 N–Q4 wins.

[6] The Queen attacks both Knights and White must win one or the other.

White to Play. Black has left a Pawn en prise, which he thinks he can recover immediately. The attempt to do so loses a piece by an exchange followed by a double attack.

WHITE	BLACK	WHITE	BLACK
1 P–K4	P–K4	SEE DIAGRAM	
2 N–KB3	N–QB3	7 BxN	QPxB
3 B–N5	P–QR3	8 NxP	Q–Q5[2]
4 B–R4	N–B3	9 N–KB3	QxKP?[3]
5 O–O	B–K2	10 QxQ	NxQ
6 Q–K2	O–O?[1]	11 R–K1[4]	....

White wins a piece

[1] Loses a Pawn. 6 . . . P–Q3 or 6 . . . P–QN4 should be played.

[2] Expecting to recover the Pawn by the simultaneous attack on White's Knight, and King Pawn.

[3] Continuing his plan, unaware that it will cost a piece.

[4] If 11 . . . P–KB4; 12 P–Q3, Knight moves; 13 RxB wins.

Black to Play. *White's King Pawn is insufficiently protected, but there is a tactical reason why the Pawn should be let alone.*

WHITE	BLACK	WHITE	BLACK
1 P–K4	P–K4	10 P–KR3	B–R4[2]
2 N–KB3	N–QB3	11 B–K3!	B–N3[3]
3 B–N5	P–QR3	12 QN–Q2	....
4 B–R4	N–B3		SEE DIAGRAM
5 O–O	B–K2	12	NxKP?[4]
6 R–K1	P–QN4	13 B–Q5	NxN
7 B–N3	P–Q3	14 NxN[5]	Q–K1
8 P–B3[1]	O–O	15 Q–B3[6]	....
9 P–Q4	B–N5		

White wins the exchange

[1] If 8 P–Q4, QNxP; 9 NxN, PxN, and White must avoid 10 QxP as that would land him in the Noah's Ark trap.

[2] 10 . . . BxN leads to equality.

[3] If 11 . . . NxKP; 12 B–Q5, Q–Q2; 13 BxKN, P–Q4; 14 PxP wins for White, as the Queen Pawn is pinned.

[4] This loses material, but Black's game is not good in any case. After 12 . . . Q–Q2 (or K1); 13 B–Q5 is strong.

[5] 14 BxQN would permit Black to wriggle out by 14 . . . NxNch.

[6] After this there is no saving move. If 15 . . . P–K5; 16 NxP, R–Q1; 17 BxN, QxB; 18 N–B6ch wins Black's Queen.

White to Play. B l a c k ' s *Queen is overburdened as it is doing a double job in protecting both the Queen Knight and the King Pawn—but can White play to win the Pawn?*

WHITE	BLACK	WHITE	BLACK
1 P–K4	P–K4	13 PxKP	PxP
2 N–KB3	N–QB3	SEE DIAGRAM	
3 B–N5	P–QR3	14 NxP?[1]	QxN
4 B–R4	N–B3	15 RxN	N–N5
5 O–O	B–K2	16 P–B4[2]	Q–B2
6 R–K1	P–QN4	17 R–R1	P–B5!
7 B–N3	P–Q3	18 R–K2[3]	Q–N3ch
8 P–B3	N–QR4	19 K–B1	NxPch
9 B–B2	P–B4	20 K–K1	Q–N8ch
10 P–Q4	Q–B2	21 K–Q2	N–B8ch
11 P–QR4	QR–N1	22 K–K1	N–K6ch
12 RPxP	RPxP		

Black wins the Queen

[1] The right move is 14 QN–Q2.
[2] 16 P–KN3 fails because of 16 . . . Q–R4; 17 P–R4, P–N4 with a winning attack, for example 18 BxP, BxB; 19 Q–Q6, BxP; 20 QxR, B–Q1; 21 K–B1, N–R7ch!; 22 K–N1, N–B6ch; 23 K–B1, B–R6ch; 24 K–K2, O–O; 25 RxP, B–N4! and Black wins, as he threatens 26 . . . RxQ, as well as 26 . . . N–K4ch.
[3] Black has too many threats. If 18 B–K3, NxB; 19 RxN, B–QB4 wins for Black.

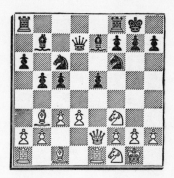

White to Play. White can remove the King Pawn with his Knight, seemingly winning a Pawn. If he does so, he will become the victim of a series of subtle moves ending in the gain of a piece for Black.

WHITE	BLACK	WHITE	BLACK
1 P–K4	P–K4	13 PxP	QxP
2 N–KB3	N–QB3	14 Q–K2	B–N2
3 B–N5	P–QR3	15 B–N3	Q–Q2
4 B–R4	N–B3		SEE DIAGRAM
5 O–O	B–K2	16 NxP?	NxN
6 R–K1	P–QN4	17 QxN	QR–K1[1]
7 B–N3	P–Q3	18 B–KB4	Q–B3[2]
8 P–B3	O–O	19 N–K3[3]	P–B5
9 P–Q3	N–QR4	20 PxP	B–B4
10 B–B2	P–B4	21 Q–N5[4]	P–R3
11 QN–Q2	N–B3	22 Q–N3	N–R4
12 N–B1	P–Q4	23 Q–N4	NxB[5]

Black has won a piece

[1] With the threat of 18 ... B–Q3.
[2] Gaining time in view of 19 ... QxP mate.
[3] If 19 Q–N5, N–R4; 20 Q–B5, NxB and Black wins.
[4] The only chance; the Queen must be able to prevent mate after 21 ... BxN. The Queen is an easy target, however.
[5] After 24 QxN, RxN, White must not recapture, as he is still threatened with 25 ... QxP mate.

White to Play. *Black is offering the sacrifice of his Knight. If White captures the piece, he will be exposed to an 'irresistible attack, leading to mate.*

WHITE	BLACK	WHITE	BLACK
1 P–K4	P–K4	13 R–K1	N–N5
2 N–KB3	N–QB3	14 P–KR3	Q–R5
3 B–N5	P–QR3	SEE DIAGRAM	
4 B–R4	N–B3	15 PxN?[3]	Q–R7ch
5 O–O	B–K2	16 K–B1	Q–R8ch
6 R–K1	P–QN4	17 K–K2	BxPch
7 B–N3	O–O	18 K–Q2	QxP
8 P–B3	P–Q4[1]	19 Q–B2[4]	QxPch
9 PxP	NxP	20 K–Q3	B–B4ch
10 NxP	NxN	21 R–K4	BxRch
11 RxN	N–B3[2]	22 KxB	QR–K1ch
12 P–Q4	B–Q3		

Black mates in two moves

[1] Marshall's famous attack, which must be met with the greatest care.

[2] Recent analysis suggests 11 . . . P–QB3 as best for Black; but the tricky text move also requires good defense.

[3] White should not accept the sacrifice, but defend by 15 Q–B3!

[4] If 19 R–K2, QR–K1 wins for Black.

White to Play. *Black tempts his opponent by the offer of a Knight. Unless White realizes what is behind the offer, the capture seems safe. Why would it be disastrous for White to accept the sacrifice?*

WHITE	BLACK	WHITE	BLACK
1 P–K4	P–K4	12 P–Q4	B–Q3
2 N–KB3	N–QB3	13 R–K1	N–N5
3 B–N5	P–QR3	14 P–KR3	Q–R5
4 B–R4	N–B3	15 Q–B3	NxP!?
5 O–O	B–K2		SEE DIAGRAM
6 R–K1	P–QN4	16 QxN?[1]	B–R7ch[2]
7 B–N3	O–O	17 K–B1	B–N6[3]
8 P–B3	P–Q4	18 Q–K2	BxP!
9 PxP	NxP	19 PxB	QR–K1
10 NxP	NxN	20 QxR	QxPch
11 RxN	N–B3	21 K–K2[4]	RxQch

And Black wins

[1] White should play 16 R–K2.

[2] A trap within a trap. If 16 ... B–N6 (which looks good) White wins by 17 QxPch!, RxQ; 18 R–K8 mate.

[3] Black's finesse to get White's King on B1 prevents 18 QxPch, as after 18 ... RxQch White would have to get out of check first, and have no time for his mating ideas.

[4] Or 21 K–N1, Q–R7ch; 22 K–B1, Q–B7 mate.

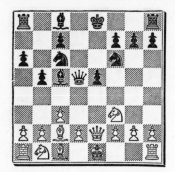

White to Play. *Black's pieces are loosely placed. How can White win a piece? Hint—he forces the exchange of Queens, and then a Bishop fork wins one of the Knights.*

WHITE	BLACK	WHITE	BLACK
1 P–K4	P–K4	8 PxP	QxP
2 N–KB3	N–QB3	SEE DIAGRAM	
3 B–N5	P–QR3	9 P–Q4!	B–Q3[4]
4 B–R4	N–B3	10 B–N3!	Q–K5
5 Q–K2	B–B4	11 QxQ	NxQ
6 P–B3[1]	P–QN4[2]	12 B–Q5	....
7 B–B2	P–Q4?[3]		

White wins a Knight

[1] White can play to win a Pawn by 6 BxN, QPxB; 7 NxP, Q–Q5; 8 N–Q3, for if 8 ... NxP; 9 NxB wins a piece.

[2] Stronger is 6 ... Q–K2; 7 P–Q3, O–O; 8 QN–Q2, KN–N5!; 9 O–O, P–Q3.

[3] A premature advance.

[4] The King Pawn needs protection, as it is attacked three times. 9 ... P–K5 would not do, as after 10 PxB, the pinned King Pawn cannot recapture.

Black to Play. *In order to win the exchange, White's Queen has gone afield. The neglected King will now be subjected to a devastating assault.*

WHITE	BLACK	WHITE	BLACK
1 P–K4	P–K4	10 NxP	N–B5
2 N–KB3	N–QB3	11 Q–K4	NxN
3 B–N5	P–QR3	12 QxR?[2]	....
4 B–R4	N–B3		SEE DIAGRAM
5 Q–K2	P–QN4	12	Q–Q6[3]
6 B–N3	B–K2	13 B–Q1	B–KR6!
7 P–B3	O–O	14 QxP	BxP
8 O–O	P–Q4?[1]	15 R–K1	Q–B6!
9 PxP	NxP	16 BxQ[4]	NxB

White has been checkmated

[1] A speculative sacrifice with many interesting possibilities.

[2] Much too greedy. The right move is 12 P–Q4.

[3] Threatening 13 . . . N–K7ch; 14 K–R1, N–N6ch; 15 RPxN, QxRch; 16 K–R2, N–N5ch; 17 K–R3, Q–R8 mate.

[4] Black was threatening . . . N–R6 mate. If 16 P–KR4, N–R6ch; 17 K–R2, N–N5 mate.

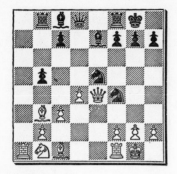

Black to Play. White expects to regain his piece with a satisfactory game, but he has overlooked a subtle finesse which spoils his hopes.

WHITE	BLACK	WHITE	BLACK
1 P–K4	P–K4	11 PxP	NxP
2 N–KB3	N–QB3	12 NxP	N–B5
3 B–N5	P–QR3	13 Q–K4	NxN
4 B–R4	N–B3	14 P–Q4[1]	....
5 Q–K2	P–QN4		SEE DIAGRAM
6 B–N3	B–K2	14	NxP!
7 P–QR4	QR–N1	15 PxN[2]	B–N2
8 PxP	PxP	16 Q–KN4	N–R5
9 O–O	O–O	17 B–Q1	Q–Q4[3]
10 P–B3	P–Q4?		

Black wins a Pawn

[1] If 14 QxN(B4), N–Q6; 15 Q–N3 (or 15 Q–K3, B–QB4), B–Q3; 16 Q–K3, R–K1, with a winning game for Black. And if 14 QxN(K5), B–Q3; 15 Q–K3, B–N2; 16 P–B3, N–Q6; 17 K–R1 (the threat was 17 . . . B–B4), Q–R5; 18 P–R3, Q–N6 kills White.

[2] If 15 QxN(K5), B–Q3, followed by 16 . . . B–N2 with a decisive assault against White's weakened King side. Or if 15 KxN, B–N2; 16 P–Q5, N–B5 with a winning game.

[3] If 18 P–KB4 (to stop mate, and save the King Pawn) B–B4ch mates quickly.

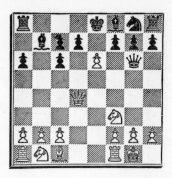

Black to Play. If he captures White's King Pawn with either of his Pawns, White can play 10 N–K5 attacking his Queen, and threatening mate at the same time. What should Black do?

WHITE	BLACK	WHITE	BLACK
1 P–K4	P–K4	8 O–O	B–N2[2]
2 N–KB3	N–QB3	9 P–K6[3]	....
3 B–N5	P–QR3	SEE DIAGRAM	
4 BxN	NPxB[1]	9	BPxP!
5 P–Q4	PxP	10 N–K5	QxPch!![4]
6 QxP	Q–B3	11 KxQ	P–B4ch[5]
7 P–K5	Q–N3		

Black wins two Pawns

[1] Inferior; 4 . . . QPxB is usual here.

[2] Sets a trap, tempting White to play 9 P–K6, seemingly a powerful move.

[3] If 9 . . . QxKP; 10 R–K1 wins the Queen. Or if 9 . . . QPxP (or 9 . . . BPxP); 10 N–K5 attacks the Queen, and threatens mate at White's Q7 square. And if 9 . . . O–O–O; 10 PxPch, RxP; 11 QxRch!, KxQ; 12 N–K5ch regains the Queen, and wins.

[4] Black saw further ahead. This is the saving move he had in mind.

[5] The discovered check regains the Queen and Black wins easily with his two extra Pawns.

White to Play. *Black's 5th move was made with the intention of offering an exchange of Pawns. Actually, he loses a Pawn, and the attempt to regain the lost Pawn costs him a piece.*

WHITE	BLACK	WHITE	BLACK
1 P–K4	P–K4	SEE DIAGRAM	
2 N–KB3	N–QB3	7 Q–K2	QxP[3]
3 B–N5	P–QR3	8 N–KB3	Q–Q4[4]
4 BxN	QPxB	9 N–N5	B–KB4
5 P–Q4	N–B3?[1]	10 P–KB3	....
6 NxP	NxP?[2]		

White wins the Knight

[1] Loses a Pawn. Best is 5 ... PxP; 6 QxP, QxQ; 7 NxQ, B–Q2!
[2] Throws good money after bad, as the Knight can be pinned. Black should have reconciled himself to the loss of the Pawn.
[3] Black's Knight cannot move away, as discovered check (by 8 NxQBPch) would follow, winning Black's Queen.
[4] If 8 . . . Q–N5ch; 9 KN–Q2, and White wins the pinned Knight.

Black to Play. *White is offering the sacrifice of a Knight. If Black takes the Knight, he will lose a Rook in a novel way. Can you see how?*

WHITE	BLACK	WHITE	BLACK
1 P–K4	P–K4	9 B–K3	RxP[1]
2 N–KB3	N–QB3	10 PxP	BPxP[2]
3 B–N5	P–QR3	11 NxP!	....
4 B–R4	P–Q3	*SEE DIAGRAM*	
5 BxNch	PxB	11	PxN?[3]
6 P–Q4	P–B3	12 QxQch	KxQ
7 N–B3	R–N1	13 O–O–Och![4]	....
8 Q–Q3	N–K2		

White wins the exchange

[1] 9 . . . N–N3 is solid and safe.
[2] 10 . . . QPxP would lose a whole Rook by the same device.
[3] Black can hardly be blamed for overlooking the threat.
[4] A double attack by the castling move—a most unusual method of winning material. Black must of course get out of check, whereupon White plays 14 KxR, remaining the exchange ahead.

Black to Play. *White has succumbed to a familiar trap motif — "fencing-in" of a Bishop. A simple trap, but important in this opening, as it comes up in various ways.*

WHITE	BLACK	WHITE	BLACK
1 P–K4	P–K4	8 QxP?[2]	....
2 N–KB3	N–QB3	SEE DIAGRAM	
3 B–N5	P–QR3	8	P–QB4
4 B–R4	P–Q3	9 Q–Q5[3]	B–K3[4]
5 P–Q4[1]	P–QN4	10 Q–B6ch	B–Q2
6 B–N3	NxP	11 Q–Q5	P–B5[5]
7 NxN	PxN		

Black wins the Bishop

[1] Simple and strong is 5 BxNch, PxB; 6 P–Q4, PxP; 7 NxP, B–Q2; 8 N–QB3.

[2] The right way is 8 B–Q5, R–N1; 9 QxP, B–Q2; 10 P–QB3, N–B3; 11 O–O, B–K2; 12 P–B3.

[3] Looks good, as it threatens mate, as well as the Rook.

[4] Parries both threats.

[5] Another form of the "Noah's Ark" trap.

White to Play. *Black has just captured a Pawn with his Knight. The capture is unsound, though it does set up a little trap. How does White evade the trap, and force a win?*

WHITE	BLACK	WHITE	BLACK
1 P–K4	P–K4	6 P–Q4	NxP?[2]
2 N–KB3	N–QB3		SEE DIAGRAM
3 B–N5	P–QR3	7 BxPch!	KxB[3]
4 B–R4	P–QN4[1]	8 NxPch	K–K1
5 B–N3	B–N2	9 QxN[4]	....

White has won a Pawn

[1] Premature. 4 . . . N–B3; 5 O–O, B–K2 (or 5 . . . NxP) is the usual procedure.

[2] Black hopes for 7 NxN, PxN; 8 QxP, P–QB4; 9 Q–K5ch (on other moves 9 . . . P–B5 wins the Bishop), Q–K2; 10 QxQch, NxQ, and White has no time to save his King Pawn, as Black still threatens 11 . . . P–B5.

[3] Forced, as 7 . . . K–K2 is answered by 8 BxN winning a piece, for if 8 . . . RxN; 9 B–N5ch wins Black's Queen.

[4] White's extra Pawn and superior position give him a winning advantage.

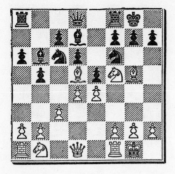

White to Play. Black's inferior opening play has led to a position in which White can win a piece by force.

WHITE	BLACK	WHITE	BLACK
1 P–K4	P–K4	10 B–Q5	B–Q2
2 N–KB3	N–QB3	11 N–R4	O–O
3 B–N5	P–QR3	12 N–B5	Q–Q1[3]
4 B–R4? [1]	B–B4? [1]		SEE DIAGRAM
5 P–B3	Q–K2	13 PxP	PxP
6 O–O	P–QN4	14 BxQN	BxB
7 B–N3	N–B3	15 QxQ	RxQ[4]
8 P–Q4	B–N3 [2]	16 N–K7ch	....
9 B–N5	P–Q3		

White wins a Bishop

[1] Not best, as the Bishop will be driven away from this square when White plays P–B3 followed by P–Q4.

[2] If 8 . . . PxP; 9 PxP, B–N3; 10 P–K5 etc. and Black's position is in ruins.

[3] If 12 . . . Q–K1; 13 B(Q5)xN, BxB; 14 BxN, PxB; 15 Q–N4ch, K–R1; 16 Q–N7 mates Black.

[4] It makes no difference which Rook recaptures.

White to Play. *Black has won the Pawn he was after, but now White retaliates with a sacrifice which releases his Queen. With Queen and Bishop in Black's territory, the win is easy.*

WHITE	BLACK	WHITE	BLACK
1 P–K4	P–K4	7 N–QR4	PxP
2 N–KB3	N–QB3	SEE DIAGRAM	
3 B–N5	P–QR3	8 NxP!	NxN[2]
4 B–R4	P–B4	9 Q–R5ch	N–N3[3]
5 N–B3	P–QN4?[1]	10 BxN[4]	RxB
6 B–N3	P–N5?	11 Q–Q5	....

White wins the exchange

[1] This attempt to win a Pawn loses. Better is 5 . . . N–B3, and an interesting continuation would be 6 Q–K2, P–QN4; 7 B–N3, PxP; 8 NxP(K4), P–Q4; 9 NxNch, PxN; 10 P–Q4, P–K5; 11 N–K5!, NxN; 12 PxN, B–K3.

[2] If 8 . . . N–R3; 9 Q–R5ch, P–N3 (9 . . . K–K2; 10 NxNch, PxN; 11 Q–K5ch, K–Q2; 12 Q–K6 mate) 10 NxNP, PxN; 11 QxPch, K–K2; 12 P–Q3, and White's next move 13 B–N5ch wins.

[3] If 9 . . . K–K2; 10 QxN is mate.

[4] 10 Q–Q5 at once also wins.

White to Play. Black h a s developed his Queen prematurely, and neglected necessary defensive measures.

WHITE	BLACK	WHITE	BLACK
1 P–K4	P–K4	7 N–B3	P–Q5[3]
2 N–KB3	N–QB3		SEE DIAGRAM
3 B–N5	N–B3	8 P–QR3	QxNP?[4]
4 P–Q3	P–Q4?[1]	9 N–B4!	QxNch
5 NxP	Q–Q3	10 B–Q2	....
6 B–KB4!	Q–N5ch[2]		

Black's Queen is trapped

[1] A pointless gambit which does not deserve to succeed. 4 ... P–Q3 is the proper move.

[2] Playing for the win of a piece.

[3] Continuing in consistent fashion. However, White has a clever resource.

[4] Still pursuing his own plans without considering the consequences.

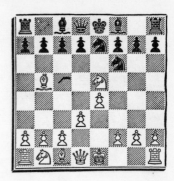

Black to Play. *White has swallowed the Pawn bait, and now he must lose a piece.*

WHITE	BLACK	WHITE	BLACK
1 P–K4	P–K4		SEE DIAGRAM
2 N–KB3	N–QB3	5	P–B3[3]
3 B–N5	N–B3	6 N–B4[4]	N–N3
4 P–Q3	N–K2[1]	7 B–R4	P–N4
5 NxP[2]	....		

Black wins a piece by the fork

[1] Abandoning his King Pawn to tempt White.

[2] Additional development, say with 5 N–B3, would leave White with the better game.

[3] Now, if White moves his Bishop, Black wins the Knight with 6 ... Q–R4ch.

[4] Trying to avoid the loss of a piece. If Black captures 6 ... PxB, then 7 N–Q6 is checkmate.

White to Play. White wins by capitalizing on the immobility of Black's Queen.

WHITE	BLACK	WHITE	BLACK
1 P–K4	P–K4	9 BxN!	NPxB[4]
2 N–KB3	N–QB3	10 NxP[5]	P–Q3[6]
3 B–N5	N–B3	11 NxP	Q–Q2
4 P–Q4	PxP	12 Q–B4ch	R–B2[7]
5 O–O	B–K2[1]	13 P–K6!	QxP
6 Q–K2	O–O[2]	14 QxQ	BxQ
7 P–K5	N–K1	15 R–K1	B–Q2
8 R–Q1	P–B3?[3]	16 NxBch	....

SEE DIAGRAM

White has gained a piece

[1] The safe course is 5 . . . P–Q3.
[2] 6 . . . P–Q3 was still available.
[3] Black's best chance is 8 . . . P–Q4.
[4] If 9 . . . QPxB; 10 RxP, B–Q2; 11 P–K6, winning a piece.
[5] Threatening to win the Queen by 11 NxP or 11 N–K6.
[6] If 10 . . . P–Q4; 11 NxP, Q–Q2; 12 NxBch, QxN; 13 RxP
with two Pawns to the good.
[7] 12 . . . K–R1 loses in the same way.

White to Play. *Black soon discovers that the pin on his Queen Knight cannot be neglected so airily.*

WHITE	BLACK	WHITE	BLACK
1 P–K4	P–K4	7 B-Q3	N–B3
2 N–KB3	N–QB3	8 PxN	P–K5[2]
3 B–N5	N–B3	9 R–K1!	P–Q4
4 O–O	P–Q3	10 B–K2!	PxN[3]
5 P–Q4	NxP[1]	11 PxNP!	BxP[4]
SEE DIAGRAM		12 B–QN5![5]	....
6 P–Q5	P–QR3		

Black has been checkmated

[1] Loses a piece. Black regains it, but with a fatal loss of time.
[2] The move on which Black relied.
[3] Else he forfeits his chance to regain the lost piece.
[4] If 11 . . . PxB; 12 PxR(Q) and Black cannot reply 12 . . . PxQ because his King Pawn is pinned.
[5] In many of these traps, Black loses because he commences operations before adequately protecting himself on the King file.

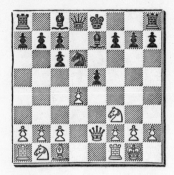

White to Play. *In recapturing with the Queen Pawn, Black thought he was aiding his development—but the opening of the Queen file exposes Black to attack.*

WHITE	BLACK	WHITE	BLACK
1 P–K4	P–K4	8 PxP	N–B4
2 N–KB3	N–QB3	9 R–Q1	B–Q2
3 B–N5	N–B3	10 P–K6![2]	PxP
4 O–O	NxP	11 N–K5	B–Q3
5 P–Q4	B–K2	12 Q–R5ch	P–N3[3]
6 Q–K2	N–Q3	13 NxNP	N–N2
7 BxN	QPxB?[1]	14 Q–R6	N–B4
SEE DIAGRAM		15 Q–R3[4]	....

White wins the Rook Pawn

[1] A mistake. The right move is 7 . . . NPxB.
[2] Disorganizes Black's position.
[3] Black's last four moves have been forced.
[4] Black must move his attacked King Rook, when White plays 16 QxP, and retains a lasting attack.

White to Play. With t h e King file about to be opened, the position of Black's uncastled King will prove disastrous.

WHITE	BLACK	WHITE	BLACK
1 P–K4	P–K4	SEE DIAGRAM	
2 N–KB3	N–QB3	7 BxN	QPxB
3 B–N5	N–B3	8 RxPch	K–B2[3]
4 O–O	NxP	9 B–N5	Q–Q2[4]
5 R–K1	P–B4?[1]	10 R–K7ch!	BxR
6 P–Q3	N–Q3[2]	11 N–K5ch	....

White wins the Queen

[1] Dangerous. Retreating the Knight is better.

[2] After 6 . . . N–B3; 7 NxP, NxN; 8 P–KB4! is strong.

[3] If 8 . . . B–K2; 9 B–N5 wins at once; while 8 . . . K–Q2 is answered by 9 B–N5, B–K2; 10 RxBch, and Black's game is in ruins.

[4] He has no choice.

Black to Play. *Black is a piece ahead, but he must not attempt to retain this advantage. It is essential for Black to close the King file by playing 7 . . . B–K2.*

WHITE	BLACK	WHITE	BLACK
1 P–K4	P–K4	SEE DIAGRAM	
2 N–KB3	N–QB3	7	NxQN?[1]
3 B–N5	N–B3	8 NxNch	B–K2
4 O–O	NxP	9 NxB![2]	NxQ
5 R–K1	N–Q3	10 N–N6ch	Q–K2
6 N–B3	NxB	11 NxQ[3]	....
7 NxP!	....		

White wins a piece

[1] Hoping to stay a piece ahead by attacking White's Queen. If 7 . . . NxKN?; 8 RxNch, B–K2; 9 N–Q5!, O–O; 10 NxBch, K–R1; 11 Q–R5 (threatening 12 QxPch and 13 R–R5 mate), P–KN3; 12 Q–R6, P–Q3; 13 R–R5!, PxR; 14 Q–B6 mate.

[2] This, and not 9 NxQ is the way to win!

[3] After 11 . . . K–Q1; 12 N–B5, White wins the imprisoned Black Knight.

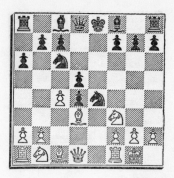

White to Play. Black has exposed himself to danger on the King file, which is open to his opponent's pieces. White can take advantage of this to win a piece.

WHITE	BLACK	WHITE	BLACK
1 P–K4	P–K4	6 B–Q3	P–Q4
2 N–KB3	N–QB3	7 P–B4!	KPxP[2]
3 B–N5	N–B3	SEE DIAGRAM	
4 O–O	NxP	8 PxP	QxP
5 P–Q4	P–QR3?[1]	9 BxN[3]	....

White has won a piece

[1] This move, which is excellent as Black's third move, is out of place here. 5 ... B–K2 (developing a piece, and also averting danger on the King file) should be played.

[2] Fatal, but the position would have been difficult, no matter what Black played.

[3] The Queen cannot recapture because of the pin by 10 R–K1, so Black must lose a piece.

White to Play. *The position appears placid. After Black develops his Bishop, and castles, he will have equalized. Before this can happen, however, White hits out with a surprising sacrifice which wins.*

WHITE	BLACK	WHITE	BLACK
1 P–K4	P–K4	7 NxP!	KxN
2 N–KB3	N–QB3	8 Q–R5ch	K–K3[1]
3 B–N5	N–B3	9 N–B3	N–K2[2]
4 O–O	NxP	10 NxN	BxB[3]
5 P–Q4	P–Q4?	11 N–B5ch	K–Q3[4]
6 NxP	B–Q2	12 NxPch	....

SEE DIAGRAM

White wins the Queen

[1] If 8 . . . P–N3; 9 QxQPch followed by 10 QxKN wins. On 8 . . . K–B3; 9 P–KB3, P–KN3 (if the Knight moves, 10 B–N5ch wins the Queen); 10 PxNch wins. Or if 8 . . . K–K2; 9 QxQP, N–B3; 10 R–K1ch wins quickly. Finally, if 8 . . . K–N1; 9 QxQPch, B–K3; 10 QxB is mate.

[2] To protect the Queen Pawn. Insufficient is 9 . . . NxN; 10 R–K1ch, N–K5 (10 . . . K–Q3; 11 B–B4ch, etc.); 11 RxNch, PxR; 12 B–B4ch, and White forces mate.

[3] Or 10 . . . PxN; 11 B–B4ch, K–B3 (if 11 . . . K–Q3; 12 Q–B5 mate); 12 Q–B7 mate.

[4] 11 . . . K–B3 permits mate in two by 12 B–N5ch, and 13 P–N4 mate.

White to Play. *Black castled without analyzing the forthcoming series of exchanges.*

WHITE	BLACK	WHITE	BLACK
1 P–K4	P–K4	10 QxQ	QRxQ[2]
2 N–KB3	N–QB3	11 NxP	BxP[3]
3 B–N5	P–Q3	12 NxB	NxN
4 P–Q4	B–Q2	13 N–Q3[4]	P–KB4
5 N–B3	N–B3	14 P–KB3	B–B4ch
6 0–0	B–K2	15 NxB	NxN
7 R–K1	0–0?[1]	16 B–N5	R–Q4[5]
SEE DIAGRAM		17 B–K7	R–K1
8 BxN	BxB	18 P–QB4	RxB[6]
9 PxP	PxP	19 RxR	....

White has won the exchange

[1] The most plausible move on the board—yet it loses! The correct move is 7 . . . PxP.

[2] See the next trap for the win against 10 . . . KRxQ.

[3] If 11 . . . NxP; 12 NxB; NxN; 13 NxBch, K–R1; 14 PxN, and White is two pieces up.

[4] Of course not 13 RxN??, R–Q8ch, forcing mate.

[5] If 16 . . . QR–K1; 17 B–K7 wins the exchange.

[6] Black has no choice, as a move by the other Rook permits 19 BxN.

White to Play. *A variation of the previous trap, showing that Black loses material even though he varies his defense.*

	WHITE	BLACK		WHITE	BLACK
1	P–K4	P–K4	12	NxB	NxN
2	N–KB3	N–QB3	13	N–Q3	P–KB4
3	B–N5	P–Q3	14	P–KB3	B–B4ch
4	P–Q4	B–Q2	15	K–B1	R–KB1[2]
5	N–B3	N–B3	16	K–K2	B–N3
6	O–O	B–K2	17	PxN	PxP
7	R–K1	O–O?[1]	18	N–B4	P–N4
8	BxN	BxB	19	N–R3[3]	P–N5
9	PxP	PxP	20	N–B4[4]	....
10	QxQ	KRxQ			
	SEE DIAGRAM				
11	NxP	BxP			

White has gained a piece

[1] Castling, though it looks good, loses. Black must play 7 . . . PxP.

[2] So that if 16 PxN, PxPch regains the Knight.

[3] But not 19 N–R5, R–B7ch; 20 K–Q1, R–Q1ch; 21 B–Q2, QRxBch, and Black wins.

[4] The Knight is unassailable here.

White to Play. *Black's capture of the King Pawn with his Knight is unsound, as White proves by a clever series of exchanges.*

WHITE	BLACK	WHITE	BLACK
1 P–K4	P–K4	9 B–N5	NxP?[2]
2 N–KB3	N–QB3	SEE DIAGRAM	
3 B–N5	P–Q3	10 BxB	KNxN[3]
4 P–Q4	B–Q2	11 BxQ	NxQ
5 N–B3	N–B3	12 BxN![4]	PxB[5]
6 0–0	B–K2	13 B–K7	NxNP[6]
7 R–K1	PxP[1]	14 BxR[7]	....
8 NxP	0–0		

White wins the exchange

[1] As we have seen in the two previous traps, 7 . . . 0–0 loses for Black.

[2] Relatively best is 9 . . . NxN.

[3] Of course 10 . . . QxB or 10 . . . NxB loses by 11 RxN.

[4] An important move. If instead 12 QRxN, RxB, and Black is a Pawn ahead.

[5] No better is 12 . . . BxB; 13 NxB, PxN; 14 B–K7. Or if 12 . . . QRxB; 13 BxB.

[6] Or 13 . . . KR–K1; 14 QRxN winning a piece.

[7] White should win despite technical difficulties.

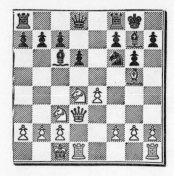

White to Play. *Black h a s disregarded the troublesome pin, and must lose material as a result.*

WHITE	BLACK	WHITE	BLACK
1 P–K4	P–K4	9 B–N5	B–N2
2 N–KB3	N–QB3	10 O–O–O	O–O?[2]
3 B–N5	P–Q3	SEE DIAGRAM	
4 P–Q4	B–Q2	11 NxB	PxN
5 N–B3	N–B3	12 P–K5	PxP[3]
6 BxN	BxB	13 QxQ	QRxQ
7 Q–Q3	PxP	14 RxR	RxR
8 NxP	P–KN3?[1]	15 N–K4[4]	....

White wins the exchange

[1] Very risky. 8 . . . B–K2 is preferable.

[2] Natural, but it loses. 10 . . . Q–Q2 is somewhat better.

[3] No better is 12 . . . P–KR3; 13 PxN, PxB; 14 PxB, winning a piece.

[4] The pinned Knight cannot be defended. Black must lose the exchange with 15 . . . NxN; 16 BxR.

White to Play. *The combination of a cramped development and weak black squares gives Black a lost game.*

WHITE	BLACK	WHITE	BLACK
1 P–K4	P–K4	8 B–KN5	B–N2
2 N–KB3	N–QB3	9 N–Q5[4]	BxN
3 B–N5	P–Q3	10 QxB!	O–O[5]
4 P–Q4	B–Q2	11 N–B6ch	K–R1
5 N–B3	KN–K2	12 N–N4ch	NxQ
6 B–QB4[1]	PxP[2]	13 B–B6ch	K–N1
7 NxP	P–KN3?[3]	14 N–R6	....

SEE DIAGRAM

Black has been checkmated

[1] Threatening 7 N–KN5.

[2] 6 . . . P–KR3 is better, but very cramping.

[3] The fianchetto development turns out badly because of the weakening of the black squares, a weakness which White immediately exploits. Best is 7 . . . NxN; 8 QxN, N–B3 etc.

[4] Threatens to win with 10 NxN(B6), followed by 11 BxN.

[5] If 10 . . . NxQ; 11 N–B6ch, K–B1; 12 B–R6 mate.

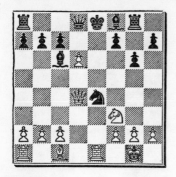

White to Play. White can win now with a brilliant display of fireworks. Can you pick the move that touches off the spark?

WHITE	BLACK	WHITE	BLACK
1 P–K4	P–K4	11 Q–Q4	R–KN1
2 N–KB3	N–QB3		SEE DIAGRAM
3 B–N5	P–Q3	12 RxNch	BxR
4 P–Q4	B–Q2	13 QxBch	K–Q2
5 N–B3	N–B3	14 N–K5ch	K–B1[4]
6 O–O	P–KN3?[1]	15 P–Q7ch	K–N1
7 BxN	BxB	16 Q–Q5	B–Q3[5]
8 PxP	NxP[2]	17 N–B6ch!	PxN
9 PxP	NxN[3]	18 Q–N3ch	B–N5
10 R–K1ch	N–K5	19 QxB[6]	....

Black has been checkmated

[1] This attempt to develop the Bishop at N2 does not fit in with the system of defense initiated by 3 ... P–Q3. Better is 6 ... B–K2; 7 R–K1, PxP; 8 NxP, O–O; 9 BxN, PxB; 10 P–QN3, P–Q4.

[2] If 8 ... PxP; 9 QxQch, RxQ; 10 NxP, NxP (10 ... BxP; 11 B–N5, B–K2; 12 KR–K1 wins); 11 NxB, NxN; 12 R–K1ch, K–Q2; 13 NxR wins for White.

[3] If 9 ... NxQP; 10 Q–Q4 is decisive.

[4] On 14 ... KxP; 15 NxPch wins Black's Queen.

[5] To prevent White from playing 17 NxBP followed by Queening the Pawn. If instead 16 ... P–QB3; 17 B–B4!, PxQ; 18 N–B6 mates nicely.

[6] A beautiful long-range mate!

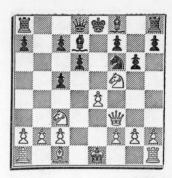

White to Play. The King side fianchetto is often risky for Black in open positions of this type.

WHITE	BLACK	WHITE	BLACK
1 P–K4	P–K4	9 N–B5	P–N3?[1]
2 N–KB3	N–QB3		SEE DIAGRAM
3 B–N5	P–Q3	10 B–N5![2]	PxN[3]
4 P–Q4	PxP	11 P–K5[4]	PxP
5 NxP	B–Q2	12 BxN	P–K5[5]
6 N–QB3	N–B3	13 NxP	PxN
7 BxN	PxB	14 QxPch	B–K2[6]
8 Q–B3	P–B4	15 BxR	....

White has won the exchange

[1] A weakening move, but it is not easy to see how White will take advantage of it. 9 . . . BxN is much better, although White's game remains preferable.

[2] Threatening to win at once with 11 N–Q5.

[3] Of course not 10 . . . B–K2; 11 NxB followed by 12 BxN, and White wins.

[4] With the intention of playing 12 BxN, winning the exchange.

[5] On 12 . . . QxB; 13 QxRch wins.

[6] Hoping for 15 BxB?, QxB and White's pinned Queen cannot capture the Rook.

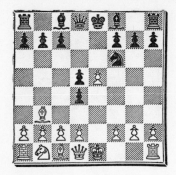

Black to Play. *White h a s lost time, and his King lacks defenders. Black wins this in brilliant style.*

WHITE	BLACK	WHITE	BLACK
1 P–K4	P–K4	11 K–R1	N–N6ch
2 N–KB3	N–QB3	12 PxN	Q–N4[3]
3 B–N5	N–Q5	13 R–B5	P–KR4!![4]
4 NxN	PxN	14 PxRP	QxR[5]
5 B–B4[1]	N–B3	15 P–N4	RxPch!
6 P–K5	P–Q4	16 PxR	Q–K5[6]
7 B–N3	....	17 Q–B3	Q–R5ch
SEE DIAGRAM		18 Q–R3	Q–K8ch
7	B–KN5	19 K–R2	B–N8ch
8 P–KB3	N–K5!	20 K–R1	B–B7ch
9 O–O[2]	P–Q6!!	21 K–R2	Q–N8
10 PxB	B–B4ch		

White has been checkmated

[1] Castling is best here.

[2] If 9 PxB, Q–R5ch; 10 K–K2 (or 10 P–N3, NxNP), Q–B7ch; 11 K–Q3, N–B4 mate.

[3] Threatening 13 . . . Q–R3 mate.

[4] If 13 . . . Q–R3ch; 14 R–R5, but after 13 . . . P–KR4; 14 RxQ, PxPch; 15 R–R5, RxR is mate.

[5] Renewing the mating threat by 15 . . . RxPch.

[6] Intending 17 . . . Q–R5 mate.

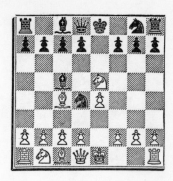

Black to Play. *White has won a Pawn, and threatens to win the exchange. Black proves this plan to be faulty, by an effective Queen maneuver.*

WHITE	BLACK	WHITE	BLACK
1 P–K4	P–K4		SEE DIAGRAM
2 N–KB3	N–QB3	5	Q–N4![4]
3 B–N5	N–Q5[1]	6 NxBP[5]	QxNP
4 B–B4[2]	B–B4	7 R–B1[6]	QxKPch
5 NxP[3]	....	8 B–K2	N–B6

White has been checkmated

[1] A trappy defense favored by Bird.

[2] A strong alternative is 4 NxN, PxN; 5 O–O, P–QB3; 6 B–B4, N–B3; 7 R–K1, P–Q3; 8 P–Q3.

[3] Snaps at the offered Pawn—instead of simply castling, with a good game.

[4] Attacks Knight and Knight Pawn, forcing White to go through with his plan to win the exchange.

[5] If 6 BxPch, K–K2 wins, or if 6 P–KB4, QxNP; 7 R–B1, QxKPch; 8 K–B2, N–B4ch wins for Black.

[6] If 7 NxR, QxRch; 8 B–B1, QxPch; 9 B–K2, NxPch; 10 K–B1, Q–R8 mate.

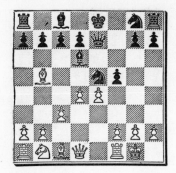

White to Play. *Temporarily, White is a piece down. The natural tendency would be to play 8 PxN immediately, as otherwise the Knight could move away. Nevertheless this would be fatal.*

WHITE	BLACK	WHITE	BLACK
1 P–K4	P–K4	7 O–O[1]	B–Q3
2 N–KB3	N–QB3		SEE DIAGRAM
3 B–N5	B–B4	8 PxN?[2]	QxP[3]
4 P–B3	P–B4	9 P–KB4	QxB
5 NxP	NxN	10 P–K5	B–B4ch
6 P–Q4	Q–K2		

Black has won a piece

[1] White can recover the piece immediately, but the text is even better.

[2] White should play 8 P–KB4 followed by 9 P–K5, after Black's Knight moves away.

[3] With the double threat of 9 ... QxP mate, as well as capture of the exposed Bishop.

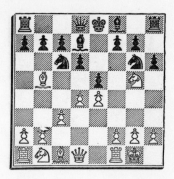

White to Play. *A smashing attack has been made possible by Black's timid and ineffectual development.*

WHITE	BLACK	WHITE	BLACK
1 P–K4	P–K4	SEE DIAGRAM	
2 N–KB3	N–QB3	8 NxP!	KxN
3 B–N5	KN–K2?[1]	9 B–B4ch	K–K2
4 P–B3	P–Q3	10 Q–R5	Q–K1[3]
5 P–Q4	B–Q2	11 Q–N5ch!	PxQ
6 O–O	N–N3	12 BxP	....
7 N–N5	P–KR3[2]		

Black has been checkmated

[1] This leaves Black with too constricted a position. The natural 3 . . . P–QR3 or 3 . . . N–B3 is best.

[2] A difficult position for Black. 7 . . . N–R4 seems to be about the only move to prevent the attack on his KB2 from assuming decisive proportions.

[3] If 10 . . . N–B5; 11 Q–B7 mate. If 10 . . . B–K1; 11 B–N5ch, PxB; 12 QxPch, K–Q2; 13 Q–B5ch, K–K2; 14 Q–K6 mate.

White to Play. *Black pays the maximum penalty for having moved his Queen out prematurely—he loses the Queen.*

WHITE	BLACK	WHITE	BLACK
1 P–K4	P–K4	7 PxB	QxP
2 N–KB3	N–QB3	8 B–KB4	P–Q3[4]
3 N–B3	B–B4[1]	SEE DIAGRAM	
4 NxP	NxN[2]	9 P–QN4!	Q–B3
5 P–Q4	Q–K2?[3]	10 B–QN5!	QxB
6 N–Q5!	Q–Q3	11 NxPch[5]	....

White wins the Queen

[1] Much stronger is 3 . . . B–N5.

[2] If 4 . . . BxPch; 5 KxB, NxN; 6 P–Q4, Q–B3ch; 7 K–N1, N–N5; 8 Q–Q2, N–K2; 9 P–KR3 and White has the edge.

[3] Black should play 5 . . . B–Q3.

[4] Black's position is not happy, but who would suspect that this move—protecting the Knight, and releasing the Queen Bishop—loses on the spot?

[5] This combination of a pin, followed by a Knight fork, is one which is frequently available to the alert player.

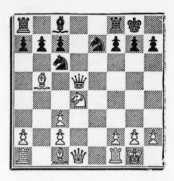

White to Play. *Black's position may look solid, but the fact that his Queen is protected by a Knight which is also guarding another piece forebodes a combination.*

WHITE	BLACK	WHITE	BLACK
1 P–K4	P–K4	8 PxP	BxN
2 N–KB3	N–QB3	9 PxB	QxP²
3 N–B3	B–N5		SEE DIAGRAM
4 B–N5	KN–K2	10 NxN!	PxN³
5 0–0	0–0	11 QxQ	PxQ⁴
6 P–Q4	PxP	12 B–R3	....
7 NxP	P–Q4?¹		

White wins the exchange

¹ The advance of the Queen Pawn two squares opens up the position prematurely, with disastrous effect on Black's game. The quiet 7 ... P–Q3 is better.

² Now he is in the trap and must lose some material.

³ If 10 ... QxQ; 11 NxNch, K–R1; 12 RxQ, and White has won two pieces. **Or,** if 10 ... QxB; 11 NxNch wins a piece.

⁴ On 11 ... NxQ; 12 BxP, B–K3; 13 BxR wins the exchange.

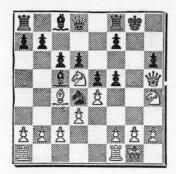

White to Play. *Black's loss of time in the opening permitted White to initiate a series of threats, which now culminate in a startling finish.*

WHITE	BLACK	WHITE	BLACK
1 P–K4	P–K4	12 Q–R5	P–QB3
2 N–KB3	N–QB3	SEE DIAGRAM	
3 N–B3	N–B3	13 N–K7ch!	QxN
4 B–N5	B–N5	14 Q–N6ch	K–R1
5 O–O	O–O	15 QxPch	K–N1
6 P–Q3	P–Q3	16 N–N6	Q–B3[5]
7 B–N5	P–KR3?[1]	17 QxRch	K–R2
8 BxKN	PxB[2]	18 BxP	B–K3
9 N–Q5[3]	B–QB4	19 B–N8ch	KxN
10 N–R4	N–Q5	20 B–R7ch	K–N4
11 B–B4	P–B4[4]	21 P–R4ch	....

White wins the Queen

[1] Weakening and a loss of time in most openings, and in this position a definite mistake.

[2] If 8 .... QxB; 9 N–Q5, Q–Q1; 10 BxN, PxB; 11 NxB wins two Pawns: 11 ... P–QR4; 12 NxP, Q–K1; 13 QNxP.

[3] Threatening to win a piece by 10 BxN, PxB; 11 NxB.

[4] Otherwise White plays 12 P–QB3 followed by 13 N–B5, so that his King Knight is powerfully posted.

[5] Forced, as White attacked the Queen and also threatened mate at R8.

White to Play. *Apparently Black has left his Bishop (at QN5) en prise. What is the trap?*

WHITE	BLACK	WHITE	BLACK
1 P–K4	P–K4	7 B–N5	B–N5[1]
2 N–KB3	N–QB3	8 N–Q5	N–Q5
3 N–B3	N–B3	9 B–QB4[2]	Q–Q2
4 B–N5	B–N5		SEE DIAGRAM
5 O–O	O–O	10 NxB?	BxN
6 P–Q3	P–Q3	11 PxB[3]	Q–R6[4]

Black wins the Queen

[1] This policy of imitation can become dangerous, if White replies properly.

[2] Best is 9 P–B3.

[3] If 11 Q–Q2, Q–N5; 12 P–KN3, Q–R6, and Black forces mate.

[4] Black threatens 12 .... NxPch followed by 13 .... QxP mate, to prevent which White must give up his Queen.

White to Play. *White is a Pawn up, and it would seem that he can maintain his material advantage by playing 9 NxP or 9 PxP — but either capture loses the game.*

WHITE	BLACK	WHITE	BLACK
1 P–K4	P–K4	SEE DIAGRAM	
2 N–KB3	N–QB3	9 NxP?[1]	NxP[2]
3 N–B3	N–B3	10 N–K3	BxN
4 B–N5	N–Q5	11 BPxB[3]	Q–R5ch
5 B–R4	B–B4	12 P–N3[4]	NxNP[5]
6 NxP	O–O	13 PxN[6]	QxRch
7 N–B3	P–Q4	14 K–K2	B–N5ch
8 NxN	BxN		

Black wins the Queen

[1] For 9 PxP see the next trap.

[2] Threatening 10 . . . . QxN, as well as 10 . . . . NxBP.

[3] If 11 QPxB, QxQch; 12 KxQ, NxPch wins the Rook.

[4] If 12 K–K2, B–N5ch wins the Queen at once.

[5] With the double threat of 13 . . . . NxRch as well as 13 . . . . B–N5.

[6] No better is 13 R–KN1, B–N5; 14 PxN, Q–R4 etc.

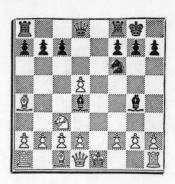

White to Play. *White's Queen is attacked, and he has only two replies—both equally ineffective.*

WHITE	BLACK	WHITE	BLACK
1 P–K4	P–K4	SEE DIAGRAM	
2 N–KB3	N–QB3	10 P–B3[2]	N–R4
3 N–B3	N–B3	11 PxB[3]	Q–R5ch
4 B–N5	N–Q5	12 K–K2[4]	N–B5ch
5 B–R4	B–B4	13 K–B3	Q–B7ch
6 NxP	O–O	14 K–K4	P–B4ch
7 N–B3	P–Q4	15 PxP	KR–K1ch
8 NxN	BxN	16 BxR	RxB
9 PxP?[1]	B–N5		

White has been checkmated

[1] The safest course is to return the Pawn with 9 O–O.

[2] If 10 N–K2, QxP; 11 O–O Q–KR4; 12 R–K1, N–K5 (threatening to win the Queen by 13 . . . NxBP); 13 P–B3, BxPch; 14 K–R1 (if 14 K–B1, QxP wins), BxN; 15 RxB, N–N6 mate.

[3] If 11 P–KN3, Q–B3; 12 R–B1, B–R6 wins.

[4] Or 12 P–N3, KR–K1ch; 13 BxR, RxBch; 14 N–K2 (if 14 K–B1, Q–R6 mate), NxP; 15 PxN, QxR mate.

White to Play. Black has fallen into a deep trap, in which the continuation is far from obvious.

WHITE	BLACK	WHITE	BLACK
1 P–K4	P–K4	9 P–Q4	Q–KB4[1]
2 N–KB3	N–QB3	10 R–K1	B–K3
3 N–B3	N–B3	11 B–N5	B–Q3?[2]
4 B–N5	P–QR3	SEE DIAGRAM	
5 BxN	QPxB	12 P–KN4!	Q–N3[3]
6 NxP	NxP	13 P–KB4	P–KB4[4]
7 NxN	Q–Q5	14 NxBch	PxN
8 O–O	QxN(K4)	15 P–Q5![5]	....

White wins a piece

[1] Not 9 . . . QxN; 10 R–K1 winning the Queen.

[2] Correct is 11 . . . P–R3; 12 Q–Q3, K–Q2! (not 12 . . . PxB?; 13 N–Q6ch winning the Queen.)

[3] If 12 . . . . QxPch; 13 QxQ, BxQ; 14 NxBch wins.

[4] To stop 14 P–B5.

[5] Winning a piece, as after 15 . . . PxQP; 16 QxP, K–B2 (if 16 . . . . K–Q2; 17 QxNPch, K–K1; 18 Q–K7 mate); 17 QxNPch, K–N1; 18 QxRch wins easily for White.

White to Play. Black has imitated too long. The positions are symmetrical, but the fact that it is White's move makes all the difference.

WHITE	BLACK	WHITE	BLACK
1 P–K4	P–K4	9 Q–Q2!	Q–Q2[3]
2 N–KB3	N–QB3		SEE DIAGRAM
3 N–B3	N–B3	10 BxN	BxN[4]
4 B–B4	B–B4	11 N–K7ch	K–R1[5]
5 O–O	O–O[1]	12 BxPch	KxB
6 P–Q3	P–Q3	13 Q–N5ch	K–R1
7 B–KN5	B–KN5?[2]	14 Q–B6	....
8 N–Q5	N–Q5		

Black has been checkmated

[1] Better is 5 ... P–Q3.

[2] This imitating process is risky. 7 ... B–K3 is safer.

[3] If 9 ... BxN; 10 BxN, PxB; 11 Q–R6, and the threat of 12 NxPch wins Black's Queen.

[4] On 10 ... PxB; 11 NxPch wins the Queen.

[5] If 11 ... QxN; 12 BxQ, N–K7ch; 13 K–R1, and White wins.

White to Play. The correct continuation is not obvious. Too much mental concentration on attacking Black's KBP makes it psychologically difficult to see the winning line.

WHITE	BLACK	WHITE	BLACK
1 P–K4	P–K4	6 Q–R5[2]	N–K4?[3]
2 N–KB3	N–QB3		SEE DIAGRAM
3 P–Q4	PxP	7 N–K6!	PxN[4]
4 B–QB4	B–B4	8 QxN(K5)[5]	....
5 N–N5[1]	N–R3		

White wins a piece

[1] 5 O–O, N–B3 transposes into the Max Lange, while 5 P–B3, N–B3; 6 PxP is the Moeller attack in the Giuoco Piano.

[2] If 6 NxBP, NxN; 7 BxNch, KxB; 8 Q–R5ch, P–N3; 9 QxB, R–K1, and Black has the better game.

[3] An instinctive reply which seems excellent at first sight— it simultaneously defends the KBP and attacks White's Bishop. And yet it is a decisive blunder! The proper move is 6 . . . Q–K2.

[4] The Knight must be captured, as it menaces too many pieces.

[5] White's threats—9 QxB, or 9 QxNP, or 9 BxN—cannot all be parried.

Black to Play. As a result of one weak move (5 Q–Q3), White has been forced to follow up with unnatural defensive maneuvers—and his game collapses!

WHITE	BLACK	WHITE	BLACK
1 P–K4	P–K4	7 P–KN3	Q–B3[3]
2 N–KB3	N–QB3	8 N(4)–B3	QN–K4
3 P–Q4	PxP	9 Q–B3[4]	B–N5!
4 NxP	Q–R5	10 QxB[5]	NxNch
5 Q–Q3?[1]	N–B3	11 NxN	QxN
6 N–Q2	....	12 R–KN1	QxBPch
	SEE DIAGRAM	13 K–Q1	QxR
6	N–KN5![2]		

Black has won a Rook

[1] Using the powerful Queen to protect a Pawn is poor policy. 5 N–N5!, as in the next trap, is the right move.

[2] Hitting at the weak point, White's KBP.

[3] Still menacing the KBP, and the King Knight as well. If now 8 N(2)-B3, NxN! wins.

[4] If 9 NxN, QxPch; 10 K–Q1, N–K6ch wins the Queen. Or if 9 Q–K2, B–B4 is decisive.

[5] If 10 Q–N3, NxNch wins a piece, for after 11 QxN, QxQ, and the pinned Knight cannot recapture.

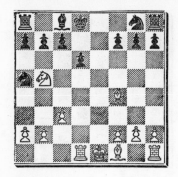

White to Play. Despite the absence of the Queens, White has a surprisingly virulent attack.

WHITE	BLACK	WHITE	BLACK
1 P–K4	P–K4	11 NxB	NxN
2 N–KB3	N–QB3	12 B–KB4	P–Q3[3]
3 P–Q4	PxP	SEE DIAGRAM	
4 NxP	Q–R5	13 NxBP!	KxN
5 N–N5![1]	B–N5ch	14 RxP[4]	N–QB3[5]
6 P–B3	QxKPch	15 R–Q5ch	K–N3
7 B–K3	B–R4	16 R–N5ch	K–R3
8 N–Q2	Q–Q4?	17 B–B7	P–QN3
9 N–B4	QxQch	18 RxPch	K–R4
10 RxQ	K–Q1[2]	19 R–R6	....

Black has been checkmated

[1] 5 N–QB3 is inferior, but then Black must not play 5 . . . N–B3, as he will lose his Queen after 6 N–B5, Q–R4; 7 B–K2, Q–N3; 8 N–KR4.

[2] White threatened 11 NxB, NxN; 12 NxPch, winning the Queen Rook.

[3] To stop 13 BxPch, but now comes an unexpected sacrifice.

[4] Threatening 15 R–QR6ch, regaining the piece.

[5] On 14 . . . P–QN3, White forces the win neatly with 15 P–QN4! If then 15 . . . N–QB3; 16 B–QN5, QN–K2; 17 R–Q7 mate. Or if 15 . . . N–N2; 16 R–Q1ch, K–B3; 17 P–N5ch, K–B4; 18 B–K3 mate.

Black to Play. *Temporarily a piece up, Black can apparently win two Pawns by playing QxP, etc. What is the trap?*

WHITE	BLACK	WHITE	BLACK
1 P–K4	P–K4	7 N–Q2?	NxN
2 N–KB3	N–QB3	8 P–K5[1]	....
3 P–Q4	PxP	SEE DIAGRAM	
4 NxP	B–B4	8	QxP?[2]
5 B–K3	Q–B3	9 PxN	BxP
6 P–QB3	KN–K2	10 N–B4[3]	....

White wins a piece

[1] About to lose a Pawn, White deliberately sets a snare.

[2] Loses a piece. Instead, 8 ... N–B7ch; 9 QxN, QxP is good enough to win.

[3] White wins the Bishop, which is twice attacked, as soon as Black's Queen moves. White's Knight not only threatens the Queen, but prevents Black from gaining time by a check at QR4.

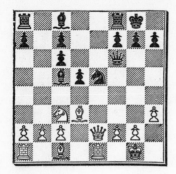

White to Play. *Black castled on his last move, and has apparently left his Knight en prise. Can White take the piece?*

WHITE	BLACK	WHITE	BLACK
1 P–K4	P–K4	10 P–KR3	NxKP[2]
2 N–KB3	N–QB3	11 R–K1	Q–B3
3 P–Q4	PxP	12 Q–K2	O–O![3]
4 NxP	N–B3		SEE DIAGRAM
5 N–QB3	B–N5	13 QxN	QxPch
6 NxN	NPxN	14 K–R1	BxP!
7 B–Q3	P–Q4	15 PxB[4]	Q–B6ch
8 P–K5?[1]	N–N5	16 K–R2	B–Q3
9 O–O	B–QB4		

Black wins the Queen

[1] An unfortunate advance which proves disastrous to White, in this and the next trap. 8 PxP, PxP; 9 O–O gives an equal game.

[2] Black seems to have fallen into a trap. The Knight can be pinned.

[3] Now it is Black's turn to trap his opponent. If White captures the Knight he will at least lose his Queen!

[4] If 15 Q–K2, BxPch; 16 K–R2, B–Q3ch wins at once for Black.

White to Play. *If White removes the annoying Knight, which exerts so much pressure on his position, Black will get more than enough compensation in the open Rook file.*

WHITE	BLACK	WHITE	BLACK
1 P–K4	P–K4	12 P–KR3?[2]	P–KR4!
2 N–KB3	N–QB3		SEE DIAGRAM
3 P–Q4	PxP	13 PxN?	PxP
4 NxP	N–B3	14 P–KN3	Q–B1![3]
5 NxN	NPxN	15 K–N2[4]	R–R7ch!!
6 B–Q3	P–Q4	16 KxR	Q–R3ch
7 P–K5?	N–N5	17 K–N1	Q–R6[5]
8 B–KB4	B–QB4	18 B–Q4	O–O–O[6]
9 O–O	P–N4!	19 B–R7	R–R1
10 B–Q2[1]	Q–K2	20 Q–Q3	BxB
11 B–B3	B–K3	21 N–Q2	RxB[7]

Black wins the Queen

[1] If 10 B–N3, P–KR4 gives Black a strong attack.

[2] Tempting fate. Here, or at the next move, Q–K2 should be played.

[3] Threatening 15 . . . Q–R3 followed by mate at R8.

[4] In order to reply to 15 . . . Q–R3 with 16 R–R1.

[5] Threatens 18 . . . QxPch; 19 K–R1, Q–R6ch; 20 K–N1, P–N6, and wins.

[6] White had hoped for 18 . . . BxB; 19 B–K4, QxPch; 20 B–N2!

[7] White must give up his Queen, or be mated.

Black to Play. *Black is a piece up, but both his Knights are attacked. If he tries to hold on to his extra material, he will leave himself open to a mating attack.*

WHITE	BLACK	WHITE	BLACK
1 P–K4	P–K4		SEE DIAGRAM
2 N–KB3	N–QB3	11	N(B5)–Q3[2]
3 B–B4	B–B4	12 QxNP	Q–B3
4 P–B3	N–B3	13 QxQ	NxQ
5 P–Q4	PxP	14 R–K1ch	K–Q1[3]
6 PxP	B–N5ch	15 B–N5	N–K1
7 N–B3	NxKP	16 RxNch!	KxR[4]
8 O–O	BxN	17 R–K1ch	K–B1
9 P–Q5![1]	N–K4	18 B–R6ch![5]	K–N1
10 PxB	NxB	19 R–K5![6]	....
11 Q–Q4	....		

White mates next move

[1] The Moeller attack, particularly rich in trappy play.
[2] This move loses. The right defense, and not an easy one to find, is to give the piece back by 11 . . . P–KB4.
[3] For the win against 14 . . . K–B1, see the next trap.
[4] If 16 . . . RxR; 17 BxNch, R–K2; 18 R–K1, and White wins.
[5] Much stronger than taking Black's Knight.
[6] White threatens 20 R–N5 mate; but if Black's Knight moves, then 20 R–K8 is mate.

White to Play. White is still a piece down, but he has a forced win by a spectacular combination, which ends in checkmate.

WHITE	BLACK	WHITE	BLACK
1 P–K4	P–K4	14 R–K1ch	K–B1
2 N–KB3	N–QB3	SEE DIAGRAM	
3 B–B4	B–B4	15 B–R6ch	K–N1
4 P–B3	N–B3	16 R–K5	N(B3)–K5[3]
5 P–Q4	PxP	17 R–K1[4]	P–KB4
6 PxP	B–N5ch	18 R–K7	P–N3
7 N–B3	NxKP	19 N–R4!	B–N2
8 O–O	BxN	20 P–B3	N–B2
9 P–Q5!	N–K4[1]	21 NxP	N(K5)–Q3
10 PxB	NxB	22 R–K8ch!	RxR
11 Q–Q4	N(B5)–Q3?[2]	23 RxRch	NxR
12 QxNP	Q–B3	24 N–K7	....
13 QxQ	NxQ		

Black has been checkmated

[1] A safer line for Black is 9 . . . B–B3; 10 R–K1, N–K2; 11 RxN, P–Q3; 12 B–N5, BxB; 13 NxB, O–O.

[2] Correct is 11 . . . P–KB4; 12 QxN, P–Q3; 13 N–Q4, O–O.

[3] If 16 . . . N(Q3)–K5; 17 N–Q2, P–Q3; 18 NxN wins at once: e.g. if 18 . . . PxR; 19 NxN mate, or if 18 . . . NxN; 19 R–K8 mate.

[4] Threatening 18 QRxN, NxR; 19 R–K8 mate.

Black to Play. *Black's Queen is attacked, but White's Bishop is unprotected, and subject to capture. Why would the capture of the Bishop be fatal?*

	WHITE	BLACK		WHITE	BLACK
1	P–K4	P–K4	11	RxN	O–O
2	N–KB3	N–QB3	12	P–Q6	PxP
3	B–B4	B–B4	13	QxP	N–B4
4	P–B3	N–B3	14	Q–Q5	P–Q3?[1]
5	P–Q4	PxP	15	N–N5	BxN
6	PxP	B–N5ch	16	BxB	....
7	N–B3	NxKP		SEE DIAGRAM	
8	O–O	BxN	16	....	QxB?[2]
9	P–Q5!	B–B3	17	QxPch!	RxQ
10	R–K1	N–K2	18	R–K8	....

Black has been checkmated

[1] Black should take the draw by repetition: 14 . . . N–K2; 15 Q–Q6, N–B4; 16 Q–Q5, N–K2 etc.

[2] Black grabs the Bishop, because he does not see the mating threat. His best defense was 16 . . . Q–B2; 17 Q–Q3, B–Q2; 18 P–KN4, P–KR3; 19 B–B4, but his extra Pawn does not compensate for White's better attacking prospects.

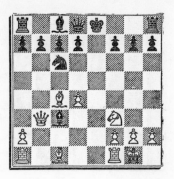

Black to Play. *Black c a n win a Rook with his Bishop. Can he risk this capture, with his King still in the center, vulnerable to attack by the opponent, who is far ahead of him in development?*

WHITE	BLACK	WHITE	BLACK
1 P–K4	P–K4	11 BxPch	K–B1[2]
2 N–KB3	N–QB3	12 B–N5	N–K2
3 B–B4	B–B4	13 N–K5	BxP
4 P–B3	N–B3	14 B–N6[3]	P–Q4
5 P–Q4	PxP	15 Q–B3ch	B–B4
6 PxP	B–N5ch	16 BxB	BxN
7 N–B3	NxKP	17 B–K6ch	B–B3
8 O–O	NxN	18 BxB	Q–N1[4]
9 PxN	BxP	19 B–N5ch	K–K1
10 Q–N3!	....	20 Q–B7ch	K–Q1
SEE DIAGRAM		21 BxN[5]	....
10	BxR?[1]		

Black has been checkmated

[1] Black can equalize by 10 . . . P–Q4; 11 BxP, O–O; 12 BxPch, K–R1; 13 QxB, RxB; 14 N–K5, NxN; 15 PxN, B–K3.

[2] On 11 . . . K–K2; 12 B–N5ch wins the Queen.

[3] Threatening 15 Q–B7 mate.

[4] 18 . . . PxB permits mate in two by 19 QxPch, K–K1; 20 Q–B7 mate.

[5] A 300 year old trap, but still an important one!

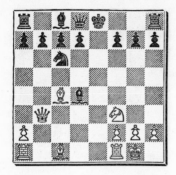

White to Play. *In this variation of the preceding trap, Black refuses the Rook, but captures instead the important center Pawn. Can he get away with it?*

WHITE	BLACK	WHITE	BLACK
1 P–K4	P–K4	11 BxPch	K–B1
2 N–KB3	N–QB3	12 B–N5	B–B3
3 B–B4	B–B4	13 QR–K1[1]	N–K2[2]
4 P–B3	N–B3	14 B–R5	N–N3
5 P–Q4	PxP	15 N–K5[3]	NxN
6 PxP	B–N5ch	16 RxN[4]	P–KN3
7 N–B3	NxKP	17 B–R6ch	B–N2
8 O–O	NxN	18 R–B5ch!	K–K2[5]
9 PxN	BxP	19 R–K1ch	K–Q3
10 Q–N3!	BxP?	20 Q–Q5	....

SEE DIAGRAM

Black has been checkmated

[1] Threatening to win the Queen by 14 R–K8ch.
[2] Of course not 13 . . . BxB; 14 NxB, QxN; 15 R–K8 mate.
[3] Aiming for 16 Q–B7 mate.
[4] Renewing the threat.
[5] If 18 . . . PxR; 19 Q–B7 mate.

Black to Play. *Black has avoided the Moeller attack, but there are still dangerous traps in the position. The good-looking defensive move 9 . . . B–K2 leads to trouble.*

WHITE	BLACK	WHITE	BLACK
1 P–K4	P–K4	10 P–Q5	N–R4
2 N–KB3	N–QB3	11 P–Q6!	BxP[2]
3 B–B4	B–B4	12 R–K1ch	B–K2
4 P–B3	N–B3	13 B–KN5	P–KB3[3]
5 P–Q4	PxP	14 BxP!	PxB
6 PxP	B–N5ch	15 N–K5[4]	P–KR4
7 N–B3	NxKP	16 Q–Q3[5]	R–R3
8 O–O	NxN	17 Q–Q5	R–R2
9 PxN	....	18 Q–N8ch	B–B1
	SEE DIAGRAM	19 N–N6ch	R–K2
9	B–K2?[1]	20 Q–B7	....

Black has been checkmated

[1] Permits a powerful attack. Correct is either 9 . . . P–Q4, or 9 . . . BxP; 10 Q–N3, P–Q4.

[2] If 11 . . . NxB; 12 PxB, KxP (on 12 . . . QxP; 13 R–K1 wins the Queen); 13 Q–K2ch, and White wins a piece. 11 . . . PxP avoids the ensuing brilliant attack, but Black's game would be difficult.

[3] Black cannot afford 13 . . . NxB; 14 BxB, QxB; 15 RxQch, KxR; 16 Q–K2ch, followed by 17 QxN.

[4] Threatening 16 Q–R5ch, and mate next move.

[5] Heading for N6 with the same object.

Black to Play. A timid player would castle at this point — and therein lies the trap. Black must not permit White to build up a strong Pawn center.

WHITE	BLACK	WHITE	BLACK
1 P–K4	P–K4	9 P–K5[2]	N–K1
2 N–KB3	N–QB3	10 P–Q6	PxP
3 B–B4	B–B4	11 PxP	N–N3
4 P–B3	N–B3	12 B–KN5	N–B3
5 P–Q4	PxP	13 N–B3	P–KR3
6 O–O	....	14 Q–Q3	K–R2[3]
SEE DIAGRAM		15 BxBP[4]	RxB
6	O–O?[1]	16 N–K5	PxB
7 PxP	B–N3	17 QxNch	K–N1
8 P–Q5	N–K2	18 QxRch[5]	....

White has won the exchange

[1] Black should play 6 . . . NxP, and if 7 R–K1, P–Q4.

[2] White's control of the center gives him an overwhelming advantage.

[3] No better is 14 . . . PxB; 15 QxN, followed by 16 NxP.

[4] Now White threatens 16 QxNch.

[5] White wins easily as he has a decisive attack, in addition to his extra material.

White to Play. *White selects an unusual move to get out of check, in order to take advantage of the plight of Black's stranded Bishop.*

WHITE	BLACK	WHITE	BLACK
1 P–K4	P–K4	7 K–B1![3]	B–Q2
2 N–KB3	N–QB3	8 Q–N3[4]	B–R4
3 B–B4	B–B4	9 BxPch	K–B1[5]
4 P–B3	P–Q3[1]	10 BxN	RxB
5 P–Q4	PxP	11 N–N5	Q–K1[6]
6 PxP	B–N5ch?[2]	12 NxPch	K–K2
SEE DIAGRAM		13 B–N5	....

Black has been checkmated

[1] Played to avoid the perils of the Moeller attack, which would follow 4 . . . N–B3; 5 P–Q4, PxP; 6 PxP etc.

[2] This, which is correct against the Moeller attack, loses in this line. Best for Black is 6 . . . B–N3.

[3] White does not interpose, as that would permit Black to exchange his Bishop. Now White threatens to win a piece by 8 P–Q5 followed by 9 Q–R4ch and 10 QxB.

[4] Threatening 9 P–Q5 and 10 QxB.

[5] If 9 . . . K–K2, 10 B–N5ch, N–B3; 11 P–K5, PxP; 12 PxP, P–KR3; 13 PxNch, and White wins a piece.

[6] If 11 . . . Q–B3 (White's threat was 12 Q–B7 mate); 12 NxPch wins the Queen.

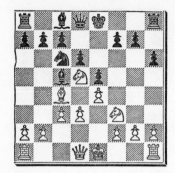

Black to Play. *Black has several good moves at his disposal, but if he plays the tempting 9 . . . B–K3, he will lose a piece. Can you see how?*

WHITE	BLACK	WHITE	BLACK
1 P–K4	P–K4		SEE DIAGRAM
2 N–KB3	N–QB3	9	B–K3?[2]
3 B–B4	B–B4	10 P–Q4!	PxP[3]
4 P–Q3	N–B3	11 PxP	B–N3[4]
5 N–B3	P–Q3	12 NxB	RPxN
6 B–KN5	P–KR3	13 P–Q5	N–R4
7 BxN[1]	QxB	14 B–Q3	B–N5
8 N–Q5	Q–Q1	15 P–QN4	....
9 P–B3	....		

White wins the Knight

[1] A line of play that has been revived with some success in modern tournament play.

[2] This is what White was angling for. Black can get an even game by 9 . . . N–K2; 10 P–Q4, PxP; 11 NxP, NxN; 12 BxN, O–O etc.

[3] If 10 . . . BxN; 11 KPxB, N–R4; 12 PxB, NxB; 13 Q–R4ch followed by 14 QxN wins a piece.

[4] If 11 . . . BxN; 12 KPxB, B–N5ch; 13 K–B1, N–K2; 14 Q–R4ch wins the stranded Bishop.

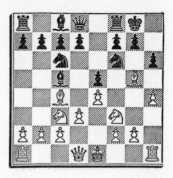

Black to Play. White offers his Bishop, but Black should refuse the sacrifice, as the opening of White's King Rook file is fatal.

WHITE	BLACK	WHITE	BLACK
1 P–K4	P–K4	8 PxP	N–KN5
2 N–KB3	N–QB3	9 P–N6!	NxP
3 B–B4	B–B4	10 NxP!	NxQ[4]
4 P–Q3	N–B3	11 PxPch	RxP
5 N–B3	O–O[1]	12 BxRch	K–B1
6 B–KN5	P–KR3[2]	13 R–R8ch	K–K2
7 P–KR4!?[3]	....	14 N–Q5ch	K–Q3
SEE DIAGRAM		15 N–QB4	....
7	PxB?		

Black has been checkmated

[1] In the Giuoco Piano it is often dubious policy to castle before the opponent's intentions have become clear.

[2] It is generally best to avoid moving the Pawns surrounding the castled King.

[3] 7 B–KR4 would be objectively more accurate, for it would lead to a further weakening of Black's castled position by 7 ... P–KN4, or else White would force such a weakening with 8 N–Q5.

[4] If 10 ... NxN; 11 R–R8ch!, KxR; 12 Q–R5ch, K–N1; 13 Q–R7 mate. Or if 10 ... NxR; 11 Q–R5, R–K1; 12 PxPch, K–B1; 13 N–N6 mate.

White to Play. *Almost the same situation as in the previous trap, but with colors reversed. White should not capture the Bishop, as the recapture clears the way for Black's King Rook.*

WHITE	BLACK	WHITE	BLACK
1 P–K4	P–K4	8 PxB?[2]	PxP[3]
2 N–KB3	N–QB3	9 N–KN5	P–N6
3 B–B4	B–B4	10 NxP	NxP!
4 P–Q3	N–B3	11 NxQ[4]	PxPch
5 N–B3	P–Q3	12 RxP	BxRch
6 O–O[1]	B–KN5	13 K–B1	R–R8ch
7 P–KR3?	P–KR4!?	14 K–K2	N–Q5

SEE DIAGRAM

White has been checkmated

[1] This time it is White who makes the mistake of castling too soon. 6 B–K3 is preferable; if Black replies by 6 . . . BxB, then 7 PxB will give White an open file for his King Rook after castling. The doubled Pawns in the center are not weak in this type of position.

[2] 8 B–K3 is still correct. It is important to cut down the scope of Black's Bishop; or, in the event of an exchange of Bishops, to reduce Black's attacking prospects.

[3] The opening of the King Rook file is decisive.

[4] If 11 PxN, R–R8ch!; 12 KxR, Q–R5ch; 13 K–N1, Q–R7 mate.

Black to Play. *Black's Queen and Rook are menaced by White's Knight, but the open lines are all Black needs to win. What is his winning move in this position?*

WHITE	BLACK	WHITE	BLACK
1 P–K4	P–K4	10 NxP?	....
2 N–KB3	N–QB3	SEE DIAGRAM	
3 B–B4	B–B4	10	PxB!
4 P–Q3	P–Q3	11 NxQ	B–KN5
5 O–O?[1]	N–B3	12 Q–Q2	N–Q5[4]
6 B–KN5?	P–KR3	13 N–B3[5]	N–B6ch!
7 B–R4?[2]	P–KN4!	14 PxN	BxP
8 B–KN3	P–KR4!	15 PxP	R–R8
9 NxNP[3]	P–R5!		

White has been checkmated

[1] As in the two previous examples, castling should be delayed until more pieces are brought into play.

[2] The Bishop should have gone instead to K3.

[3] 9 P–KR4 was the only chance.

[4] Threatening 13 . . . N–B6ch; 14 PxN, BxP; 15 PxP (otherwise 15 . . . PxRP mate follows), R–R8 mate.

[5] If 13 P–KR3, N–K7ch; 14 K–R1, RxPch; 15 PxR, B–B6 mate. Or if 13 RPxP, N–B6ch; 14 PxN, BxP, and Black mates next move by 15 . . . R–R8. Finally, if 13 BPxP, N–K7ch; 14 K–R1, NxP is checkmate.

Black to Play. W h i t e threatens to win the Queen by 6 NxBP. The attempt to meet this threat by castling would be a serious error, leading to loss of material or checkmate.

WHITE	BLACK	WHITE	BLACK
1 P–K4	P–K4	5	O–O?[2]
2 N–KB3	N–QB3	6 Q–R5[3]	P–KR3
3 B–B4	B–B4	7 NxP	Q–K1[4]
4 P–Q3	KN–K2?[1]	8 NxRPch	K–R2
5 N–N5	....	9 N–B7ch	K–N1
SEE DIAGRAM		10 Q–R8	....

Black has been checkmated

[1] This constricting move may lead to serious trouble. The normal development of the King's Knight to B3 is correct in almost every variation of every opening—and if a player intends to castle King side, then the Knight at B3 is a tower of defensive strength.

[2] Black's only chance is 5 . . . P–Q4; 6 PxP, N–R4, with the hope of playing it out on the lines of the Two Knights' Defense.

[3] Notice that with the Knight at B3, the opposing Queen can never get to R5.

[4] Black could prolong the game by 7 . . . RxN, giving up the exchange, but his game would of course be hopeless.

White to Play. White uses his powerful Pawn center to break up the opposing position, and clear the way for an irresistible attack on Black's King.

WHITE	BLACK	WHITE	BLACK
1 P–K4	P–K4	11 R–K1ch	K–B1[3]
2 N–KB3	N–QB3	12 B–R3ch	K–N1
3 B–B4	B–B4	13 P–Q5	N–R4
4 P–QN4	BxP	14 B–K7!	Q–Q2
5 P–B3	B–B4[1]	15 PxP	KxP
6 O–O	N–B3?[2]	16 Q–Q2[4]	Q–N5[5]
7 P–Q4	PxP	17 Q–B3ch	K–N1
8 PxP	B–N3	18 QxRch!	KxQ
SEE DIAGRAM		19 B–B6ch	Q–N2
9 P–K5	P–Q4	20 R–K8	....
10 PxN	PxB		

Black has been checkmated

[1] 5 . . . B–R4 is to be preferred, if only for the reason that the Bishop is not attacked when White plays P–Q4.

[2] Instinctive, but weak. Best is 6 . . . P–Q3, and if 7 P–Q4, B–N3!, as recommended by Dr. Lasker.

[3] If 11 . . . B–K3; 12 P–Q5 wins a piece, or if 11 . . . K–Q2; 12 P–Q5, N–R4; 13 N–K5ch, K–Q3 (if 13 . . . K–K1; 14 N–B6ch wins the Queen): 14 NxKBPch wins the Queen.

[4] Threatening 17 Q–N5 mate.

[5] If 16 . . . P–KB3; 17 BxPch, KxB; 18 Q–N5ch, K–B2; 19 N–K5ch wins the Queen.

Black to Play. *White has played a faint-hearted gambit. After giving up a Pawn for the attack, he changed his mind and won back his Pawn. Black punishes this vacillation by forcing the win of a piece — or more.*

WHITE	BLACK	WHITE	BLACK
1 P–K4	P–K4	SEE DIAGRAM	
2 N–KB3	N–QB3	5	Q–B3![3]
3 B–B4	B–B4	6 P–Q4	BxP[4]
4 P–QN4	NxP[1]	7 QxB[5]	NxPch
5 NxP?[2]	....		

Black wins the Queen

[1] The usual way of accepting the gambit Pawn is by 4 . . . BxP, but sometimes the unusual way is good for a point on the score-sheet.

[2] Correct is 5 P–B3; N–QB3; 6 P–Q4, leading into the regular lines of this opening.

[3] Attacking White's Knight (and the Rook behind the Knight) as well as threatening 6 . . . QxP mate.

[4] Still threatening Knight, Rook, and mate!

[5] Loses, but so does every other move.

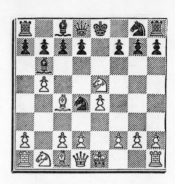

Black to Play. *White's attack is premature. He has won a Pawn at the expense of permitting Black's pieces to enter his territory with decisive effect.*

WHITE	BLACK	WHITE	BLACK
1 P–K4	P–K4		
2 N–KB3	N–QB3	SEE DIAGRAM	
3 B–B4	B–B4	6	Q–N4![1]
4 P–QN4	B–N3	7 NxBP[2]	QxKNP
5 P–N5	N–Q5	8 R–B1[3]	QxKPch
6 NxP?	....	9 B–K2	N–B6

White has been checkmated

[1] Black begins by attacking the Knight, as well as the important Knight's Pawn.

[2] If 7 N–N4, P–Q4 wins either the Knight or the Bishop. If 7 N–KB3, QxKNP wins.

[3] If 8 NxR, QxRch; 9 B–B1, QxPch; 10 B–K2, NxPch winning the Queens, for if 11 K–B1, Q–R8 is mate.

White to Play. W h i t e ' s Queen is attacked, and if he plays 11 QxN, or 11 Q–K3, Black wins the Queen by 11 . . . NxPch. White seems to be in trouble—but there is a good solution.

WHITE	BLACK	WHITE	BLACK
1 P–K4	P–K4	8 BxP	N–B3
2 N–KB3	N–QB3	9 B–R3	NxKP?[2]
3 B–B4	B–B4	10 Q–K2	NxBP
4 P–QN4	B–N3	11 NxP	N–Q5[3]
5 P–QR4[1]	P–QR3		SEE DIAGRAM
6 P–R5	B–R2	12 NxQPch!	NxQ
7 P–N5	PxP	13 N–B6	....

Black has been checkmated

[1] Threatening to win the Bishop by 6 P–R5, B–Q5; 7 P–B3.
[2] A risky capture. The quiet 9 . . . P–Q3 would be safer.
[3] Apparently seizing the initiative—but White has a stunning surprise.

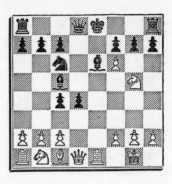

Black to Play. *White has a dangerous Pawn at B6. The natural impulse would be to remove this Pawn. Why would the capture lose?*

WHITE	BLACK	WHITE	BLACK
1 P–K4	P–K4	8 R–K1ch[1]	B–K3
2 N–KB3	N–QB3	9 N–N5	....
3 B–B4	N–B3		SEE DIAGRAM
4 P–Q4	PxP	9	QxP?[2]
5 O–O	B–B4	10 NxB	PxN
6 P–K5	P–Q4	11 Q–R5ch	Q–B2
7 PxN	PxB	12 QxB	....

White has won a piece

[1] An important position, as it can be reached from several openings, such as the Giuoco Piano, Scotch Gambit, Two Knights' Defense, Bishop's Opening and Center Game.

[2] The correct move is 9 . . . Q–Q4. If Black takes the Pawn by 9 . . . PxP; 10 NxB, PxN; 11 Q–R5ch, and White wins a piece the same way as in the text.

White to Play. *Black has attempted to defend against White's threats by guarding his KNP with his Bishop, but the safety of his King was more important.*

WHITE	BLACK	WHITE	BLACK
1 P–K4	P–K4	10 N–QB3	Q–B4[1]
2 N–KB3	N–QB3	11 QN–K4	B–KB1?[2]
3 B–B4	N–B3	SEE DIAGRAM	
4 P–Q4	PxP	12 NxBP!	KxN[3]
5 O–O	B–B4	13 N–N5ch	K–N1[4]
6 P–K5	P–Q4	14 P–KN4	QxNPch?[5]
7 PxN	PxB	15 QxQ	BxQ
8 R–K1ch	B–K3	16 P–B7	....
9 N–N5	Q–Q4		

Black has been checkmated

[1] 10 ... PxN would be a blunder, as after 11 QxQ, Black could not recapture.

[2] White's threat was 12 PxP, KR–N1; 13 P–KN4, Q–K4 (if 13 ... QxNPch; 14 QxQ, BxQ; 15 N–B6ch wins); 14 P–B4, Q–Q4; 15 N–B6ch and wins the Queen. Black's best move is 11 ... O–O–O.

[3] Not 12 ... BxN; 13 N–Q6ch winning the Queen.

[4] If 13 ... KxP; 14 RxBch wins.

[5] Loses at once. However, if 14 ... Q–Q4; 15 RxB wins for White.

White to Play. *Black has moved his King to avoid the dangers resulting from 8 . . . B–K3, but he finds himself the victim of a terrific attack.*

WHITE	BLACK	WHITE	BLACK
1 P–K4	P–K4	SEE DIAGRAM	
2 N–KB3	N–QB3	9 B–N5	PxP[2]
3 B–B4	N–B3	10 B–R6ch	K–N1
4 P–Q4	PxP	11 N–B3	B–KN5[3]
5 O–O	B–B4	12 N–K4	B–N3?[4]
6 P–K5	P–Q4	13 Q–K2[5]	N–K4
7 PxN	PxB	14 NxN!	BxQ[6]
8 R–K1ch	K–B1?[1]	15 N–Q7!![7]	....

White forces checkmate

[1] Inferior, as White quickly demonstrates. 8 . . . B–K3 should be played.

[2] White threatened to win the Queen with 10 PxPch. If 10 . . . P–KN3; 11 B–R6ch, K–N1; 12 B–N7 wins the exchange.

[3] Not 11 . . . PxN; 12 QxQch, NxQ; 13 R–K8ch, B–B1; 14 RxB mate.

[4] 12 . . . B–K2 puts up more resistance, although White still has a strong attack.

[5] With this idea: 14 NxPch!, QxN; 15 Q–K8ch, RxQ; 16 RxR mate.

[6] If 14 . . . PxN; 15 QxBch etc.

[7] There is no defense to White's threat of 16 NxPch, QxN; 17 NxQ mate. A lovely finish.

White to Play. Black has been lured into making an "aggressive" move with his Queen, and White unleashes a bewildering attack.

WHITE	BLACK	WHITE	BLACK
1 P-K4	P-K4	SEE DIAGRAM	
2 N-KB3	N-QB3	9 N-Q2!	Q-N5[2]
3 B-B4	N-B3	10 N-Q5!	Q-R4[3]
4 P-Q4	PxP	11 P-QB4!	B-Q3[4]
5 O-O	NxP	12 NxN	O-O
6 R-K1	P-Q4	13 B-Q2	Q-R3
7 BxP	QxB	14 NxB	PxN
8 N-B3	Q-B5?[1]	15 N-B7	....

White wins the exchange

[1] The best retreats for the Queen are QR4, KR4 or Q1. The text spells trouble for Black, as his Queen is exposed to harrying attacks.

[2] If 9 ... Q-K3; 10 RxN, N-K4; 11 P-B4, P-KB3; 12 N-K2, and White wins a piece. Or 9 ... Q-R3; 10 N-Q5, B-Q3; 11 NxN, K-Q1; 12 B-N5ch, P-B3 (if 12 ... N-K2; 13 NxN, BxN; 14 BxBch, KxB; 15 N-B5ch wins); 13 KNxP, P-R3; 14 Q-R5, B-Q2; 15 NxBch, KxN; 16 Q-B7ch, and White wins.

[3] If 10 ... Q-B4, or 10 ... Q-Q3; 11 NxN decides at once.

[4] If 11 ... P-KB4; 12 P-B3 with a winning game. Or 11 ... PxP e.p.; 12 N-QB4 wins. Finally, if 11 ... B-K3; 12 N-N3! wins.

White to Play. *White is temporarily a piece behind. If he now plays NxP, in the belief that Black's pinned Knight can be regained later, he will lose the game.*

WHITE	BLACK	WHITE	BLACK
1 P–K4	P–K4	11 B–N5²	Q–B4
2 N–KB3	N–QB3	12 Q–Q8ch	K–B2
3 B–B4	N–B3	13 NxN	PxN
4 P–Q4	PxP	14 QR–Q1³	B–Q4⁴
5 O–O	NxP	15 QxR	QxB⁵
6 R–K1	P–Q4	16 P–KB4	Q–R5
7 BxP	QxB	17 RxP⁶	B–KR6!
8 N–B3	Q–QR4	18 QxR	B–B4ch
SEE DIAGRAM		19 K–R1⁷	BxPch!
9 NxP?¹	NxN	20 KxB	Q–N5ch
10 QxN	P–KB4!		

Black checkmates in two moves

¹ Correct is 9 NxN, B–K3; 10 QN–N5, O–O–O; 11 NxB, PxN; 12 RxP.

² White cannot play 11 P–B3, as 11 . . . B–B4 would win his Queen. He therefore tries to work up a compensating attack.

³ But not 14 RxP, B–KB4!

⁴ A nice sacrifice to seize the attack.

⁵ Threatening 16 . . . B–KR6, either mating or winning the Queen.

⁶ If 17 P–KN3, B–B4ch; 18 K–R1, B–KN5! finishes White.

⁷ Or 19 R–Q4, BxRch; 20 RxB, Q–K8 mate.

White to Play. Black h a s missed this important point. When you threaten something, and your opponent lets you carry out your threat—watch out!

WHITE	BLACK	WHITE	BLACK
1 P–K4	P–K4	11 NxB	PxN
2 N–KB3	N–QB3	12 RxP	B–Q3
3 B–B4	N–B3	13 B–N5	QR–B1[2]
4 P–Q4	PxP[1]	14 Q–K2!	RxN?[3]
5 O–O	NxP		SEE DIAGRAM
6 R–K1	P–Q4	15 R–K8ch	N–Q1[4]
7 BxP	QxB	16 RxR	R–B1[5]
8 N–B3	Q–QR4	17 Q–N4ch	K–N1[6]
9 NxN	B–K3	18 RxR	BxR
10 QN–N5	O–O–O	19 BxN	....

White has won a Rook

[1] If 4 ... QNxP; 5 BxPch, KxB; 6 NxPch followed by 7 QxN wins a Pawn for White.

[2] In order to win two pieces for a Rook with 14 ... RxN; 15 QxR, QxB.

[3] Paying no attention to White's threats.

[4] If 15 ... RxR; 16 QxRch, N–Q1; 17 QxN mate.

[5] To stop 17 RxN mate. If 16 ... QxB; 17 QxR with two exchanges ahead.

[6] If 17 ... Q–B4; 18 QxQch, RxQ; 19 RxN mate, or 18 RxR, QxQ; 19 RxN mate.

White to Play. Instead of defending h i m s e l f against White's obvious threats, Black has captured a Pawn with his Knight. White can take immediate advantage of this mistake.

WHITE	BLACK	WHITE	BLACK
1 P–K4	P–K4	5 BxPch	K–K2
2 N–KB3	N–QB3	6 NxN[2]	KxB
3 B–B4	N–B3	7 Q–B3ch	K–N1?[3]
4 N–N5	NxP?[1]	8 N–N5![4]	QxN[5]
SEE DIAGRAM		9 Q–Q5	....

Black has been checkmated

[1] Best is 4 . . . P–Q4; 5 PxP, N–QR4.

[2] A good alternative is 6 P–Q4, P–Q3; 7 B–N3.

[3] With 7 K–K1 Black would have the inferior game, but he could still put up a fight.

[4] A pretty sacrifice. Black must do something about the threat of 9 Q–B7 mate.

[5] But what can he do? If 8 . . . Q–K2, or 8 . . . Q–B3; 9 Q–Q5ch, Q–K3; 10 NxQ wins.

White to Play. Black is quickly punished for exposing his King to attack, via the open King file.

WHITE	BLACK	WHITE	BLACK
1 P–K4	P–K4	8 R–K1	Q–Q2
2 N–KB3	N–QB3	SEE DIAGRAM	
3 B–B4	N–B3	9 NxBP![3]	KxN[4]
4 N–N5	P–Q4	10 Q–B3ch	K–N3[5]
5 PxP	NxP?[1]	11 RxBch	QxR
6 P–Q4!	PxP[2]	12 B–Q3ch	....
7 O–O	B–K3		

White checkmates next move

[1] Safest and best is 5 . . . N–QR4.

[2] Better is 6 B–N5ch; 7 P–B3, B–K2 with a fair game.

[3] A beautiful move.

[4] If 9 . . . QxN; 10 BxN recovers the piece with a strong attack.

[5] If 10 . . . K–K1; 11 BxN wins easily (11 . . . QxB? ; 12 QxQ). Or if 10 . . . K–N1; 11 RxB, QxR; 12 BxN, and Black's Queen is pinned.

White to Play. *Seemingly Black has a more solid defense than in the previous trap, but White's developed Rook, Knight and Bishop each makes a capture, and White forces a decisive gain of material.*

WHITE	BLACK	WHITE	BLACK
1 P–K4	P–K4	7 O–O	B–K3
2 N–KB3	N–QB3	8 R–K1	B–K2
3 B–B4	N–B3	SEE DIAGRAM	
4 N–N5	P–Q4	9 RxB![2]	PxR
5 PxP	NxP?	10 NxKP	Q–Q2
6 P–Q4!	PxP?[1]	11 BxN[3]	....

White has won two pieces for a Rook

[1] 6 . . . B–N5ch is the right move.
[2] An unpleasant surprise for Black.
[3] Black dare not play 11 . . . QxB, because of 12 NxBPch winning the Queen.

Black to Play. *White h a s placed two unprotected pieces in exposed positions, thereby giving Black the opportunity to bring his Queen into the game with terrific effect.*

WHITE	BLACK	WHITE	BLACK
1 P–K4	P–K4	10 N–K5[2]	....
2 N–KB3	N–QB3	SEE DIAGRAM	
3 B–B4	N–B3	10	Q–Q5
4 N–N5	P–Q4	11 BxPch	NxB
5 PxP	N–QR4	12 NxN	Q–Q4
6 B–N5ch	P–B3	13 NxP[3]	B–KN5![4]
7 PxP	PxP	14 P–KB3	PxP[5]
8 B–R4?[1]	P–KR3	15 O–O[6]	B–B4ch
9 N–KB3	P–K5	16 K–R1	PxP[7]

White has been checkmated

[1] The right place for the Bishop is K2.

[2] 10 N–N1 would leave White with a badly backward game.

[3] White has enough Pawns for the piece, but Black has the attack.

[4] Much stronger than 13 . . . RxN.

[5] Threatening to win White's Queen with 15 . . . P–B7ch, or 15 . . . PxP.

[6] If 15 K–B2, Q–Q5ch; 16 K–N3, N–R4ch; 17 K–R4, B–K2 mate.

[7] A pretty finish.

White to Play. B l a c k i s
threatening the Queen and has
based his hopes on this tempo-
gaining attack—but White has
a subtle and powerful reply.

WHITE	BLACK	WHITE	BLACK
1 P-K4	P-K4	8 QxB	N-Q5
2 N-KB3	N-QB3	SEE DIAGRAM	
3 B-B4	N-B3	9 Q-K4![3]	NxP
4 P-Q3	P-Q4[1]	10 BxN	NxR[4]
5 PxP	NxP	11 BxP	R-QN1
6 O-O	B-KN5	12 B-B6ch	K-K2
7 P-KR3	BxN?[2]	13 QxP	....

Black has been checkmated

[1] It is risky to open the position at so early a stage.

[2] Black should be content with 7 . . . B-R4.

[3] Much stronger than 9 QxN, QxQ; 10 BxQ, NxP winning the
Rook.

[4] Allowing a quick finish, but if 10 . . . P-QB3; 11 BxQBPch,
PxB; 12 QxBPch, K-K2; 13 QxN, and White is a piece to
the good.

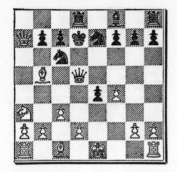

Black to Play. *White has won a Pawn with his Queen. In doing so he has given Black the opportunity to win a piece in an interesting manner.*

WHITE	BLACK	WHITE	BLACK
1 P–K4	P–K4	SEE DIAGRAM	
2 N–KB3	N–QB3	10	QxB!
3 P–B3	P–Q4	11 NxQ	NxQ
4 Q–R4	PxP	12 NxN	P–QB3[3]
5 NxP	Q–Q4	13 P–Q3	R–R1
6 B–N5	N–K2[1]	14 B–K3	N–Q4
7 P–KB4	B–Q2[2]	15 B–N1[4]	P–K6
8 NxB	KxN	16 P–B4	N–N5[5]
9 N–R3	R–Q1	17 K–Q1	RxN
10 QxRP?	....		

Black has won a piece

[1] If 6 ... QxN; 7 BxNch, K–Q1; 8 QxKP wins a Pawn for White.

[2] Threatening to win a piece with 8 ... NxN; 9 BxBch (if 9 PxN, BxB wins) NxB etc.

[3] Closing the exit gate!

[4] If 15 B–Q4, P–QB4 attacks two pieces, and wins. Or if 15 B–B2, P–K6 wins, as Knight and Bishop are threatened.

[5] Intending 17 ... N–B7ch and 18 ... NxR.

Black to Play. *Black could win quickly if he could bring his Bishop to B4—but White's Knight Pawn controls that square. How does Black accomplish his object?*

WHITE	BLACK	WHITE	BLACK
1 P–K4	P–K4	9 O–O	N–B4
2 N–KB3	N–QB3	10 P–QN4[1]	P–QR4![2]
3 P–B3	P–Q4	11 K–R1	....
4 Q–R4	PxP	SEE DIAGRAM	
5 NxP	Q–Q4	11	PxP!
6 B–N5	N–K2	12 QxR	B–B4
7 P–KB4	B–Q2	13 QxR	N–N6ch
8 NxB	KxN	14 PxN	Q–R4

White has been checkmated

[1] To stop Black from winning with 10 ... B–B4ch; 11 K–R1 (11 P–Q4, PxPe.p.ch doesn't help the situation), N–N6ch; 12 PxN, Q–R4 mate.

[2] Combining against White's Queen and King. The threat is 11 ... PxP; 12 QxR, B–B4ch; 13 R–B2 (on 13 K–R1, Black mates in two), RxQ, and Black wins.

Black to Play. *W h i t e ' s Bishop at K2 is pinned and his Knight blocks his other Bishop. Black now finds an ingenious way to make advantage of these weaknesses without loss of time.*

WHITE	BLACK	WHITE	BLACK
1 P–K4	P–K4	9 QxPch	B–Q2
2 N–KB3	N–QB3	10 Q–R6	O–O
3 P–B3	P–Q4	11 B–K2	R–K1
4 Q–R4	N–B3	12 N–Q2?[2]	....
5 NxP[1]	B–Q3	SEE DIAGRAM	
6 NxN	PxN	12	R–N1[3]
7 P–K5	BxP	13 P–QR4[4]	Q–K2
8 P–Q4	B–Q3	14 N–B1	B–N4![5]

Black wins the Queen

[1] This line is of dubious value. White loses valuable time with the Queen's gallivanting.

[2] White should castle before the pin on his Bishop is intensified. He intends to unpin with 13 N–B1 and 14 N–K3, but this is far too slow.

[3] Threatening 13 . . . B–N4. Now if 13 O–O, Q–K2; 14 R–K1 (or 14 B–B3, B–N4 winning the exchange), B–N4 wins. Or if 13 O–O, Q–K2; 14 B–Q3, R–N3; 15 QxP, B–B3, followed by 16 . . . R–R1 wins White's Queen.

[4] Apparently preventing 13 . . . B–N4.

[5] If 15 PxB (White's Queen is now shut off), QxB mate.

White to Play. Black's attempt to win a Pawn recoils on him, as White springs a startling winning combination, beginning with a Queen sacrifice.

WHITE	BLACK	WHITE	BLACK
1 P–K4	P–K4	SEE DIAGRAM	
2 N–KB3	N–QB3	8 BxN!	NxQ[4]
3 P–B3	N–B3	9 BxPch	K–K2
4 P–Q4	NxKP[1]	10 B–N5ch	K–Q3
5 P–Q5	N–K2	11 N–B4ch	K–B4
6 NxP	N–N3	12 QN–R3	NxNP[5]
7 B–Q3![2]	NxKBP?[3]	13 B–K3	....

Black has been checkmated

[1] 4 . . . P–Q4 is the simplest equalizing move.

[2] Setting a beautiful trap.

[3] Black succumbs: he counts on winning a Pawn by 8 KxN, NxN. Instead he should play the simple 7 . . . NxN, or 7 . . . Q–R5.

[4] If 8 . . . RPxB; 9 KxN, and White is a piece ahead. If 8 . . . Q–B3; 9 Q–K2 (threatening a ruinous discovered check) NxR; 10 BxPch (not 10 N–N4ch, Q–K2) K–Q1 (if 10 . . . K–K2; 11 N–N4ch wins the Queen); 11 N–B6ch, QPxN; 12 Q–K8 mate.

[5] To stop 13 P–QN4 mate. If 12 . . . P–QR4; 13 BxQ wins easily.

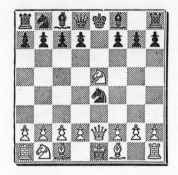

Black to Play. *Black's open-ing mistake must cost him material; but he can hold his loss down to a Pawn—if he plays well. What happens if he moves his attacked Knight?*

WHITE	BLACK	WHITE	BLACK
1 P–K4	P–K4	SEE DIAGRAM	
2 N–KB3	N–KB3	4	N–KB3?[2]
3 NxP	NxP?[1]	5 N–B6ch[3]	....
4 Q–K2	....		

White wins the Queen

[1] Black's last move is a serious error; the policy of imitation can be carried too far. The safe way is 3 ... P–Q3; 4 N–KB3, NxP and if 5 Q–K2, Q–K2 etc.

[2] Completely overlooking the threat. The only way to avoid the loss of more than a Pawn is to play 4 ... Q–K2, as in the next trap.

[3] Black must get out of check, and White plays 6 NxQ.

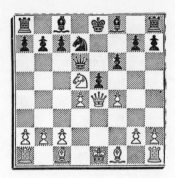

White to Play. *Black's attempt to avoid the loss of a Pawn, will cost him at least the exchange.*

WHITE	BLACK	WHITE	BLACK
1 P–K4	P–K4	9 N–Q5	Q–Q3?
2 N–KB3	N–KB3		SEE DIAGRAM
3 NxP	NxP?	10 BPxP	PxP
4 Q–K2	Q–K2	11 PxP[2]	Q–QB3[3]
5 QxN	P–Q3	12 B–QN5!	Q–KN3[4]
6 P–Q4	P–KB3	13 QxQch	PxQ
7 P–KB4	N–Q2[1]	14 NxPch	....
8 N–QB3!	QPxN		

White wins the exchange and two Pawns

[1] The immediate capture of the Knight would have left Black a Pawn down. He tries for more—and the result is a catastrophe.

[2] Now Black cannot recover the Pawn. If 11 . . . QxP; 12 NxPch, K–Q1 (Black's Queen is pinned) 13 QxQ followed by 14 NxR. Or if 11 . . . NxP; 12 B–KB4 and the pinned Knight is lost.

[3] To guard against the threatened 12 NxPch.

[4] If 12 . . . QxB; 13 NxPch, or if 12 . . . Q–B4; 13 B–K3 and White wins the Queen.

Black to Play. *White's last move was a blunder, as Black breaks out of the pin with winning threats.*

WHITE	BLACK	WHITE	BLACK
1 P–K4	P–K4	6 B–N5?[2]	....
2 N–KB3	N–KB3	SEE DIAGRAM	
3 NxP	N–B3[1]	6	NxP!
4 NxN	QPxN	7 BxQ[3]	BxPch
5 P–Q3	B–QB4	8 K–K2	B–N5

White has been checkmated

[1] Black gives up a Pawn to get his pieces into play quickly.
[2] A premature pin, as Black demonstrates brilliantly. 6 B–K2 and then 7 O–O is correct.
[3] If 7 PxN, Black wins the Queen with 7 . . . BxPch; 8 K–K2, B–N5ch; 9 KxB, QxQ.

Black to Play. *White has fallen into a clever trap, and loses to a Queen fork combination.*

WHITE	BLACK	WHITE	BLACK
1 P–K4	P–K4	10 R–K1?[2]	....
2 N–KB3	N–KB3	SEE DIAGRAM	
3 NxP	P–Q3	10	BxPch!
4 N–KB3	NxP	11 KxB	NxP
5 P–Q4	P–Q4	12 Q–K2	NxB
6 B–Q3	B–Q3	13 QxN[3]	BxN[4]
7 O–O	B–KN5	14 QxB	Q–R5ch
8 P–B4	O–O!?[1]	15 Q–R3	QxR
9 PxP	P–KB4		

Black has won the exchange

[1] Marshall's tricky variation; Black sacrifices a Pawn (and in some cases two Pawns) in order to get ingenious attacking chances.

[2] 10 N–B3 is correct. The text allows a neat reply.

[3] Now the Queen, one of the guards of White's King Rook, has been lured away.

[4] And now the other guard has been removed.

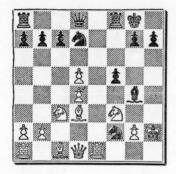

White to Play. If White moves his Queen, which is attacked, Black wins as in the previous trap. But White has a winning line of play.

WHITE	BLACK	WHITE	BLACK
1 P–K4	P–K4	10 N–B3	N–Q2
2 N–KB3	N–KB3	11 R–K1	BxPch?[1]
3 NxP	P–Q3	12 KxB	NxP
4 N–KB3	NxP	SEE DIAGRAM	
5 P–Q4	P–Q4	13 B–KN5	NxQ[2]
6 B–Q3	B–Q3	14 BxQ	NxN[3]
7 O–O	B–KN5	15 B–K7	NxQP
8 P–B4	O–O!?	16 BxR	RxB
9 PxP	P–KB4	17 N–K5[4]	....

White has won the exchange

[1] Black is deceived by the apparent similarity of this position to that of the previous trap.

[2] If 13 ... QxB; 14 NxQ, BxQ; 15 QRxB, NxR, 16 NxN, and White has won two pieces for a Rook.

[3] If 14 ... QRxB; 15 QRxN and White is a piece ahead.

[4] White has a probable but technically difficult win.

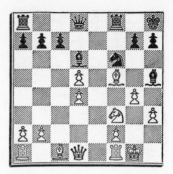

Black to Play. *Black may retreat his attacked Bishop, or he may try a counter-attack. No matter what his choice is, he loses.*

WHITE	BLACK	WHITE	BLACK
1 P–K4	P–K4	12 NxN	PxN
2 N–KB3	N–KB3	13 BxP	N–B3
3 NxP	P–Q3	14 B–B5	K–R1
4 N–KB3	NxP	15 P–KN4!	....
5 P–Q4	P–Q4	SEE DIAGRAM	
6 B–Q3	B–Q3	15	NxQP[1]
7 O–O	B–KN5	16 B–K6!	B–B2[2]
8 P–B4	O–O!?	17 N–N5!	BxB[3]
9 PxP	P–KB4	18 NxB	Q–R5[4]
10 N–B3	N–Q2	19 Q–N3![5]	....
11 P–KR3!	B–R4		

White wins the exchange

[1] So that if 16 PxB, RxB with good chances. On 15 . . . B–B2, White continues with 16 B–K6, either remaining two Pawns ahead or transposing into the text line.

[2] Forced, as two pieces are attacked.

[3] If 17 . . . B–N1; 18 BxB, KxB (18 . . . RxB; 19 N–B7 is mate); 19 N–K6 wins the exchange.

[4] Hoping for 19 NxR, QxP; 20 P–B4, Q–N6ch forcing a draw.

[5] White guards the Rook Pawn, keeps the Rook under observation, and threatens to win the Queen with 20 B–N5.

Black to Play. White offers his Queen Pawn as bait. On the surface, 9 ... NxQP looks good for Black, as he will then be hitting again at White's pinned Knight. What is wrong with this capture?

WHITE	BLACK	WHITE	BLACK
1 P–K4	P–K4	8 R–K1	B–KN5
2 N–KB3	N–KB3	9 P–B4	....
3 NxP	P–Q3	SEE DIAGRAM	
4 N–KB3	NxP	9	NxQP?[1]
5 P–Q4	P–Q4	10 BxN	PxB[2]
6 B–Q3	N–QB3	11 QxN	PxN[3]
7 O–O	B–K2	12 QxB	....

White has won a piece

[1] 9 ... N–B3 should be played.
[2] Or 10 ... NxNch; 11 BxN, and White wins a piece.
[3] If 11 ... QxQ; 12 NxQ leaves White a piece up. Or if 11 ... BxN; 12 QxQch, RxQ; 13 PxB with the same result.

Black to Play. *Black is a Pawn ahead, but behind in development — and White threatens to recover his Pawn. What is Black's best move?*

WHITE	BLACK	WHITE	BLACK
1 P–K4	P–K4	6 N–N5!	B–K3
2 N–KB3	N–KB3	7 BxB	PxB
3 B–B4	NxP	8 Q–B3[2]	Q–Q2[3]
4 N–B3	NxN	9 QxP	Q–B3[4]
5 QPxN	....	10 Q–B8ch	K–K2
SEE DIAGRAM		11 QxKPch	K–Q1
5	P–Q3?[1]	12 N–B7	....

Black has been checkmated

[1] Strangely enough, this natural move is bad, and the unnatural 5 . . . P–KB3 is correct.

[2] Threatening 9 Q–B7 mate, as well as 9 QxP,N–Q2; 10 NxKP, Q–B1; 11 QxR, QxQ; 12 NxBPch winning a Rook.

[3] If 8 . . . Q–B1; 9 Q–B7ch, K–Q1; 10 NxPch wins the Queen.

[4] Black saves his Rook—but walks into a mate.

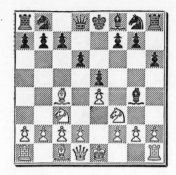

White to Play. *Black h a s violated opening principles by making time - wasting Pawn moves, instead of developing his pieces. And his Bishop "pin" was premature.*

WHITE	BLACK	WHITE	BLACK
1 P-K4	P-K4	SEE DIAGRAM	
2 N-KB3	P-Q3	5 NxP![2]	BxQ[3]
3 B-B4	B-N5	6 BxPch	K-K2
4 N-B3	P-KR3?[1]	7 N-Q5[4]	....

Black has been checkmated

[1] Better is bringing out one of the Knights to B3.

[2] This brilliant move is possible because Black has neglected his development so flagrantly.

[3] If 5 . . . PxN; 6 QxB, and White is a Pawn to the good, with a position which should win easily.

[4] One of the oldest, and still one of the most frequently seen traps.

White to Play. Black hoped that his last move, attacking White's Queen, would give him time to play 8 . . . N–N4—but he failed to foresee White's mating combination.

WHITE	BLACK	WHITE	BLACK
1 P–K4	P–K4	SEE DIAGRAM	
2 N–KB3	P–Q3	8 B–B7ch	K–K2
3 B–B4	P–KB4?[1]	9 QxNch!!	KxQ[4]
4 P–Q4	N–KB3	10 N–Q5ch	K–K4
5 N–B3	KPxP[2]	11 N–B3ch	KxP
6 QxP	B–Q2	12 N–B3[5]	....
7 N–KN5	N–B3[3]		

Black has been checkmated

[1] Too risky. 3 . . . B–K2, followed by 4 . . . N–KB3, is better.

[2] Only facilitates White's development.

[3] A very natural move, as it brings out a piece, attacks White's Queen, and threatens to occupy the center. But Black has walked into a beautifully constructed trap.

[4] Or 9 . . . PxQ; 10 N–Q5 mate.

[5] The mate, accomplished by retreating both Knights, is unique.

White to Play. Black's exposure of his own king is a fatal mistake and leads to an early checkmate.

WHITE	BLACK	WHITE	BLACK
1 P–K4	P–K4	7 Q–B5ch	K–B3
2 N–KB3	P–Q3	8 QxP(K5)	P–QR3[3]
3 B–B4	P–KB4?	9 P–Q5ch	K–B4[4]
4 P–Q4	BPxP?[1]	10 B–K3ch	KxB[5]
SEE DIAGRAM		11 Q–Q4ch	K–N4
5 NxP!	PxN	12 N–B3ch	K–R4
6 Q–R5ch	K–Q2[2]	13 Q–R4	....

Black has been checkmated

[1] Intensifying the error of the previous move.

[2] If 6 ... K–K2; 7 QxPch, B–K3; 8 QxB mate. Or if 6 ... P–N3; 7 QxKPch wins the King Rook.

[3] To stop White's threat of 9 Q–N5ch, K–Q3; 10 Q–Q5ch, K–K2; 11 Q–K5ch, B–K3; 12 QxB mate.

[4] 9 ... K–N3 also loses quickly.

[5] If 10 ... K–N5; 11 Q–B3ch, K–R5; 12 P–N3 mate.

White to Play. *White takes advantage of Black's cramped position, and plays a combination to win the Queen.*

WHITE	BLACK	WHITE	BLACK
1 P–K4	P–K4	7 N–K6!!	Q–K1[2]
2 N–KB3	P–Q3	8 NxBP	Q–Q1
3 B–B4	B–K2	9 Q–R5ch![3]	P–N3
4 P–Q4	PxP	10 Q–Q5ch	K–B3
5 NxP	N–Q2?[1]	11 B–N5ch	K–N2
SEE DIAGRAM		12 N–K6ch[4]	....
6 BxPch!	KxB		

White wins the Queen

[1] Allowing a pretty combination.
[2] If 7 . . . KxN; 8 Q–Q5ch, K–B3; 9 Q–B5 mate.
[3] An important move, which deprives Black's King of a flight square at KN3.
[4] The Knight fork wins the Queen "to begin with."

White to Play. *White profits by the fact that Black has "smothered" his own Queen, and forces a quick win.*

WHITE	BLACK	WHITE	BLACK
1 P–K4	P–K4	8 P–KR3[1]	R–K1
2 N–KB3	P–Q3	9 R–K1	N–Q2?[2]
3 B–B4	B–K2		SEE DIAGRAM
4 P–Q4	PxP	10 BxPch!	KxB[3]
5 NxP	N–KB3	11 N–K6!!	KxN[4]
6 N–QB3	N–B3	12 Q–Q5ch	K–B3
7 O–O	O–O	13 Q–KB5	....

Black has been checkmated

[1] To cut down the scope of Black's Queen Bishop.

[2] Removing the most important defensive piece of a King side castled position. This is usually dangerous, and is most cases permits a decisive break-through. Better would have been 9 . . . N–K4.

[3] If Black refuses the Bishop by 10 . . . K–B1 or 10 . . . K–R1, then White does not take the Rook, but plays 11 N–K6 winning the Queen.

[4] He saves his Queen, but now he cannot prevent mate.

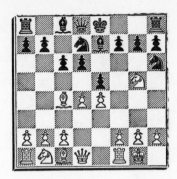

White to Play. Black's entire system of defense is inferior, but his last move leads to quick loss of the game.

WHITE	BLACK	WHITE	BLACK
1 P–K4	P–K4	SEE DIAGRAM	
2 N–KB3	P–Q3	7 N–K6!	PxN[2]
3 P–Q4	N–Q2	8 BxN	PxB[3]
4 B–QB4	P–QB3	9 Q–R5ch	K–B1
5 N–N5	N–R3	10 BxP[4]	Q–K1
6 O–O	B–K2?[1]	11 QxRP	....

Black has been checkmated

[1] 6 . . . N–N3 is better, but the outlook for Black's game remains poor.

[2] If 7 . . . Q–N3; 8 NxPch followed by 9 BxN wins for White.

[3] If 8 . . . N–N3; 9 BxNP, KR–N1; 10 Q–R5ch, K–Q2; 11 BxPch, K–B2 (if 11 . . . KxB; 12 Q–B5 is mate); 12 BxR wins the exchange.

[4] Intending 11 Q–B7 mate.

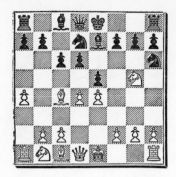

White to Play. *Black's last move seemed to be logical, but remarkably enough it leads to the loss of his Queen!*

WHITE	BLACK	WHITE	BLACK
1 P–K4	P–K4	7 BxPch!	NxB[2]
2 N–KB3	P–Q3	8 N–K6	Q–N3[3]
3 P–Q4	N–Q2	9 P–R5	Q–N5ch
4 B–QB4	P–QB3	10 B–Q2	Q–B5
5 N–N5	N–R3	11 N–B7ch	K–Q1[4]
6 P–QR4	B–K2?[1]	12 P–QN3	QxQP
SEE DIAGRAM		13 N–K6ch[5]	....

White wins the Queen

[1] That this should be the losing move, is a tribute to the subtlety of the trap. 6 . . . N–N3 is relatively best.

[2] Forced, as after 7 . . . K–B1; 8 N–K6ch wins the Queen.

[3] Or 8 . . . Q–R4ch; 9 B–Q2, Q–N3; 10 P–R5, QxNP; 11 B–B3, Q–N4; 12 N–B7ch wins the Queen.

[4] 11 . . . K–B1 loses in the same way.

[5] The number of Knight forks at White's disposal, in this trap, is remarkable.

114 Philidor Defense

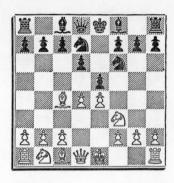

White to Play. *Black's last move threatened White's King Pawn — but the threat is not only made harmless by White's reply, but it is White who wins the Pawn!*

WHITE	BLACK	WHITE	BLACK
1 P–K4	P–K4	6 NxN	PxN
2 N–KB3	P–Q3	7 BxPch	KxB
3 P–Q4	N–Q2	8 QxQ	B–N5ch[3]
4 B–QB4	KN–B3?[1]	9 Q–Q2	BxQch
SEE DIAGRAM		10 NxB[4]	....
5 PxP	QNxP[2]		

White has won a Pawn

[1] Black's best move is 4 . . . P–QB3.

[2] If 5 . . . PxP; 6 N–N5 wins. Or if 5 . . . KNxP; 6 Q–Q5, threatening mate and the Knight, wins a piece.

[3] Regaining his Queen.

[4] As White has no positional weaknesses, the Pawn plus is enough to win.

White to Play. *Black has won a Pawn, and now threatens White's Rook. It may look good, but Black is in a trap which costs him his Queen.*

WHITE	BLACK	WHITE	BLACK
1 P–K4	P–K4	7 Q–Q3	B–N5
2 N–KB3	P–Q3	8 B–N5	QxP?³
3 P–Q4	N–Q2	SEE DIAGRAM	
4 B–QB4	N–N3?¹	9 Q–N5ch!	P–B3⁴
5 B–N3	PxP	10 BxPch	KxB
6 QxP²	Q–B3	11 QxQ	....

White has won the Queen

¹ Another deviation from the straight and narrow path. Black moves the same piece twice, to put it on a worse square!

² Disappointing Black, who would have liked 6 NxP, P–QB4; 7 N–KB3, P–B5, winning the Bishop.

³ Black soon learns to his sorrow that the "unprotected" Knight Pawn is tainted.

⁴ If 9 . . . B–Q2 (or 9 . . . N–Q2); 10 BxPch wins the Queen in the same way.

White to Play. *Black's apparently normal development of the Bishop is a mistake which loses at least a Pawn.*

WHITE	BLACK	WHITE	BLACK
1 P–K4	P–K4	6 Q–Q5	N–N3[3]
2 N–KB3	P–Q3	7 QxPch	K–Q2
3 P–Q4	N–Q2	8 NxPch	K–Q3
4 B–QB4	B–K2?[1]	9 N–Q3	NxB[4]
	SEE DIAGRAM	10 Q–Q5	....
5 PxP	PxP?[2]		

Black has been checkmated

[1] In the Hanham line of this defense, characterized by 3 . . . N–Q2, it is imperative to follow up with 4 . . . P–QB3.
[2] The lesser evil is 5 . . . NxP; 6 NxN, PxN; 7 Q–R5, and White wins a valuable Pawn.
[3] If 6 . . . N–R3; 7 BxN wins.
[4] Losing at once, but Black is two Pawns down, and has no saving alternative.

White to Play. *With his last move Black prevented a possible N–N5 by White — but the loss of time is fatal.*

WHITE	BLACK	WHITE	BLACK
1 P–K4	P–K4	7 NxPch	K–B3
2 N–KB3	P–Q3	8 Q–Q5	N–K2[3]
3 P–Q4	N–Q2	9 Q–B7ch	KxN
4 B–QB4	P–KR3?[1]	10 B–B4ch	K–Q5
SEE DIAGRAM		11 Q–K6	N–QB4
5 PxP	PxP[2]	12 B–K3	....
6 BxPch!	KxB		

Black has been checkmated

[1] As stated before, 4 . . . P–QB3 must be played.

[2] If 5 . . . NxP; 6 NxN, PxN; 7 BxPch wins.

[3] This loses quickly, as does 8 . . . Q–K2; 9 N–N4ch, K–N3; 10 Q–B5 mate. The best defense is 8 . . . Q–K1, but after 9 P–KB4 White's attack remains powerful and Black has difficulty obtaining an orderly development.

White to Play. Once again Black's "smothered" Queen is a target for White's attack.

WHITE	BLACK	WHITE	BLACK
1 P–K4	P–K4	9 BxPch!	KxB
2 N–KB3	P–Q3	10 N–K6!!	KxN
3 P–Q4	N–KB3	11 Q–B4ch	P–Q4[3]
4 N–B3	QN–Q2	12 PxPch	K–B2[4]
5 B–QB4	B–K2	13 P–Q6ch	N–Q4[5]
6 O–O	O–O	14 PxB	QxP
7 Q–K2	PxP[1]	15 NxN	Q–K3
8 NxP	R–K1?[2]	16 Q–B4ch	K–N1
	SEE DIAGRAM	17 NxP	....

White wins the exchange

[1] Surrendering the center improves White's game, not Black's.

[2] Black should play 8 . . . N–K4.

[3] If 11 . . . K–K4; 12 P–B4 mate. Or if 11 . . . N–Q4; 12 QxNch, K–B3; 13 Q–B5 mate.

[4] Other King moves lead to mate, or loss of the Queen. If 12 . . . K–K4; 13 Q–B4 mate. If 12 . . . K–B4; 13 Q–Q3ch, K–K4; 14 R–K1ch, K–Q3; 15 R–K6ch, K–B4; 16 Q–N5ch, K–Q5; 17 N–K2 mate. Finally, if 12 . . . K–Q3; 13 N–N5ch, K–K4; 14 B–B4ch, K–B4; 15 BxP wins Black's Queen.

[5] Forced, else 14 PxP follows, winning the Queen.

White to Play. *Black's King is exposed to all sorts of dangers. White can afford to sacrifice material for a mating attack.*

WHITE	BLACK	WHITE	BLACK
1 P–K4	P–K4	8 KNxKP	PxN[3]
2 N–KB3	P–Q3	9 Q–R5ch	P–N3[4]
3 P–Q4	P–KB4?[1]	10 Q–K5	R–N1
4 QPxP	BPxP	11 B–KN5	Q–Q3[5]
5 N–N5	P–Q4	12 R–Q1	QxP[6]
6 P–K6	N–KR3[2]	13 R–Q8ch	K–B2
7 N–QB3	P–B3	14 B–QB4	QxB
SEE DIAGRAM		15 Q–B6	....

Black has been checkmated

[1] An old-fashioned move which has virtually disappeared, because of the resulting weakening of the King-side.

[2] To prevent 7 N–B7. Black's position may already be considered as lost.

[3] Black could hold out longer with 8 . . . N–B4.

[4] If 9 . . . K–K2; 10 B–N5ch wins the Queen.

[5] If 11 . . . B–Q3; 12 R–Q1 regains the piece with a winning attack.

[6] Or 12 . . . QxQ; 13 R–Q8 mate.

White to Play. Black offers a Pawn, in return for which he expects to threaten an embarrassing pin, as well as a Pawn fork, winning a piece. Should White take the Pawn?

WHITE	BLACK	WHITE	BLACK
1 P–K4	P–K4	11 QxQch	KxQ
2 N–KB3	P–KB4	12 BxPch	K–K2
3 NxP!	Q–B3	13 NxR	B–K3
4 P–Q4	P–Q3	14 B–N5ch!	N–B3
5 N–B4	PxP	15 BxB!	KxB
6 N–B3	P–B3?[1]	16 O–O–O	QN–Q2[4]
SEE DIAGRAM		17 KR–K1ch	K–B4
7 NxP!	Q–K3	18 B–R4!	P–KN4
8 Q–K2	P–Q4	19 B–N3	B–N2[5]
9 N(K4)–Q6ch	K–Q2[2]	20 N–B7	....
10 N–B7!!	PxN[3]		

White has won the exchange and two Pawns

[1] More usual is 6 . . . Q–N3, when White can get the advantage with 7 N–K3, N–KB3; 8 B–B4. The text offers White a Pawn, which to all appearances, he cannot safely accept.

[2] If 9 . . . BxN; 10 NxBch, K–Q2; 11 QxQch, KxQ; 12 NxB, N–Q2; 13 NxP winning a Pawn for White.

[3] 10 . . . QxQch; 11 BxQ, PxN; 12 NxR, K–K2; 13 B–N5ch!, N–B3; 14 BxP transposes to the main-play.

[4] Still hoping to trap the Knight.

[5] If 19 . . . B–N5; 20 P–QB3 wins.

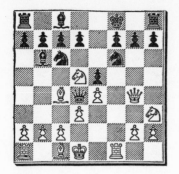

White to Play. White gives his opponent no time to consolidate his forces, but crashes through with a magnificent winning combination.

WHITE	BLACK	WHITE	BLACK
1 P–K4	P–K4	9 R–B1[4]	N–B3
2 N–QB3	N–QB3		SEE DIAGRAM
3 B–B4	B–B4	10 RxN!	P–Q3[5]
4 Q–N4	Q–B3?[1]	11 QxPch!!	KxQ
5 N–Q5!	QxPch[2]	12 B–R6ch	K–N1
6 K–Q1	K–B1	13 R–N6ch!	RPxR
7 N–R3	Q–Q5	14 N–B6	....
8 P–Q3[3]	B–N3		

Black has been checkmated

[1] Tempting, but risky. 4 ... K–B1, or 4 ... P–KN3 is much safer.

[2] Black has no choice, as he can no longer guard his King Knight Pawn and Queen Bishop Pawn.

[3] Threatening to win the Queen with 9 P–B3.

[4] Now the threat is 10 NxB, RPxN; 11 RxPch, with immediate ruin for Black.

[5] To gain time by attacking White's Queen. If instead 10 ... PxR; 11 B–R6ch, K–K1; 12 Q–N7 with an easy win. But the text leads to an exquisite finish.

White to Play. *Black's inferior opening play has led to this losing position. Now White unleashes a vicious attack which culminates in the win of Black's Queen.*

WHITE	BLACK	WHITE	BLACK
1 P–K4	P–K4	9 Q–R4	BxN[2]
2 N–QB3	N–QB3	10 QxB	N–R4[3]
3 B–B4	B–B4		SEE DIAGRAM
4 Q–N4	Q–B3?	11 R–KB1	NxB[4]
5 N–Q5!	QxPch	12 Q–Q7![5]	P–KB3
6 K–Q1	K–B1	13 NxKBP!	Q–B7[6]
7 N–R3	Q–Q5	14 RxQ	BxR
8 P–Q3	P–Q3[1]	15 N–R5[7]	....

And White wins

[1] Black varies from the previous trap.

[2] In order to be able to move his Queen to B7 after P–B3.

[3] If 10 . . . Q–B7; 11 B–Q2 with serious threats to the Queen.

[4] Guarding against the menace of 12 P–B3, which would now be answered by 12 . . . NxPch; 13 BxN, Q–R5ch.

[5] Object: mate in one.

[6] He must lose the Queen, or be mated. If 13 . . . PxN; 14 RxPch, NxR; 15 B–R6ch, K–N1; 16 Q–N7 mate.

[7] A possible finish might be: 15 . . . P–KN3 (White was threatening 16 QxNPch, or 16 Q–B5ch, or 16 PxNJ; 16 B–R6ch, NxB; 17 Q–N7ch, K–K1; 18 N–B6ch, K–Q1; 19 Q–Q7 mate.

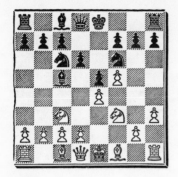

Black to Play. *White h a s exposed his King to danger by his flank attack. Black quickly demonstrates the weakness of White's position.*

WHITE	BLACK	WHITE	BLACK
1 P–K4	P–K4	6	P–Q4![3]
2 N–QB3	N–QB3	7 NxKP	NxP!
3 P–B4	B–B4	8 N–B3[4]	Q–R5ch!![5]
4 N–B3	P–Q3	9 NxQ	B–B7ch
5 P–B5[1]	N–B3	10 K–K2	N–Q5ch
6 P–KR3?[2]	....	11 K–Q3	N–B4

SEE DIAGRAM

White has been checkmated

[1] Premature, as Black demonstrates convincingly.

[2] Intending to support the advanced Bishop Pawn with 7 P–KN4.

[3] Smashing White's center.

[4] To prevent Black's Queen from checking.

[5] An unpleasant surprise.

White to Play. *Black, who has been lured into attacking prematurely, hopes to make something of his threatened discovered check — but White has ideas of his own!*

WHITE	BLACK	WHITE	BLACK
1 P–K4	P–K4		SEE DIAGRAM
2 N–QB3	N–KB3	7 N–B3	Q–R4
3 P–B4	P–Q4	8 NxP	K–Q1[3]
4 BPxP	NxP	9 N–B4!	Q–N5[4]
5 P–Q3	Q–R5ch?[1]	10 B–R3	....
6 P–N3	NxP[2]		

White wins the Queen

[1] The proper play is 5 . . . NxN; 6 PxN, P–Q5.

[2] Somewhat better was 6 . . . NxN; 7 PxN, Q–Q1, although White would still have the superior game.

[3] Leads to disaster. However, if 8 . . . NxR; 9 NxPch, K–Q1; 10 NxR, B–N5; 11 B–N2, when Black's Knight is lost, and his King is insecure.

[4] If 9 . . . Q–R3; 10 N–K2, Q–R4; 11 NxN wins a piece.

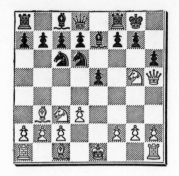

White to Play. Black is trying to escape mate by chasing White's Knight away—but the Knight stays, and takes an important part in the mating finale.

WHITE	BLACK	WHITE	BLACK
1 P–K4	P–K4	8 N–KN5	P–KR3[3]
2 N–QB3	N–KB3		SEE DIAGRAM
3 B–B4	NxP[1]	9 P–KR4![4]	N–K1[5]
4 Q–R5	N–Q3	10 N–Q5!	N–B3
5 B–N3	B–K2	11 Q–N6![6]	PxQ[7]
6 P–Q3	O–O?[2]	12 NxBch	K–R1
7 N–B3	N–B3	13 NxP	....

Black has been checkmated

[1] A less dangerous line is 3 . . . N–B3; 4 P–Q3, B–N5; 5 B–KN5, P–KR3; 6 BxN, BxNch etc.

[2] This plausible move leads to serious trouble. 6 . . . N–B3; 7 N–B3, P–KN3 is better.

[3] The alternative 8 . . . BxN; 9 BxB, Q–K1 (if 9 . . . N–K2; 10 N–Q5 wins) ; 10 N–Q5, threatening 11 NxP, is unpleasant.

[4] With this threat: 10 Q–N6, PxN; 11 PxP, R–K1; 12 Q–R7ch, K–B1; 13 Q–R8 mate.

[5] If 9 . . . PxN; 10 PxP followed by 11 Q–R8 mate.

[6] Now threatening 12 NxNch, BxN; 13 Q–R7 mate.

[7] If 11 . . . PxN; 12 NxNch, BxN; 13 PxP, R–K1; 14 QxBP mate.

Black to Play. *With two Knights in the vicinity of White's King and Queen, look at every possible capture or check, in order to force a winning Knight fork.*

WHITE	BLACK	WHITE	BLACK
1 P–K4	P–K4	6 B–N3	B–N5ch
2 P–Q4	PxP	7 P–B3[1]	B–B4![2]
3 QxP	N–QB3	8 Q–N3?[3]	....
4 Q–K3	N–B3	SEE DIAGRAM	
5 B–B4	N–K4	8	BxPch!![4]

Black wins the Queen

[1] 7 B–Q2 is better, for it creates no weaknesses and aids White's development.

[2] The Bishop retreats, but with gain of time. If now 8 QxB?, N–Q6ch wins the Queen.

[3] Loses at once, although the refutation is not too obvious. 8 Q–K2 would have prolonged the game, although Black would have had a considerable advantage in development.

[4] A beautiful move! If 9 QxB, N–Q6ch; or if 9 KxB, NxPch. In either case, a Knight fork does the trick.

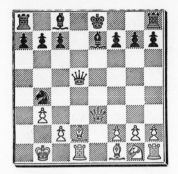

White to Play. Black's Queen seems to be safe from the threat of a discovered attack, as White's Rook is unprotected. But a combination provides the solution.

WHITE	BLACK	WHITE	BLACK
1 P–K4	P–K4	9 NxN	NxPch?[2]
2 P–Q4	PxP	10 K–N1	QxN
3 QxP	N–QB3	11 P–QN3	N–N5[3]
4 Q–K3	N–B3		SEE DIAGRAM
5 B–Q2	B–K2	12 QxBch!	KxQ
6 N–QB3	P–Q4[1]	13 BxNch	K–K3
7 PxP	N–QN5	14 B–B4[4]	....
8 O–O–O	KNxP		

White wins a piece

[1] An excellent idea in principle, but it would be wiser to delay this move, and play it after castling.

[2] Not content with 9 .... NxN, Black stops to snatch a Pawn.

[3] So far all very plausible.

[4] The pin regains the Queen, leaving White a piece up.

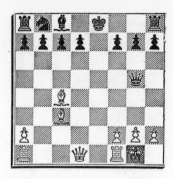

White to Play. With all the lines open to his two Bishops and open files for his Queen and two Rooks, White has an overwhelming attack.

WHITE	BLACK	WHITE	BLACK
1 P–K4	P–K4	9 NxN	BxN?
2 P–Q4	PxP	10 BxB	Q–N4[2]
3 P–QB3	PxP		SEE DIAGRAM
4 B–QB4	PxP	11 R–K1ch	K–Q1[3]
5 BxP	N–KB3[1]	12 P–B4	QxP[4]
6 N–QB3	B–N5?	13 BxNP	R–N1
7 N–K2	NxP?	14 Q–N4!	QxQ[5]
8 O–O	NxN?	15 B–B6	....

Black has been checkmated

[1] The first of a series of bad moves. Black should play 5 ....
P–Q4. Then the logical continuation would be 6 BxQP, N–KB3; 7 BxPch, KxB; 8 QxQ, B–N5ch; 9 Q–Q2, BxQch; 10 NxQ, P–B4, with a good game.

[2] If 10 .... O–O; 11 Q–N4, P–KN3; 12 Q–Q4 and 13 Q–N7 mate.

[3] If 11 .... K–B1; 12 B–N4ch, P–Q3; 13 BxPch wins at once.

[4] Or 12 .... Q–B4ch; 13 B–Q4, QxB; 14 BxNP wins.

[5] On 14 ... Q–Q3; 15 B–B6ch, QxB; 16 QxR is mate.

White to Play. White has removed Black's Knight which protected the Bishop, and now he can win a piece. If he takes it he will be mated. Can you see how?

WHITE	BLACK	WHITE	BLACK
1 P–K4	P–K4	8 Q–R4ch	N–B3
2 P–Q4	PxP	9 BxNch?[4]	PxB
3 P–QB3	PxP	SEE DIAGRAM	
4 B–QB4	PxP	10 QxB?	Q–Q8ch
5 BxP	P–Q4![1]	11 Q–K1	B–R3ch
6 BxQP	B–N5ch	12 N–K2	BxNch
7 K–B1[2]	N–KB3![3]	13 K–N1	QxQ

White has been checkmated

[1] Black has the right idea. He returns one Pawn in order to open up lines for his pieces.

[2] White is so eager to avoid exchanges, that he willingly forfeits the privilege of castling.

[3] Superficially this is merely an obvious developing move. Actually it is more, for it involves the offer of a piece.

[4] White should simply have continued his development, but he finds the lure of winning a piece irresistible.

Black to Play. *The open King file, and the menacing position of White's Queen on that file, indicate a defensive move for Black.*

WHITE	BLACK	WHITE	BLACK
1 P–K4	P–K4	6 Q–K2	....
2 P–KB4	PxP	SEE DIAGRAM	
3 N–KB3	P–Q4	6	BxN?[2]
4 N–B3	PxP	7 N–B6![3]	....
5 NxP	B–KN5?[1]		

Black has been checkmated

[1] Somewhat premature; Knights into play before Bishops is a good rule.

[2] By capturing the Knight, and thereby attacking White's Queen with his Bishop, Black expects the immediate recapture of the Bishop. Black forgets that permitting a double check is nearly always disastrous. He should have played 6 . . . Q–K2.

[3] A lightning K. O. by double check and mate.

Black to Play. *White's last move exposed him to a simultaneous Knight fork and discovered attack.*

WHITE	BLACK	WHITE	BLACK
1 P–K4	P–K4	7 O–O?¹	....
2 P–KB4	PxP	SEE DIAGRAM	
3 N–KB3	P–Q4	7	N–K6!
4 PxP	N–KB3	8 BxN²	BxB
5 P–Q4	NxP	9 BxP³	BxR
6 B–B4	B–K3		

Black has won the exchange

¹ Strangely enough, White gets into trouble with this obvious move. 7 Q–K2 avoids the ensuing embarrassment.

² Forced, as Black's Knight attacks Queen, Rook and Bishop.

³ Of course 9 R–K1, PxB is even worse for White.

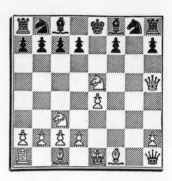

Black to Play. *Black is a Rook ahead, but far behind in development, and White has many threats. In such positions one must not attempt to hold on to material.*

WHITE	BLACK	WHITE	BLACK
1 P–K4	P–K4	9 Q–R5	....
2 P–KB4	PxP	SEE DIAGRAM	
3 N–KB3	P–KN4	9	B–K2?[2]
4 N–B3	P–N5	10 NxBP	N–KB3
5 N–K5	Q–R5ch	11 N–Q6ch	K–Q1[3]
6 P–N3!?	PxP	12 Q–K8ch!	R(or N)xQ
7 QxP![1]	P–N7ch	13 N–B7[4]	....
8 QxQ	PxR(Q)		

Black has been checkmated

[1] Very surprising.

[2] Black's best chance was to play 9 ... N–KR3; 10 P–Q4, P–Q3; 11 BxN, PxN etc.

[3] Or 11 ... K–B1; 12 Q–B7 mate.

[4] The always thrilling "smothered mate."

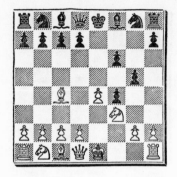

White to Play. Black has lost time, and exposed his King to attack, by making time-wasting and dangerous Pawn moves. White proceeds to rip open Black's King side position.

WHITE	BLACK	WHITE	BLACK
1 P–K4	P–K4	5 NxP!	PxN[2]
2 P–KB4	PxP	6 Q–R5ch	K–K2
3 N–KB3	P–KN4	7 Q–B7ch	K–Q3
4 B–B4	P–KB3?[1]	8 Q–Q5ch	K–K2
	SEE DIAGRAM	9 Q–K5	....

Black has been checkmated

[1] 4 . . . B–N2 is indicated. The text move is bad not only because it defies principle (in the opening one should make only one or two Pawn moves) but it exposes Black's King to an immediate and devastating attack.

[2] Black has no choice but to accept the sacrifice. On other moves White continues with 6 Q–R5ch, or 6 N–B7.

White to Play. *Black has placed his Queen on a dangerous square. White now weaves a net around the Queen, from which there is no escape.*

WHITE	BLACK	WHITE	BLACK
1 P–K4	P–K4	6 BxPch!	K–Q1[2]
2 P–KB4	PxP	7 P–KR3	Q–N6
3 B–B4	Q–R5ch	8 N–B3	B–B4[3]
4 K–B1	P–KN4	9 P–Q4	B–N5
5 N–KB3	Q–N5?[1]	10 N–K2	....

SEE DIAGRAM

White wins the Queen

[1] A fatal mistake. 5 . . . Q–R4 is in order.

[2] If 6 . . . KxB; 7 N–K5ch wins the Queen. Now that White's Bishop is at B7, Black's Queen cannot escape by way of R4.

[3] A last ray of hope against the threatened N–K2. If White is hasty and moves 9 N–K2, then 9 . . . Q–B7 is mate.

White to Play. Black's last move was played by instinct and without thought. The punishment for making a time-wasting Pawn move in a wide open position is swift and sure.

WHITE	BLACK	WHITE	BLACK
1 P–K4	P–K4		SEE DIAGRAM
2 P–KB4	PxP	7 BxPch![2]	QxB
3 B–B4	Q–R5ch	8 N–K5	Q–N2[3]
4 K–B1	P–KN4	9 Q–R5ch	K–Q1[4]
5 N–KB3	Q–R4	10 N–B7ch	K–K2
6 P–KR4	P–KR3?[1]	11 NxR[5]	....

White has a winning advantage

[1] Black need not hurry about protecting his Knight Pawn, as White's Knight and Rook Pawn are pinned, and cannot capture the Pawn. He should simply develop with 6 . . . B–N2.

[2] A surprise! Black dare not reply 7 . . . KxB as 8 N–K5ch wins Black's Queen.

[3] Or 8 . . . Q–B3; 9 Q–R5ch winning as in the text.

[4] If 9 . . . K–K2; 10 N–N6ch etc.

[5] After 11 . . . QxN; 12 PxP, White also wins the KRP and Black's two minor pieces are no match for White's Rook and Pawns.

Black to Play. *Black can win the exchange with a Knight fork by 9 ... NxPch — but what threats would he be overlooking?*

WHITE	BLACK	WHITE	BLACK
1 P–K4	P–K4	10 K–Q1	NxR[2]
2 P–KB4	B–B4	11 PxP	PxP
3 N–KB3	P–Q3	12 QxP	R–KB1
4 N–B3	N–KB3	13 R–B1	B–K2[3]
5 B–B4	N–B3	14 B–N5	N–R4
6 P–Q3	B–KN5	15 BxPch	K–Q2
7 P–KR3	BxN	16 QxKP[4]	P–B3[5]
8 QxB	N–Q5	17 B–K6ch	K–K1
9 Q–N3	....	18 RxRch	KxR
SEE DIAGRAM		19 Q–R8	....
9	NxPch?[1]		

Black has been checkmated

[1] Black should play 9 . . . Q–K2.

[2] Black has won his Rook, but now comes the counter-attack.

[3] Or 13 . . . N–Q2; 14 BxPch, K–K2; 15 B–Q5ch, K–Q3; 16 N–N5 mate.

[4] Threatening 17 Q–K6 mate.

[5] If 16 . . . N–N2; 17 BxB, QxB; 18 QxN with an easy win for White.

Black to Play. *White's King is exposed to attack from all directions. Defending Black's pseudo-threat of winning the exchange has kept White's Queen inactive.*

WHITE	BLACK	WHITE	BLACK
1 P–K4	P–K4	9 Q–Q1[3]	P–KN3
2 P–KB4	B–B4	10 PxP	....
3 N–KB3	P–Q3	SEE DIAGRAM	
4 N–B3	N–KB3	10	N–R4![4]
5 B–B4	N–B3	11 BxPch[5]	KxB
6 P–Q3	B–KN5[1]	12 O–Och	N–B6ch!
7 P–KR3	BxN	13 K–R1	N–N6
8 QxB	N–Q5[2]		

White has been checkmated

[1] Black can avoid these trappy lines of play by 6 . . . B–K3.
[2] A good alternative is 8 . . . PxP; 9 BxP, N–Q5; 10 Q–N3, N–R4. Or if 9 QxP, N–K4; 10 B–N3, N–R4 etc.
[3] A timid retreat. 9 Q–N3 is correct here.
[4] Threatening 11 . . . Q–R5ch; 12 K–B1, N–N6ch etc.
[5] Sacrificing the Bishop, so that he may castle into safety—or so he thinks!

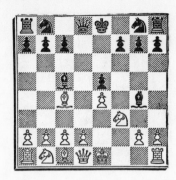

White to Play. The position illustrates an illusory pin. White breaks out of the pin with a gain of material.

WHITE	BLACK	WHITE	BLACK
1 P–K4	P–K4	SEE DIAGRAM	
2 P–KB4	B–B4	6 BxPch	KxB
3 N–KB3	P–Q3	7 NxPch	K–K3
4 B–B4	B–KN5?[1]	8 NxB[3]	....
5 PxP	PxP[2]		

White has won two Pawns

[1] Knights should be developed before Bishops. 4 . . . N–QB3 is correct here.

[2] Not much better is 5 . . . BxN; 6 QxB, when Black cannot play 6 . . . PxP on account of the mating threat at his B2.

[3] A convincing example of the danger of a premature pin.

Black to Play. *With White's King and Queen so far apart, it seems almost incredible that the Queen can be lost by a discovered attack — or a Knight fork!*

WHITE	BLACK	WHITE	BLACK
1 P–K4	P–K4	8 K–Q1	Q–R4
2 P–KB4	B–B4	9 QxP?[3]	....
3 N–KB3	P–Q3	SEE DIAGRAM	
4 B–B4	N–QB3	9	QxPch!
5 P–B3	B–KN5	10 K–B2[4]	QxKPch
6 Q–N3?[1]	BxN	11 P–Q3[5]	N–Q5ch
7 PxB[2]	Q–R5ch		

Black wins the Queen

[1] 6 P–KR3 was necessary here.

[2] If 7 BxPch, K–B1; 8 PxB, Q–R5ch; 9 K–Q1, N–R4; 10 Q–R4, KxB; 11 QxN, Q–B7; 12 QxPch, N–K2, and Black has a winning game.

[3] It is true that after 9 R–B1, KN–K2; 10 QxP, O–O, White's position would be quite bad—but the text loses by a knockout.

[4] On 10 K–K1, B–B7ch; 11 K–B1, B–N6ch; 12 K–N1, Q–B7 is mate.

[5] If 11 K–N3, N–R4ch wins the Queen by a Knight fork, and if 11 K–Q1, QxRch; 12 K–K2 (or 12 K–B2), N–Q5ch wins the Queen by discovered attack.

White to Play. *Black's errors have produced this position. Now White plays and wins the Queen, or checkmates!*

WHITE	BLACK	WHITE	BLACK
1 P–K4	P–K4	7 P–Q4	B–N3?[5]
2 P–KB4	P–Q4	SEE DIAGRAM	
3 KPxP[1]	QxP[2]	8 B–N5ch!	K–Q1[6]
4 N–QB3	Q–K3	9 R–K1	Q–B4
5 N–B3	PxPch	10 R–K8	....
6 K–B2[3]	B–B4ch?[4]		

Black has been checkmated

[1] Not 3 BPxP?, Q–R5ch; 4 P–N3, QxKPch and Black wins a Rook.

[2] 3 .... PxP is good, but best is 3 .... P–K5 as that is in keeping with the spirit of the counter-gambit.

[3] Castling is unimportant in this position, as the King is in no danger.

[4] Bad as this move is, amateurs seem to find it irresistible.

[5] The decisive mistake. 7 .... B–K2 must be played.

[6] On 8 .... P–B3 or other interpositions, 9 R–K1 wins the Queen. Against 8 .... K–B1, White still plays 9 R–K1, winning the Queen, or mating at K8.

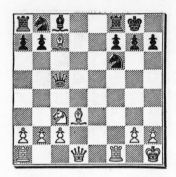

Black to Play. *White offers his Bishop in order to gain time to institute a winning combination. White's method of breaking up the adverse position is highly instructive.*

WHITE	BLACK	WHITE	BLACK
1 P–K4	P–K4	11 B–KB4	Q–QB4
2 P–KB4	P–Q4	12 BxP!	....
3 N–KB3	QPxP	SEE DIAGRAM	
4 NxP	B–Q3	12	QxB
5 P–Q4	PxPe.p.	13 RxN!	PxR
6 BxP	N–KB3	14 Q–R5	P–B4[2]
7 O–O	O–O	15 Q–N5ch	K–R1
8 N–QB3	BxN?[1]	16 Q–B6ch	K–N1
9 PxB	Q–Q5ch	17 N–Q5	Q–Q1
10 K–R1	QxP	18 N–K7ch	....

White wins the Queen

[1] Black plays to win a Pawn. 8 .... QN–Q2 is the right move.
[2] If 14 . . . R–K1; 15 QxRPch, K–B1; 16 N–Q5 and mate cannot be avoided. Or if 14 . . . R–Q1; 15 QxRPch, K–B1; 16 R–K1, B–K3; 17 RxB, and the Bishop Pawn dare not recapture.

White to Play. White has nothing better than the capture of Black's Rook, after which Black demonstrates that this capture loses.

WHITE	BLACK	WHITE	BLACK
1 P–K4	P–K4		SEE DIAGRAM
2 P–KB4	P–Q4	8 NxR	N–Q5
3 N–KB3	QPxP	9 Q–Q1	N–B6ch!
4 NxP	B–QB4	10 PxN[2]	PxPch
5 N–QB3	N–KB3	11 B–K2[3]	P–B7ch
6 Q–K2	N–B3	12 K–B1	B–R6
7 NxBP?[1]	Q–K2		

White has been checkmated

[1] In order to win a Pawn after 7 .... KxN by 8 Q–B4ch, and 9 QxB. However, this shows poor judgment. Better is 7 NxKP, or 7 Q–B4, Q–K2; 8 N–R4.

[2] If 10 K–K2, B–KN5 decides.

[3] Or 11 N–K2 when 11 .... P–B7 is mate.

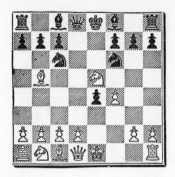

White to Play. *White can win the exchange with a Bishop fork after 6 NxN, PxN; 7 BxPch etc. Should he follow this plan, or continue his development?*

WHITE	BLACK	WHITE	BLACK
1 P–K4	P–K4	SEE DIAGRAM	
2 P–KB4	P–Q4	6 NxN[1]	PxN
3 N–KB3	QPxP	7 BxPch	B–Q2
4 NxP	N–QB3	8 BxR?[2]	B–KN5[3]
5 B–N5	N–B3		

Black wins the Queen

[1] Better is 6 O–O, B–B4ch; 7 K–R1, O–O; 8 N–QB3.

[2] Too greedy. After 8 BxBch, QxB; 9 O–O White is a Pawn ahead, in return for which Black's development is superior.

[3] This is the unexpected blow. White probably anticipated the simple recapture, 8 . . . QxB.

White to Play. *Black's exposed Knight can be imprisoned by White's Pawns.*

WHITE	BLACK	WHITE	BLACK
1 P–K4	N–KB3	6 P–Q3	N–N4
2 P–K5	N–K5?[1]	7 P–N3	Q–R3
SEE DIAGRAM		8 B–B4[7]	Q–N3[8]
3 P–QN4![2]	P–K3[3]	9 P–KR4	N–B2
4 P–QB3[4]	Q–R5[5]	10 P–R5	Q–N5
5 Q–K2[6]	P–KB4	11 P–B3[9]	....

White wins the Queen

[1] This loses at least a piece. Correct is 2 .... N–Q4.

[2] Threatening to win the Knight with 4 P–Q3.

[3] So that if 4 P–Q3, BxPch, or if 4 P–KB3, Q–R5ch.

[4] Now the idea is 5 P–Q3, N–N4; 6 P–KR4, trapping the Knight.

[5] If 4 .... P–KR3; 5 P–KR4.

[6] Now White threatens to win the Knight after 6 P–N3.

[7] Not 8 P–KR4, as Black counters with 8 .... N–B6ch; 9 K–Q1, NxN; 10 BxQ, NxQ etc.

[8] If 8 .... B–K2; 9 P–KR4 followed by 10 N–KR3 wins the Knight.

[9] Black saved his Knight, but loses his Queen.

White to Play. Black's last move (4 ... N–B3) is a blunder which results in the loss of a piece.

WHITE	BLACK	WHITE	BLACK
1 P–K4	N–KB3	SEE DIAGRAM	
2 P–K5	N–Q4	5 P–Q5!	NxKP[2]
3 P–QB4	N–N3	6 P–B5	N(N3)–B5
4 P–Q4	N–B3?[1]	7 P–B4	....

White wins one of the Knights

[1] As a rule 4....P–Q3 is played in order to exercise some restraint on White's center Pawns, and also to prepare the development of the Queen Bishop. In addition 4....P–Q3 is a necessary preliminary to the development of Black's Queen Knight.

[2] If 5....N–N1; 6 P-B5 wins the King Knight at once. Or if 5....N–N5; 6 P–B5, N(N3)xP; 7 P–QR3 winning a Knight.

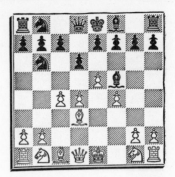

Black to Play. *White has been lured into challenging Black's Bishop. Black's next two moves clear the way for him to concentrate his fire on White's helpless Queen Pawn.*

WHITE	BLACK	WHITE	BLACK
1 P–K4	N–KB3	6........	BxB!
2 P–K5	N–Q4	7 QxB[3]	PxP
3 P–QB4	N–N3	8 BPxP	P–QB4!
4 P–Q4	P–Q3	9 P–Q5[4]	P–K3[5]
5 P–B4	B–B4[1]	10 N–QB3	Q–R5ch
6 B–Q3?[2]	....	11 P–N3	QxBP

SEE DIAGRAM

Black has won a Pawn

[1] More usual is 5 ... PxP; 6 BPxP, N–B3; 7 B–K3, B–B4 etc., but the text move is trappy.

[2] White's idea is to cut down the scope of Black's Bishop, or force him to exchange.

[3] The exchange leaves White's Queen unprotected, and his Queen Pawn will therefore be unable to do any capturing— a circumstance which Black will utilize.

[4] If 9 N–KB3, PxP; 10 NxP (10 QxP, QxQ; 11 NxQ, NxP wins a Pawn), N–B3; 11 B–K3, NxKP, and Black has won a Pawn.

[5] Theatening to win a Pawn by 10 ... PxP; 11 PxP, QxP.

White to Play. *White wins at least a Pawn, but the slightest slip-up in Black's defense will cost him his Queen.*

WHITE	BLACK	WHITE	BLACK
1 P–K4	N–KB3	10 B–K2	O–O–O
2 P–K5	N–Q4	11 O–O	B–K2?[2]
3 P–QB4	N–N3		SEE DIAGRAM
4 P–Q4	P–Q3	12 P–Q5!	PxP[3]
5 P–B4	PxP	13 BxN	RPxB
6 BPxP	N–B3	14 PxP	N–N5
7 B–K3	B–B4	15 N–Q4!	P–N3[4]
8 N–QB3[1]	P–K3	16 NxB	PxN
9 N–B3	Q–Q2	17 RxP![5]	....

White wins a Pawn

[1] 8 B-Q3? would lose a Pawn by 8 . . . . BxB; 9 QxB, NxKP etc.
[2] Black should play 11 . . . . P–B3.
[3] If 12 . . . . N–N1; 13 N–Q4 with a powerful attack.
[4] If 15 . . . . B–N3; 16 B–N4 wins the Queen. If 15 . . . . B–B4; 16 RxB!, QxR; 17 B–N4, BxNch; 18 QxB also wins the Queen.
[5] If 17 . . . . NxQP (on 17 . . . . QxR; 18 B–N4); 18 P–K6!, PxP; 19 RxN!, PxR; 20 B–N4 wins the Queen.

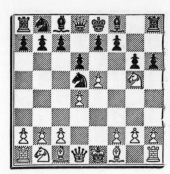

White to Play. Black thought he could chase the Knight away, but receives a nasty shock!

WHITE	BLACK	WHITE	BLACK
1 P–K4	N–KB3	6 NxP!	KxN
2 P–K5	N–Q4	7 Q–B3ch	K–K3?[4]
3 P–Q4	P–Q3	8 P–B4	N–N5
4 N–KB3	P–KN3?[1]	9 P–Q5ch	K–Q2[5]
5 N–N5[2]	P–KR3?[3]	10 P–K6ch	K–K1
	SEE DIAGRAM	11 Q–B7	....

Black has been checkmated

[1] The best move is 4....B–N5.

[2] Black's inferior move makes it possible for White to "move the same piece twice"—usually a mistake in the opening.

[3] Reacting instinctively. However if 5....PxP; 6 PxP, P–KR3; 7 P–QB4, PxN; 8 PxN, and White has a distinct advantage.

[4] Relatively better is the return of the piece with 7....N–B3; 8 PxN, PxP.

[5] Or 9....KxP; 10 Q–B4 mate.

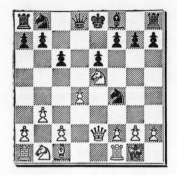

White to Play. *Black is trying to win a Pawn, but his combination is unsound, and he loses a piece.*

WHITE	BLACK	WHITE	BLACK
1 P–K4	N–KB3	7 NxP	BxB
2 P–K5	N–Q4	8 QxB	P–K3
3 P–Q4	P–Q3	9 P–QN3	N–B5?[2]
4 N–KB3	B–N5		SEE DIAGRAM
5 B–K2	P–QB3	10 Q–B3![3]	QxP[4]
6 O–O	PxP?[1]	11 QxN[5]	....

White wins a piece

[1] 6 .... BxN is much better.

[2] Black should continue his development with 9 .... B-K2.

[3] Black had hoped for 10 BxN, QxP, forking Rook and Bishop.

[4] Black must follow through, as a Knight move allows an immediate mate; while if 10 .... P–KN4; 11 BxN, QxP (after 11 .... PxB; 12 QxP, Black's game is hopeless); 12 BxP, QxN (if 12 ... QxR; 13 QxP mate); 13 B–B6 forks Queen and Rook.

[5] If 11 ... QxR; 12 QxPch, K–Q1; 13 B–N5ch, K–B1; 14 Q–K8ch, K–B2; 15 Q–Q8 mate.

White to Play. *Black's premature Queen attack has won a Rook, but White's counterattack wins the game.*

WHITE	BLACK	WHITE	BLACK
1 P–K4	N–KB3	10 N–B3	B–Q2[2]
2 P–K5	N–Q4	11 K–B2	B–B3
3 N–QB3	P–K3	12 B–KN2	BxN
4 P–Q4	P–Q3	13 QxB	QxP
5 P–B4	NxN	14 QxP[3]	B–K2
6 PxN	PxP	15 Q–B8ch!	B–Q1
7 BPxP	Q–R5ch?[1]	16 B–R3[4]	Q–R4
8 P–N3	Q–K5ch	17 QxN![5]	RxQ
9 Q–K2	QxR	18 B–B6	....

SEE DIAGRAM

Black has been checkmated

[1] Playing to win a Rook, but violating opening principles.

[2] White threatened to win the Queen with 11 K–B2 and 12 B–KN2.

[3] Threatening 15 Q–B8ch! (stronger than 15 QxR), K–K2; 16 B–R3ch, P–B4; 17 BxP mate.

[4] In order to win the Queen with 17 R–R1.

[5] A beautiful Queen sacrifice.

Black to Play. *White offers his Queen Pawn as bait. On principle Black should lose no time by Pawn-grabbing. But what happens if he snatches the Pawn?*

WHITE	BLACK	WHITE	BLACK
1 P–K4	P–QB3	9 B–Q3	....
2 P–Q4	P–Q4	SEE DIAGRAM	
3 N–QB3	PxP	9	QxP?[2]
4 NxP	B–B4	10 NxKBP!	BxB[3]
5 N–N3	B–N3	11 NxR	Q–K4ch[4]
6 P–KR4	P–KR3	12 B–K3	B–R2[5]
7 N–B3	P–K3?[1]	13 Q–Q8ch!	KxQ
8 N–K5!	B–R2	14 N–B7ch[6]	....

White wins the exchange

[1] 7 ... N–Q2, as in the next example, is better.
[2] Black should play 9 .... BxB, and then develop his pieces.
[3] Of course not 10 .... KxN; 11 B–N6ch, BxB; 12 QxQ.
[4] Black saves his Bishop, by breaking the pin with a check.
[5] How does White's Knight escape?
[6] This pretty Knight fork regains the Queen, and leaves White the exchange ahead.

White to Play. *A sacrificial Knight fork by White, either wins material or leads to checkmate.*

WHITE	BLACK	WHITE	BLACK
1 P–K4	P–QB3	9 Q–K2	B–Q3[1]
2 P–Q4	P–Q4	10 O–O	KN–B3
3 N–QB3	PxP	11 N–K5[2]	B–R2?[3]
4 NxP	B–B4	SEE DIAGRAM	
5 N–N3	B–N3	12 NxKBP![4]	KxN[5]
6 P–KR4	P–KR3	13 QxPch	K–N3[6]
7 N–B3	N–Q2	14 P–R5	....
8 B–QB4	P–K3		

Black has been checkmated

[1] Better is 9 .... B–K2, so as to answer an eventual N–K5 with .... NxN.

[2] Threatening to win a Pawn by 11 NxB followed by QxPch.

[3] A plausible counter to the threat; but 11 .... BxN would have avoided White's winning reply.

[4] This stroke smashes Black's position. It is worthy of note as it occurs frequently in the Caro-Kann.

[5] Quick death. Moving the Queen is slower, but just as certain.

[6] If 13 .... K–B1; 14 Q–B7 is mate.

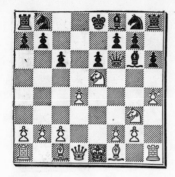

White to Play. In this apparently harmless position, White can force Black into a discovered attack.

WHITE	BLACK	WHITE	BLACK
1 P–K4	P–QB3	7 P–KR4	P–KR3
2 P–Q4	P–Q4	8 N–K5!	Q–B3?[2]
3 N–QB3	PxP		SEE DIAGRAM
4 NxP	B–B4	9 B–KN5!	PxB[3]
5 N–N3	B–N3	10 PxP	QxP
6 N–B3	P–K3?[1]	11 RxR	....

White has won the exchange

[1] The right move is 6 .... N–Q2.
[2] In order to recapture with the Queen, after 9 NxB. But White has a deadly reply.
[3] There is no choice, as the Queen has no flight-square.

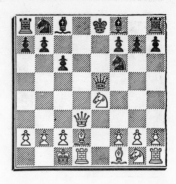

Black to Play. White has seemingly left his Knight en prise—but the subtle offer of a piece should be declined. If Black captures, he will lose instantaneously.

WHITE	BLACK	WHITE	BLACK
1 P–K4	P–QB3	7 B–Q2!	QxKP
2 P–Q4	P–Q4	8 O–O–O!	....
3 N–QB3	PxP	SEE DIAGRAM	
4 NxP	N–B3	8	NxN?[2]
5 Q–Q3	P–K4?[1]	9 Q–Q8ch!!	KxQ
6 PxP	Q–R4ch	10 B–N5ch[3]	....

White checkmates next move

[1] This premature opening up of the position is risky. 5 .... QN–Q2 followed by .... NxN and .... N–B3 is better.

[2] If 8 .... QxN?; 9 R–K1 wins the Queen.

[3] The deadly double check forces the King to move. Now if 10 .... K–K1; 11 R–Q8 is mate; or if 10 .... K–B2; 11 B–Q8 checkmates.

Black to Play. *White has apparently guarded against Black's threat of Queening— but a combination removes the guard.*

WHITE	BLACK	WHITE	BLACK
1 P–K4	P–QB3	8 B–K5³	....
2 P–Q4	P–Q4	SEE DIAGRAM	
3 N–QB3	PxP	8........	RxP!⁴
4 NxP	N–B3	9 RxR	Q–R4ch!
5 N–N3	P–KR4	10 P–B3	QxBch!⁵
6 B–KN5?¹	P–R5	11 PxQ	PxR⁶
7 BxN²	PxN		

Black has won a piece

¹ This is not the right way to answer Black's threat, and leads to trouble.   6 P–KR4 or 6 Q–Q3 is correct.

² 7 QN–K2 is obviously uncomfortable, but preferable to the text.

³ Guarding the square KR2, and thus stopping Black from carrying out his idea of winning by 8 .... RxP; 9 RxR, PxR, and Queening the Pawn.

⁴ The threat still works!

⁵ The point of the combination.

⁶ Black Queens his Pawn, and remains a piece ahead.

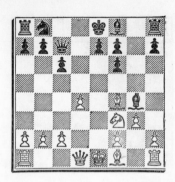

Black to Play.White neglects the defense of his pinned Knight. Disaster comes in the form of a new pin.

WHITE	BLACK	WHITE	BLACK
1 P–K4	P–QB3	7 N–B3	B–N5
2 P–Q4	P–Q4	8 B–KB4?[1]	....
3 N–QB3	PxP	SEE DIAGRAM	
4 NxP	N–B3	8........	P–K4!
5 NxNch	NPxN	9 PxP[2]	PxP
6 P–KN3	Q–B2	10 BxP	Q–K2[3]

Black wins a piece

[1] A premature counter-attack on the Queen, when the pinned Knight needed help. The safe continuation was 8 B–N2, P–K4; 9 Q–Q3.

[2] If 9 B–K3, P–K5 wins the pinned Knight.

[3] Another pin which wins the Bishop—or the Knight. White is helpless against Black's threat of 11 .... BxN; 12 QxB, QxBch.

White to Play. To win a Pawn, Black has placed his Queen in a dangerously exposed position and will suffer the usual consequences.

WHITE	BLACK	WHITE	BLACK
1 P–K4	P–QB3	7 PxP	QxNP?[2]
2 P–Q4	P–Q4		SEE DIAGRAM
3 PxP	PxP	8 R–B1!	N–QN5[3]
4 P–QB4	N–KB3	9 N–R4!	QxRP
5 N–QB3	N–B3	10 B–QB4	B–N5
6 B–N5[1]	Q–N3?	11 N–KB3[4]	....

White wins a piece

[1] A difficult move to meet. Black's safest reply is 6 .... P–K3.

[2] Pawn-grabbing with the Queen, at the expense of development, is always perilous.

[3] Other Knight moves are also unfavorable.

[4] White wins at least a piece. If 11 .... Q–R6; 12 R–B3, N–B7ch; 13 QxN etc.

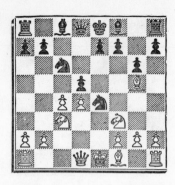

White to Play. Black sets a trap by offering his Queen Pawn. Apparently White can win a Pawn by capturing with his Queen Knight.

WHITE	BLACK	WHITE	BLACK
1 P–K4	P–QB3	6 N–B3	P–KN3
2 P–Q4	P–Q4	7 B–N5	N–K5
3 PxP	PxP	SEE DIAGRAM	
4 P–QB4	N–KB3	8 NxP?[1]	NxB
5 N–QB3	N–B3	9 NxN	P–K3[2]

Black wins a piece

[1] The wrong way to take the Pawn. The proper course is 8 PxP, NxN; 9 BPxN, QxP etc.

[2] The discovered attack threatens both Knights simultaneously, and wins one of them. If 10 Q–B3, QxKN; 11 N–B7ch, K–Q1; 12 NxR, B–N5ch, and White must give up his Queen, as a King move permits 13 .... Q–Q7 mate.

Black to Play. *Black is a piece ahead, but he is threatened with 13 QxR as well as 13 QxBPch. How can Black meet these threats?*

WHITE	BLACK	WHITE	BLACK
1 P-K4	P-QB3	11 BxNch![1]	PxB
2 P-Q4	P-Q4	12 Q-N7?[2]	....
3 PxP	PxP	SEE DIAGRAM	
4 P-QB4	N-KB3	12	N-Q4ch
5 N-QB3	N-B3	13 B-Q2	Q-N3
6 N-B3	B-N5	14 QxRch	K-Q2[3]
7 PxP	KNxP	15 O-O	N-B2
8 B-QN5	Q-R4	16 B-R5[4]	NxQ
9 Q-N3!	BxN	17 BxQ	NxB
10 PxB	NxN		

Black has won two pieces for a Rook

[2] The simple 11 PxN leaves White with a fine game.

[2] Instead of recapturing the Knight, White hopes to gain an advantage by attacking Black's Rook. But this plan is not sound.

[3] White's Queen is trapped!

[4] Other moves simply lose the Queen.

Black to Play. He can win the Queen Pawn with his Knight, or the Queen Knight Pawn with his Queen—but the capture of either Pawn loses.

WHITE	BLACK	WHITE	BLACK
1 P–K4	P–QB3	9 B–K3	Q–N3[1]
2 P–Q4	P–Q4	10 O–O!	....
3 PxP	PxP	SEE DIAGRAM	
4 N–QB3	N–KB3	10........	NxP?[2]
5 N–B3	B–N5	11 Q–B4	B–B4
6 P–KR3	BxN	12 N–R4![3]	Q–B3
7 QxB	P–K3	13 NxB	QxN
8 B–Q3	N–B3	14 BxN	....

White has won a piece

[1] An ill-advised attempt to win a Pawn, which White rightly ignores.

[2] If 10 .... QxNP; 11 N–N5 threatening to win the Queen with 12 KR–N1 as well as the Rook with 12 N–B7ch.

[3] The refutation. White proceeds to remove one of the defenders of the pinned Knight.

White to Play. *Black thinks he has set a trap to swindle his opponent, but if White sees far enough ahead, he can fall for the trap with confidence in the outcome.*

WHITE	BLACK	WHITE	BLACK
1 P–K4	P–QB3	8 BxPch!	KxB
2 P–Q4	P–Q4	9 QxQ[2]	PxPch
3 P–KB3	PxP[1]	10 K–K2	PxR(Q)[3]
4 PxP	P–K4	11 N–N5ch!	K–N3
5 N–KB3	PxP	12 Q–K8ch	K–R3[4]
6 B–QB4	B–N5ch	13 N–K6ch	P–N4
7 P–B3	PxP	14 BxP	....

SEE DIAGRAM

Black has been checkmated

[1] With this and the following four moves, Black lays the groundwork for a trap. But he allows White to get an aggressive development in an open position. The result is that Black is out-smarted when he tries a "swindle." 3 .... P–K3 followed by 4 .... P–QB4 is more prudent.

[2] Did Black overlook something?

[3] Has White missed something?

[4] If 12 .... K–B3; 13 R–B1ch, B–B4; 14 Q–K6 mate.

Black to Play. *Two careless Knight moves have brought about this predicament. Should he move his Knight a third time, or capture the Pawn?*

WHITE	BLACK	WHITE	BLACK
1 P–K4	P–QB3		SEE DIAGRAM
2 P–Q4	P–Q4	5	PxP?[4]
3 B–Q3[1]	N–B3?[2]	6 Q–R5ch	P–N3
4 P–K5	KN–Q2?[3]	7 QxPch!	PxQ
5 P–K6!	....	8 BxP[5]	....

Black has been checkmated

[1] Not the best move, as Black can develop with gain of time by 3 .... PxP; 4 BxP, N–B3 etc.

[2] The most natural post for the Knight—but in this case bad, as the Knight is immediately driven away.

[3] Again overlooking White's reply. The Knight should have returned to N1, even though that were an admission of error.

[4] By far the lesser evil was 5 .... N–B3; 6 PxPch, KxP. However with the castling privilege lost, and the King Pawn backward, Black would have a poor game.

[5] An unexpectedly drastic conclusion.

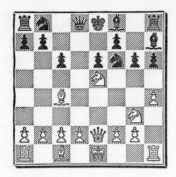

White to Play. The sacrificial Knight fork motif, which occurs frequently in the Caro-Kann, is again used here.

WHITE	BLACK	WHITE	BLACK
1 P–K4	P–QB3	8 Q–R5	P–KN3
2 N–QB3	P–Q4	9 B–B4![2]	P–K3
3 N–B3	PxP	10 Q–K2	N–B3?[3]
4 NxP	B–B4?[1]	SEE DIAGRAM	
5 N–N3	B–N3	11 NxKBP!	KxN[4]
6 P–KR4	P–KR3	12 QxPch	K–N2
7 N–K5	B–R2	13 Q–B7	....

Black has been checkmated

[1] This leads to a bad game. Black should play 4 . . . . B–N5.
[2] So that if 9 . . . . PxQ? ; 10 BxP mates Black.
[3] Overlooking White's crushing reply. However, after 10 . . . .
Q–B2; 11 P–Q4, Black's game would be hopeless.
[4] Moving the Queen would cost the exchange immediately, with more losses to follow.

Black to Play. *White's attack looks risky, but it succeeds because of Black's inferior opening moves.*

WHITE	BLACK	WHITE	BLACK
1 P–K4	P–QB3	10 Q–N3!	Q–Q4
2 N–QB3	P–Q4	11 QxP!	....
3 N–B3	PxP	SEE DIAGRAM	
4 NxP	B–B4?	11	QxNch
5 N–N3	B–N3	12 B–K2	Q–Q3[1]
6 P–KR4	P–KR3	13 QxR	Q–B2
7 N–K5	B–R2	14 P–R4![2]	B–N2
8 Q–R5	P–KN3	15 R–QR3!	O–O
9 Q–B3	N–B3	16 R–N3[3]	....

White has won the exchange

[1] Black must guard against the main threat of 13 Q–B8 mate.
[2] Now White extricates his Queen cleverly.
[3] The Queen escapes by way of QN7.

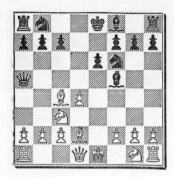

White to Play. The continuation from this point is a good example of a Knight fork combination, where threats are used in order to force the forking position.

WHITE	BLACK	WHITE	BLACK
1 P–K4	P–Q4	6 B-Q2	P–K3?[1]
2 PxP	QxP		SEE DIAGRAM
3 N–QB3	Q–QR4	7 N–Q5!	Q–R5
4 P–Q4	N–KB3	8 B–N5ch![2]	QxB
5 B–QB4	B–B4	9 NxPch	....

White wins the Queen

[1] Blissfully unaware of any danger. The position of White's Bishop at Q2 threatens a discovered attack on the Queen, and Black should either flee at once with the Queen, or as in this case where there are no good squares, prepare a shelter (at Q1) by 6 .... P–B3.

[2] A sacrificial Bishop fork, forcing the Queen to occupy a square where it becomes vulnerable to a Knight fork.

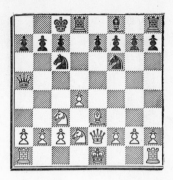

Black to Play. *White's Queen Pawn is attacked twice, guarded once—but Black should look before he leaps. An exposed Queen is always a vulnerable target.*

WHITE	BLACK	WHITE	BLACK
1 P–K4	P–Q4	8 N–Q2[1]	BxB
2 PxP	QxP	9 QxB	....
3 N–QB3	Q–QR4	SEE DIAGRAM	
4 P–Q4	N–KB3	9	NxP?
5 N–B3	B–N5	10 BxN	RxB[2]
6 B–K2	N–B3	11 N–N3	....
7 B–K3	O–O–O		

White wins the exchange

[1] White makes a kind offer of a Pawn.
[2] Now that Black's Queen and Rook are both unprotected pieces, the stage is set for a pretty Knight fork.

White to Play. White's King Knight is pinned by the Bishop and attacked by the Knight, but Black's attack is premature and the pin is broken by force.

WHITE	BLACK	WHITE	BLACK
1 P–K4	P–Q4	7 NxN![3]	BxQ
2 PxP	QxP	8 B–N5ch	P–B3
3 N–QB3	Q–Q1	9 PxP	P–QR3[4]
4 P–Q4	N–QB3?[1]	10 P–B7ch	PxB
5 N–B3	B–N5	11 PxQ(Q)ch	RxQ
6 P–Q5	N–K4?[2]	12 NxB	....

SEE DIAGRAM

White has won a piece

[1] Not best, as the Knight is subject to attack by White's Queen Pawn. 4....N–KB3 is much better.

[2] Looks good, but loses as his Queen side is deserted, and he is not yet developed enough to make such "powerful" attacking moves. There was nothing better than the return to N1.

[3] Breaking the pin brilliantly, with a Queen sacrifice.

[4] If 9....Q–B2; 10 PxPch, K–Q1; 11 NxP is mate.

White to Play. *An example of an illusory pin. Before pinning a piece, make sure that your opponent cannot break the pin with a check, winning attack, or mating threat.*

WHITE	BLACK	WHITE	BLACK
1 P–K4	P–Q4	6 N–B3	B–N5?[2]
2 PxP	QxP		SEE DIAGRAM
3 N–QB3	Q–Q1	7 N–K5![3]	BxQ?[4]
4 P–Q4	N–KB3	8 BxP	....
5 B–QB4	P–B3[1]		

Black has been checkmated

[1] Rather slow. Either 5 . . . B–N5, or 5 . . . B–B4 is playable here.

[2] But now this move is a mistake.

[3] More brilliant than the win of a Pawn by the prosaic 7 BxPch, KxB; 8 N–K5ch followed by 9 NxB.

[4] Loses at once. 7 . . . . B–R4 is refuted by 8 QxB!; but 7 . . . . B–K3 would stave off the mate—although after 8 BxB, PxB, Black's game would be seriously compromised.

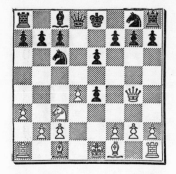

Black to Play. *In the French Defense, White can often play Q–N4 with good effect — but not in this position. A move should never be made without considering the opponent's possible replies.*

WHITE	BLACK	WHITE	BLACK
1 P–K4	P–K3	7 Q–N4?[2]	....
2 P–Q4	P–Q4		SEE DIAGRAM
3 N–QB3	B–N5	7	NxP
4 N–K2[1]	PxP	8 QxNP?[3]	NxPch
5 P–QR3	BxNch	9 K–K2	Q–Q6
6 NxB	N–QB3		

White has been checkmated

[1] More fashionable today is 4 P–K5, P–QB4; 5 P–QR3, and Black has choice of two interesting moves: 5 . . . PxP, or 5 . . . BxNch, either leading to lively play.

[2] The right continuation is 7 B–QN5, N–K2; 8 O–O, O–O.

[3] Blindly continuing his "attack" without observing Black's threat. The only chance was 8 QxKP, although Black would still have the better development and a pawn plus.

Black to Play. *Black is threatened with loss of his Rook by 9 QxP. How should he defend himself?*

WHITE	BLACK	WHITE	BLACK
1 P–K4	P–K3	7 Q–N4	BxNch
2 P–Q4	P–Q4	8 PxB	....
3 N–QB3	B–N5[1]	SEE DIAGRAM	
4 P–K5	P–QB4	8	NxP?[3]
5 P–QR3	PxP	9 QxP	Q–B3
6 QxP[2]	N–QB3	10 B–KR6![4]	....

White wins the exchange

[1] This line of play is a great favorite with the Soviet masters, who are thoroughly familiar with its fine points.

[2] White can get a fine game with the Pawn sacrifice 6 PxB, PxN; 7 N–B3!, Q–B2; 8 Q–Q4, N–K2; 9 B–Q3, N–Q2; 10 O–O.

[3] Plausible, but it loses. The right way was 8 . . . Q–B2; 9 QxP, QxPch, or if 9 P–KB4, P–B4 etc.

[4] If 10 . . . QxB; 11 QxR. If 10 . . . K–K2 (to meet the threat of 11 QxQ, NxQ; 12 B–N7); 11 B–KN5 wins Black's Queen.

White to Play. *If White captures the Knight, Black's idea is to play Q–B6ch, regain the piece, and remain a Pawn ahead. What is wrong with Black's plan?*

WHITE	BLACK	WHITE	BLACK
1 P–K4	P–K3	8 B–Q3	PxP[1]
2 P–Q4	P–Q4	9 PxP	NxQP?[2]
3 N–QB3	B–N5	SEE DIAGRAM	
4 P–K5	P–QB4	10 NxN	Q–B6ch
5 P–QR3	BxNch	11 Q–Q2![3]	QxR[4]
6 PxB	Q–B2	12 P–QB3[5]	Any
7 N–B3	N–QB3	13 N–N3	....

White wins the Queen

[1] Hoping to win a Pawn; better is 8 . . . P–B5.

[2] Starting an unsound combination. Correct is 9 . . . B–Q2, or 9 . . . KN–K2.

[3] White sees further ahead. Black will lose his Queen, if he captures either the Knight or the Rook.

[4] If 11 . . . QxN; 12 B–N5ch wins Black's Queen by discovered attack.

[5] Keeps the Queen from coming out.

Black to Play. *White has left his Queen side vulnerable to attack. Black is now in position to exploit the absence of White's Queen.*

WHITE	BLACK	WHITE	BLACK
1 P–K4	P–K3	7 QxP	PxP
2 P–Q4	P–Q4	8 P–QR3	....
3 N–QB3	B–N5	SEE DIAGRAM	
4 P–K5	P–QB4	8	Q–R4!²
5 Q–N4¹	N–K2	9 R–N1³	PxN
6 QxNP	R–N1	10 PxB	Q–R7⁴

Black wins a Rook

¹ Certainly a tempting move, with Black's King Bishop away from the defense.

² To pin White's Rook Pawn.

³ Very plausible—and bad. White expects in reply 9 . . . B–B4, when he can save his Knight by 10 P–QN4. Best was 9 PxB, losing the exchange for a Pawn.

⁴ The point of Black's combination: White's Rook is trapped.

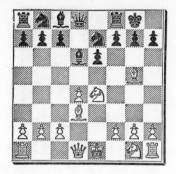

White to Play. *Weak opening moves and unsafe castling have exposed Black to a sacrificial mating attack. The snappy finish shows the power of superior mobility.*

WHITE	BLACK	WHITE	BLACK
1 P–K4	P–K3		SEE DIAGRAM
2 P–Q4	P–Q4	7 N–B6ch!	PxN[4]
3 N–QB3	PxP	8 BxP	Q–Q2[5]
4 NxP	B–Q3?[1]	9 BxPch!	KxB
5 B–Q3	N–K2?[2]	10 Q–R5ch	K–N1
6 B–N5	O–O?[3]	11 Q–R8	....

Black has been checkmated

[1] This and Black's next two moves are weak; Knights should be brought into play before Bishops. The correct way is 4 ... N–Q2 followed by 5 ... KN–B3.

[2] A poor spot for the Knight. The normal development to B3 is far superior.

[3] The final error; but Black's position was bad in any event.

[4] If 7 ... K–R1; 8 Q–R5, P–KR3; 9 BxP, PxN; 10 B–N5ch, K–N2; 11 Q–R7 mate.

[5] Black unpins the Knight in order to reply to 9 Q–N4ch with 9 ... N–N3.

Black to Play. Black is in check and must capture White's Knight. The most natural way is to do so by 7 ... QxN — but that costs Black his Queen.

WHITE	BLACK	WHITE	BLACK
1 P–K4	P–K3		SEE DIAGRAM
2 P–Q4	P–Q4	7	QxN?[2]
3 N–QB3	PxP	8 B–KN5	BxN[3]
4 NxP	B–Q2?[1]	9 Q–Q2!	QxP
5 N–KB3	B–B3	10 B–N5ch	N–B3
6 B–Q3	N–B3	11 QxQ[4]	....
7 NxNch	....		

White has won the Queen

[1] Not a good idea. A better course is 4 ... N–Q2; 5 N–KB3, KN–B3; 6 NxNch, NxN; 7 B–Q3, P–B4.

[2] 7 ... PxN offers fighting chances. The text move unexpectedly loses the Queen.

[3] Black's Queen had no flight square, but this capture seems to save everything, as the Knight, protector of White's Queen Bishop, is removed.

[4] Black's pinned Knight cannot recapture.

White to Play. In opening the diagonal leading to his Queen Rook, at the wrong time, Black becomes the victim of a Queen fork. White can now win the Rook.

WHITE	BLACK	WHITE	BLACK
1 P-K4	P-K3	7 B-Q3¹	B-K2
2 P-Q4	P-Q4	8 Q-K2	O-O
3 N-QB3	PxP	9 B-KN5	P-QN3?²
4 NxP	N-Q2	SEE DIAGRAM	
5 N-KB3	KN-B3	10 BxN	BxB
6 NxNch	NxN	11 Q-K4³	....

White wins the Queen Rook

¹ Capablanca in one of his greatest games, played against Blanco 7 N-K5, B-Q3; 8 Q-B3; P-B3; 9 P-B3, O-O; 10 B-KN5, B-K2; 11 B-Q3 and built up a beautiful attack against Black's King side.

² A natural developing move, but it loses instantly. Better is 9 ... P-KR3; 10 BxN, BxB; 11 Q-K4, P-KN3; 12 P-KR4, although White still has the superior game.

³ Black must stop the threat of 12 QxP mate.

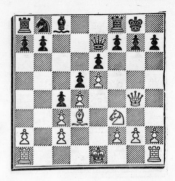

White to Play. *Black's last move, attacking the Bishop with a Pawn, is a common mistake. Not only does Black overlook the mating threat, but he almost forces White to play the winning combination!*

WHITE	BLACK	WHITE	BLACK
1 P–K4	P–K3	9 PxN	P–QB4
2 P–Q4	P–Q4	10 N–B3	P–B5?[4]
3 N–QB3	N–KB3		SEE DIAGRAM
4 B–N5	B–K2	11 BxPch	KxB
5 P–K5	N–K5[1]	12 Q–R5ch	K–N1
6 BxB	QxB[2]	13 N–N5	R–Q1
7 Q–N4	O–O	14 Q–R7ch	K–B1
8 B–Q3[3]	NxN	15 Q–R8	....

Black has been checkmated

[1] The retreat to Q2 is more usual—and safer.

[2] A good alternative is 6 ... NxN; 7 BxQ, NxQ; 8 BxP, NxNP; 9 R–N1, N–B5 etc.

[3] If 8 NxN, PxN; 9 QxP(K4), Q–N5ch regains the Pawn.

[4] Black should play either 10 ... P–B4, or 10 ... P–B3.

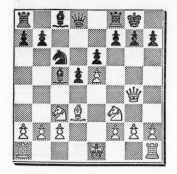

White to Play. *Black has been caught off-guard. A mating attack at such an early stage is so unexpected, that this trap inveigles even the wiliest.*

WHITE	BLACK	WHITE	BLACK
1 P–K4	P–K3		SEE DIAGRAM
2 P–Q4	P–Q4	11 BxPch	KxB²
3 N–QB3	N–KB3	12 Q–R5ch	K–N1
4 B–N5	B–K2	13 N–KN5	R–K1³
5 BxN	BxN	14 QxPch	K–R1
6 P–K5	B–K2	15 Q–R5ch	K–N1
7 B–Q3	P–QB4	16 Q–R7ch	K–B1
8 PxP	BxP	17 Q–R8ch	K–K2
9 Q–N4	O–O	18 QxP	....
10 N–B3	N–B3?¹		

Black has been checkmated

¹ The same neglect to provide against a sacrificial mating attack, as in the previous trap. Black should play 10 . . . P–B4, which stops the mate, and incidentally cuts down the scope of White's Bishop.

² If 11 . . . K–R1; 12 Q–R5, threatening mate by discovered check as well as 13 N–KN5, wins for White.

³ To make room for the King, but it is too late.

White to Play. *Black believed his last Pawn move would defend his King side position, but White tears through with a whirlwind attack, sacrificing three pieces to force checkmate.*

WHITE	BLACK	WHITE	BLACK
1 P–K4	P–K3	SEE DIAGRAM	
2 P–Q4	P–Q4	10 N–KN5!	PxN[3]
3 N–QB3	N–KB3	11 BxPch	KxB[4]
4 B–N5	B–K2	12 PxPch	K–N1[5]
5 BxN	BxB	13 R–R8ch	KxR[6]
6 N–B3	O–O	14 Q–R5ch	K–N1
7 P–K5	B–K2	15 P–N6	R–K1
8 B–Q3	B–Q2?[1]	16 Q–R7ch	K–B1
9 P–KR4	P–KB3?[2]	17 Q–R8	....

Black has been checkmated

[1] This is out of place here. 8 . . . P–QB4 should be played.

[2] 9 . . . P–KB4 is necessary.

[3] If 10 . . . P–KN3; 11 NxRP, KxN; 12 Q–R5ch, K–N1; 13 QxPch, K–R1; 14 Q–R7 is mate.

[4] If 11 . . . K–B2; 12 Q–R5ch, P–N3; 13 QxP mate.

[5] On 12 . . . K–N3; 13 Q–R5ch leads to a quick mate.

[6] No better is 13 . . . K–B2; 14 Q–R5ch, P–N3; 15 Q–R7ch, K–K1; 16 QxP mate.

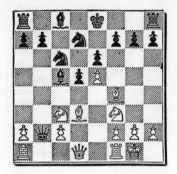

White to Play. *Black's win of a Pawn with his Queen seems playable, but the perennial warning against the capture of the Queen Knight Pawn still holds good.*

WHITE	BLACK	WHITE	BLACK
1 P–K4	P–K3	8 B–Q3	Q–N3[2]
2 P–Q4	P–Q4	9 O–O	QxP?
3 N–QB3	N–KB3		SEE DIAGRAM
4 P–K5	KN–Q2	10 N–QN5[3]	K–Q1
5 N–B3[1]	P–QB4	11 B–Q2[4]	P–Q5
6 PxP	BxP	12 Q–K2[5]	....
7 B–KB4	N–QB3		

White wins the Queen next move

[1] Better is 5 QN–K2, P–QB4; 6 P–QB3, N–QB3; 7 P–KB4, Q–N3; 8 N–B3, P–B3; 9 P–QR3.

[2] Threatening two of White's Pawns, one by 9 ... BxPch, and the other by 9 ... QxP.

[3] One idea is to win the exchange by 11 N–B7ch, and the other is to cut off the retreat of Black's Queen.

[4] In order to win the Queen by 12 B–B3.

[5] Black cannot prevent White from playing 13 KR–N1, winning the Queen.

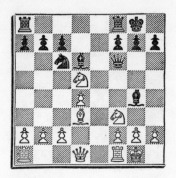

Black to Play. *White has won a Pawn, but in doing so, he permitted Black's Queen to get into the game. Black's well-posted pieces now rip up White's King side position.*

WHITE	BLACK	WHITE	BLACK
1 P–K4	P–K3	10	Q–R3[3]
2 P–Q4	P–Q4	11 P–KR3[4]	NxP![5]
3 PxP	PxP	12 B–K2	NxNch
4 N–KB3	N–KB3	13 BxN	BxP![6]
5 B–Q3	B–Q3	14 R–K1	B–K3
6 O–O	O–O	15 P–KN3	QR–Q1
7 B–KN5	B–KN5	16 Q–K2	BxN
8 N–B3	N–B3[1]	17 BxB	BxP
9 BxN[2]	QxB	18 B–K4	R–Q7
10 NxP?	....	19 Q–B3	Q–R7ch
SEE DIAGRAM		20 K–B1	RxPch

Black mates next move

[1] Baiting the trap with a Pawn.

[2] If at once 9 NxP, BxPch; 10 KxB, QxN, regains the Pawn with advantage to Black.

[3] Threatening 11 . . . BxN; 12 QxB, QxP mate.

[4] If 11 P–KN3, Q–R4; 12 N–B4, B(Q3)xN; 13 PxB, BxN wins for Black.

[5] So that he can reply to 12 PxB by 12 . . . NxNch; 13 QxN, Q–R7 mate.

[6] Now if 14 PxB, QxP; 15 R–K1, B–R7ch; 16 K–R1, B–N6ch, and mate in two more moves.

White to Play. Black has made a hazardous capture of a Pawn. It is instructive to see how White utilizes the awkward position of Black's Queen to force a decisive gain of material.

WHITE	BLACK	WHITE	BLACK
1 P–K4	P–QB4		SEE DIAGRAM
2 N–KB3	P–K3	9 N–B3![4]	N–K2
3 P–Q4	PxP	10 R–Q1	N–B3
4 NxP	P–QR3	11 Q–K3	N–K4
5 P–KN3[1]	Q–B2[2]	12 R–Q2[5]	N–B5
6 B–N2	N–QB3	13 RxQ	NxQ
7 O–O!	NxN[3]	14 BxN	....
8 QxN	QxBP?		

White has won a piece

[1] Another strong move for White is 5 P–QB4.
[2] Better is 5 ... P–Q4; 6 B–N2, PxP; 7 BxP, N–KB3; 8 B–N2, B–B4; 9 B–K3, Q–N3 etc.
[3] Black sees a chance to snatch a Pawn.
[4] Cuts off the Queen's retreat.
[5] The simplest way; a piece ahead is enough to win.

White to Play. The displacement of Black's King Knight, and the absence of his King Bishop, weaken his King side position, and he can put up little resistance to White's onslaught.

WHITE	BLACK	WHITE	BLACK
1 P–K4	P–QB4	8 Q–N4	BxNch[3]
2 N–KB3	P–K3	9 PxB	K–B1?[4]
3 P–Q4	PxP		SEE DIAGRAM
4 NxP	N–KB3	10 B–R3ch	K–N1[5]
5 N–QB3	B–N5?[1]	11 NxP[6]	PxN
6 B–Q3	P–Q4[2]	12 QxKP	....
7 P–K5!	KN–Q2		

Black has been checkmated

[1] Black's last move is questionable, as it allows White to work up a powerful attack. 5 . . . P–Q3 is preferable.

[2] And here 6 . . . P–K4 is better.

[3] No improvement on 8 . . . B–B1. Black's best chance is 8 . . . P–KN3.

[4] 9 . . . P–KN3 is not inviting, but it is better than the text, which turns out to be catastrophic.

[5] If 10 . . . K–K1; 11 QxP wins easily.

[6] With two powerful threats: 12 QxP mate, and 12 NxQ.

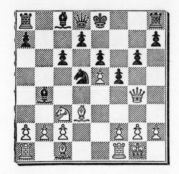

White to Play. *Black has just advanced his KBP two squares, attempting to drive away White's Queen, but this loses quickly.*

WHITE	BLACK	WHITE	BLACK
1 P–K4	P–QB4	8 P–K5	N–Q4
2 N–KB3	P–K3	9 Q–N4!	P–N3
3 P–Q4	PxP	10 O–O	P–KB4?
4 NxP	N–KB3		SEE DIAGRAM
5 N–QB3	B–N5?	11 PxPe.p.	BxN[3]
6 B–Q3	N–B3[1]	12 BxPch[4]	....
7 NxN	NPxN[2]		

White mates quickly

[1] This also leads to a difficult game. Black should play 6 . . . P–K4.

[2] Too slow; 7 . . . QPxN offers better prospects, although Black's position is uncomfortable.

[3] If 11 . . . QxP; 12 NxN followed by 13 QxB wins a piece. Or if 11 . . . NxP; 12 QxB. Finally, if 11 . . . NxN; 12 BxPch, PxB (12 . . . K–B1; 13 B–R6ch, K–N1; 14 P–B7 is mate); 13 QxNPch, K–B1; 14 Q–N7ch, K–K1; 15 P–B7ch; K–K2; 16 P–B8(Q) mates Black.

[4] After 12 . . . PxB; 13 QxNPch, K–B1; 14 B–R6ch, RxB; 15 Q–N7ch, K–K1; 16 Q–N8 is checkmate.

White to Play. Black *has been ultra-careful in his defense, instead of trying for counter-play. The result is that White sacrifices two pieces, and tears through his opponent's position.*

WHITE	BLACK	WHITE	BLACK
1 P–K4	P–QB4	9 NxKP!	PxN[3]
2 N–KB3	P–K3	10 B–N6ch!	PxB[4]
3 P–Q4	PxP	11 QxNPch	K–K2
4 NxP	N–KB3	12 B–N5ch	N–B3
5 N–QB3	B–N5	13 PxNch	K–Q2[5]
6 B–Q3	P–Q4[1]	14 PxP	B–K2
7 P–K5!	KN–Q2	15 PxR(Q)	QxQ
8 Q–N4	B–B1?[2]	16 Q–B7	....

SEE DIAGRAM

White has won the exchange

[1] 6 ... P–K4 is better.

[2] The best defense is 8 ... P–KN3; 9 NxP, BxNch; 10 PxB, NxP (not 10 ... PxN; 11 BxPch, PxB; 12 QxPch, K–B1; 13 B–R3ch and White wins); 11 Q–Q4, Q–K2; 12 QxN, but White, with his two Bishops, has somewhat the better game.

[3] If 9 ... NxP; 10 NxPch, K–K2; 11 B–N5ch, P–B3; 12 BxPch etc.

[4] If 10 ... K–K2; 11 B–N5ch, N–B3; 12 PxNch, PxP (if 12 ... K–Q2; 13 PxP wins); 13 BxPch, KxB; 14 Q–R4ch and White wins the Queen.

[5] Or 13 ... PxP; 14 BxPch wins Black's Queen.

Black to Play. *White has failed to realize that his apparently well-posted Knight (supported by Pawn and Bishop) might have the props knocked out from under him!*

WHITE	BLACK	WHITE	BLACK
1 P–K4	P–QB4		SEE DIAGRAM
2 N–KB3	P–K3	8	P–Q4![3]
3 P–Q4	PxP	9 PxP	P–K5
4 NxP	N–KB3	10 BxP[4]	R–K1[5]
5 N–QB3	B–N5	11 N–N3	NxB!
6 B–Q3	P–K4	12 BxQ[6]	NxN(B6)ch
7 N–B5[1]	O–O	13 K–Q2	NxQch
8 B–KN5?[2]	....	14 KxN	RxB

Black has won two pieces

[1] This leads to trouble. 7 N–K2 is better.

[2] The Knight should return to K3, in order to exert pressure on Q5.

[3] Threatens 9 ... P–Q5, as well as 9 ... PxP; 10 BxP, QxQch; 11 KxQ (if 11 RxQ, NxB wins) NxB; 12 NxN, BxN, and Black wins a piece.

[4] If 10 BxN, QxB; 11 BxP, BxN wins a piece.

[5] Threatening 11 ... RxBch, as well as 11 ... BxN.

[6] There is nothing better, for on 12 NxN, QxB wins, the "protecting" Knight being pinned.

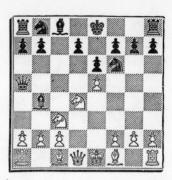

White to Play. *Black has left his Knight en prise, believing that his Queen-side attack will prevent White from capturing his Knight—or gain material if he does.*

WHITE	BLACK	WHITE	BLACK
1 P–K4	P–QB4	10 P–QB3!	Q–N8
2 N–KB3	P–K3	11 B–Q3	Q–N3
3 P–Q4	PxP	12 PxP	R–N1
4 NxP	N–KB3	13 Q–R6	P–B4
5 N–QB3	B–N5?	14 QxP	K–B2
6 P–K5![1]	Q–R4?[2]	15 NxBP	PxN[5]
SEE DIAGRAM		16 B–B4ch	K–K2
7 PxN[3]	BxNch	17 QxR	Q–KB3
8 PxB	QxPch	18 B–KN5	QxB
9 Q–Q2	QxR[4]		

White mates next move

[1] Stronger than 6 B–Q3.

[2] Looking forward to winning a Pawn, or the exchange. Had Black seen what was coming, he would have played 6 . . . N–Q4.

[3] Leaving Black no choice. If, instead, 7 B–Q2, QxPch wins a Pawn.

[4] This is what Black planned when he moved 6 . . . Q–R4. But now it is White's turn to attack.

[5] Otherwise 16 N–R6ch wins Black's Rook.

White to Play. In this trap Black loses because he misses completely the most obvious reply.

WHITE	BLACK	WHITE	BLACK
1 P–K4	P–QB4	7 Q–N4	P–KN3
2 N–KB3	P–K3	8 P–QR3	Q–R4?[1]
3 P–Q4	PxP		SEE DIAGRAM
4 NxP	N–KB3	9 PxB![2]	QxR
5 N–QB3	B–N5?	10 N–N3	....
6 P–K5	N–Q4		

White wins the Queen

[1] To strengthen the pressure on White's pinned Knight, which is now attacked three times. Black isn't worried about the attack on his Bishop, as White's Rook Pawn is pinned.
[2] Teaching Black that it is dangerous for chess players to take things for granted!

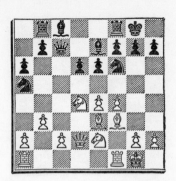

Black to Play. *White's minor pieces are jumbled together awkwardly. The following stroke by Black highlights this difficulty.*

WHITE	BLACK	WHITE	BLACK
1 P–K4	P–QB4	12 P–QN3	R–N1
2 N–KB3	P–K3	13 QN–K2?[2]	....
3 P–Q4	PxP	SEE DIAGRAM	
4 NxP	N–KB3	13	P–K4!
5 N–QB3	P–Q3	14 PxP[3]	PxP
6 B–K2	N–B3	15 N–B5	BxN
7 O–O	B–K2	16 PxB	P–K5
8 B–K3	P–QR3	17 B–B4	Q–N3ch
9 P–B4	Q–B2	18 B–K3[4]	B–B4!
10 B–B3	O–O	19 BxB	QxBch
11 Q–Q2[1]	N–QR4	20 N–Q4	N–B3!

Black wins a piece

[1] More exact is 11 Q–K2, allowing for 12 QR–Q1 and 13 B–B1, in case Black plays . . . N–QR4 followed by . . . N–B5.
[2] This loses a piece. White should play 13 P–KN4.
[3] If 14 N–B5, BxN; 15 PxB, P–K5, and Black wins the Bishop.
[4] If 18 K–R1, PxB wins.

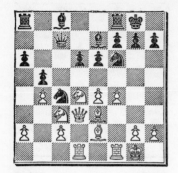

White to Play. Seemingly Black's Knight is firmly entrenched at B5, supported by Queen and Pawn. But a sacrifice by White removes the Pawn support, and nets him two Pawns.

WHITE	BLACK	WHITE	BLACK
1 P–K4	P–QB4	10 P–B4	Q–B2
2 N–KB3	P–K3	11 QR–Q1	N–QR4[1]
3 P–Q4	PxP	12 Q–Q3	P–QN4?[2]
4 NxP	N–KB3	13 P–QN4!	N–B5[3]
5 N–QB3	P–Q3		SEE DIAGRAM
6 B–K2	N–B3	14 N(Q4)xNP[4]	PxN
7 O–O	B–K2	15 NxP	Q–B3
8 B–K3	P–QR3	16 QxN	....
9 Q–Q2	O–O		

White has won two Pawns

[1] Black wants to plant the Knight at B5, at which square it would exert tremendous pressure.

[2] More accurate would be 12 ... B–Q2; 13 P–QN4, QR–B1!

[3] A difficult situation. If 13 ... N–B3; 14 NxN, QxN; 15 P–K5 with the better game for White; or 13 ... N–N2; 14 P–QR4, again with advantage to White. But the square B5 looks appetizing to Black!

[4] A temporary loan, which White gets back with interest.

White to Play. *Black has carried out his plan of getting "the two Bishops" but he has neglected securing his King against attack. Now White rips apart Black's King side position.*

WHITE	BLACK	WHITE	BLACK
1 P–K4	P–QB4	11 BxN	QxB
2 N–KB3	P–K3	12 PxP	PxP[3]
3 P–Q4	PxP		SEE DIAGRAM
4 NxP	N–KB3	13 RxN!	PxR
5 N–QB3	P–Q3	14 Q–R5ch	K–Q1[4]
6 B–K2	N–B3	15 Q–B7!	B–K2
7 O–O	P–QR3	16 N–B5!	R–K1[5]
8 B–K3	Q–B2	17 NxP!	BxN
9 P–B4?[1]	N–QR4?[1]	18 B–N6ch	B–B2
10 P–B5	N–B5?[2]	19 R–Q1ch	....

White checkmates in two moves

[1] Premature; 9 ... B–K2 is best here.

[2] Again, 10 ... B–K2 is safer. On 10 ... P–K4; 11 N–N3, N–B5; 12 BxN, QxB; 13 Q–B3, B–K2; 14 B–N5 is strong for White.

[3] 12 ... BxP was his best chance.

[4] If 14 ... K–K2; 15 N–B5ch!, PxN; 16 N–Q5ch, K–Q1 (16 ... K–K3; 17 Q–K8ch wins); 17 B–N6ch, K–Q2; 18 Q–B7ch, K–B3; 19 Q–B7ch, K–N4; 20 P–R4ch, QxP; 21 P–B4ch, QxP; 22 R–R5 mate. Or if 14 ... K–Q2; 15 Q–B7ch, B–K2; 16 N–B5!, R–K1; 17 R–Q1, and White's threats of 18 NxP or 18 RxPch cannot be met.

[5] If 16 ... Q–B2; 17 N–QR4 (threatening 18 B–N6) wins.

White to Play. *If White now captures the Knight, Black has a clever combination in mind; but he fails to reckon with an even more subtle refutation.*

WHITE	BLACK	WHITE	BLACK
1 P–K4	P–QB4	9 Q–N4!	NxN[2]
2 N–KB3	P–K3		SEE DIAGRAM
3 P–B4	N–QB3	10 P–QR3![3]	B–R4[4]
4 N–B3	N–B3	11 QxP	R–B1
5 P–Q4	PxP	12 P–QN4	B–B2
6 NxP	B–N5	13 B–N5	BxP[5]
7 NxN	NPxN[1]	14 QxRch!	KxQ
8 P–K5	N–K5	15 BxQ	....

White has won the exchange

[1] The recapture with the Queen Pawn is almost always preferable in such positions.

[2] Black is playing for this beautiful win: 10 PxN, BxPch; 11 K–Q1, BxR; 12 QxP, R–B1; 13 B–R3, P–Q3; 14 BxP, QxBch!; 15 PxQ, BxQ, and Black is a Rook and Bishop ahead.

[3] But White does not recapture. Instead he attacks the Bishop.

[4] If 10 ... Q–R4; 11 QxP, R–B1; 12 B–Q3, N–K5ch; 13 PxB, QxR; 14 O–O and White has a terrific attack. However, 10 ... N–Q4ch is relatively better than the text.

[5] Hoping for 14 QxB, P–B3; 15 QxN, PxB; but White refuses to be swindled.

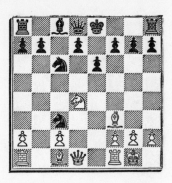

White to Play. *Black has won two Pawns, but lines have been opened for White's pieces. They spring into action, and their sharp attack forces the win of Black's Queen.*

WHITE	BLACK	WHITE	BLACK
1 P–K4	P–QB4	10 Q–Q3	N–Q4[3]
2 N–KB3	N–QB3	11 BxN	PxB
3 P–Q4	PxP	12 R–K1ch	K–B1
4 NxP	N–B3	13 N–B5!	P–Q3
5 N–QB3	P–K3	14 NxNP!	N–K4[4]
6 B–K2	B–N5	15 N–R5!!	B–K3[5]
7 O–O[1]	BxN	16 RxN!	PxR
8 PxB	NxP	17 B–R3ch	K–K1
9 B–B3	NxQBP?[2]	18 Q–N5ch!	Q–Q2[6]
SEE DIAGRAM		19 N–B6ch	

White wins the Queen

[1] 7 B–B3 is the safer course.

[2] But this is too much of a good thing. 9 ... P–Q4 is better.

[3] If 10 ... N–R5; 11 B–R3 gives White a powerful game; or if 10 ... NxN; 11 QxN(Q4), N–Q4; 12 BxN, PxB; 13 QxNP, R–B1; 14 R–K1ch is sheer murder.

[4] If 14 ... KxN; 15 Q–N3ch, K–B3 (15 ... K–B1; 16 B–R6 mate) 16 Q–N5 is mate.

[5] If 15 ... NxQ; 16 B–R6ch, K–N1; 17 R–K8ch!,QxR; 18 N–B6 mates Black.

[6] Or 18 ... B–Q2; 19 N–N7 mate.

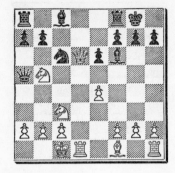

Black to Play. *White has captured an attractive-looking center Pawn with his Queen, but he will pay for it with one of his Bishops.*

WHITE	BLACK	WHITE	BLACK
1 P-K4	P-QB4	10 KN-N5	Q-R4!
2 N-KB3	N-QB3	11 QxP?[1]	....
3 P-Q4	PxP		SEE DIAGRAM
4 NxP	N-B3	11	P-QR3
5 N-QB3	P-Q3	12 N-R3[2]	BxN
6 B-KN5	P-K3	13 N-B4[3]	B-N5!
7 Q-Q2	B-K2	14 NxQ	BxQ
8 O-O-O	O-O	15 NxN[4]	B-B5ch![5]
9 BxN	BxB	16 K-N1	PxN

Black has won a piece

[1] It is hard to resist taking so important a Pawn!

[2] If 12 N-B7, B-K4; 13 Q-Q3, QxN(B2) wins a piece.

[3] If 13 PxB, R-Q1 forces White's Queen to give up the protection of the Knight, and Black wins a piece.

[4] 15 RxB will not do, as 15 . . . NxN leaves Black a Knight up.

[5] Disappointing White, whose last hope was that Black might play 15 . . . PxN, when 16 RxB would save him.

White to Play. *In offering a series of exchanges, which can be carried out in different ways, every possible capture must be carefully studied. Here Black's neglect of this principle proves expensive.*

WHITE	BLACK	WHITE	BLACK
1 P–K4	P–QB4	7 B–K3	B–N2
2 N–KB3	N–QB3	8 O–O	N–KN5?[1]
3 P–Q4	PxP	SEE DIAGRAM	
4 NxP	N–B3	9 BxN!	BxB[2]
5 N–QB3	P–Q3	10 NxN[3]	BxQ[4]
6 B–K2	P–KN3	11 NxQ	....

White has won a piece

[1] 8 . . . O–O should be played. The text is a premature attempt to simplify by exchanging, which costs a piece.

[2] If 9 . . . NxN or 9 . . . BxN; 10 B(N4)xB wins for White.

[3] Not 10 QxB, NxN with equality.

[4] No better is 10 . . . PxN; 11 QxB, and White is a piece up.

White to Play. *Black should have been more careful about protecting his Q4 square. Now White can win a piece by force.*

WHITE	BLACK	WHITE	BLACK
1 P–K4	P–QB4	9 Q–Q2	P–QR3
2 N–KB3	N–QB3	10 R–Q1	Q–B2
3 P–Q4	PxP	11 P–KN4	P–QN4?[1]
4 NxP	N–B3		SEE DIAGRAM
5 N–QB3	P–Q3	12 P–N5	N–Q2[2]
6 B–K2	P–KN3	13 N–Q5!	Q–N2
7 B–K3	B–N2	14 NxN	QxN[3]
8 P–KR3	O–O	15 NxPch	....

White wins the Queen

[1] Loses a piece. 11 ... B–K3 is a playable alternative.

[2] The Knight must leave, for if 12 ... P–N5; 13 PxN, PxN; 14 QxP, and White threatens two pieces (15 QxN as well as 15 PxB).

[3] Else Black is a piece down—which would mean a longer, but still a futile resistance.

White to Play. *Black has fatally weakened his black squares. White pounces on the weakness, even giving up a Rook to maintain his strangle-hold.*

WHITE	BLACK	WHITE	BLACK
1 P–K4	P–QB4	SEE DIAGRAM	
2 N–KB3	N–QB3	9 Q–Q6!	QxPch
3 N–B3	P–K3	10 K–Q1![2]	QxRch
4 P–Q4	PxP	11 K–Q2	K–Q1
5 NxP	B–N5	12 Q–B8ch	K–B2
6 NxN	BxNch?	13 B–Q6ch	K–N3[3]
7 PxB	NPxN?[1]	14 Q–Q8ch	K–N2
8 B–R3!	Q–R4	15 Q–B7	....

Black has been checkmated

[1] 7 . . . QPxN is better. The text gives White altogether too much scope on the diagonal QR3–KB8.

[2] Allowing the Queen Rook to be captured, and with check!

[3] If 13 . . . K–N2; 14 B–R6ch, KxB; 15 RxQ wins for White.

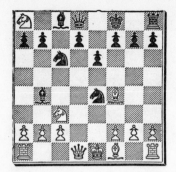

Black to Play. *White has won a Rook by a premature attack. The waste of time leaves him helpless against a fierce counter-attack.*

WHITE	BLACK	WHITE	BLACK
1 P–K4	P–QB4		SEE DIAGRAM	
2 N–KB3	N–QB3	9	Q–B3[3]
3 N–B3	P–K3	10 Q–B3[4]	NxN
4 P–Q4	PxP	11 B–Q2	N–Q5
5 NxP	N–B3	12 Q–Q3[5]	Q–K4ch
6 KN–N5	B–N5	13 B–K3[6]	N–R5ch
7 B–KB4?[1]	NxP	14 P–B3[7]	NxNP
8 N–B7ch	K–B1	15 QxN[8]	BxPch
9 NxR[2]	....		

Black wins the Queen

[1] The safe move is 7 P–QR3.

[2] White cannot afford to take the Rook. 9 Q–B3 offered better defensive chances.

[3] With a double attack on the Queen Knight and the Queen Bishop.

[4] If 10 B–Q2, QxP mate.

[5] If 12 QxQ, NxBP is mate.

[6] If 13 B–K2, N(Q5)xB; 14 BxN (or 14 PxN, N–B5ch; 15 Q–K3, NxPch), NxBch wins for Black.

[7] On 14 K–Q1, NxPch wins White's Queen.

[8] If 15 Q–Q2, N–B6ch; 16 PxN, BxP wins the Queen.

White to Play. *Black has made the mistake of choosing an opening variation which permits a combined attack on his King Bishop Pawn, before castling is available as a defense.*

WHITE	BLACK	WHITE	BLACK
1 P–K4	P–QB4		SEE DIAGRAM
2 N–KB3	N–KB3	7 Q–B3!	P–B3³
3 N–B3	P–Q4	8 Q–R5ch	P–N3
4 PxP	NxP	9 NxP	K–B2
5 B–N5ch¹	B–Q2	10 N–K5ch!⁴	....
6 N–K5!	NxN?²		

White wins the Queen

¹ A tricky line of play which must be met with care.

² 6 . . . BxB is better, but not quite good enough: 7 Q–B3!, P–B3; 8 NxB, PxN; 9 QxN, QxQ; 10 N–B7ch, K–Q2; 11 NxQ, N–B3; 12 P–Q3, and Black's doubled King Pawn will prove a fatal weakness. The conservative 6 . . . N–KB3 is much safer.

³ The lesser evil is 7 . . . Q–B2; 8 BxBch, NxB; 9 QxPch, K–Q1; 10 NxN, and White wins a pawn.

⁴ If 10 . . . K–K3 (10 . . . K–N2; 11 Q–B7ch, K–R3; 12 QPxN is mate); 11 B–B4ch, N–Q4 (11 . . . K–Q3; 12 N–B7ch wins the Queen); 12 BxNch, KxB; 13 N–B7ch, and Black's Queen goes.

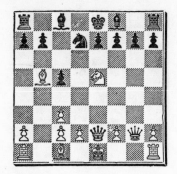

White to Play. *Black has violated sound opening principles by neglecting his development to win a Pawn with his Queen. The refutation is astonishing.*

WHITE	BLACK	WHITE	BLACK
1 P–K4	P–QB4	10 K–K2	P–K3
2 N–KB3	N–KB3	11 BxNch	K–K2
3 N–B3	P–Q4	12 BxB	RxB
4 PxP	NxP	13 Q–Q7ch	K–B3
5 N–K5	NxN	14 QxBPch!!	KxN³
6 NPxN	Q–Q4	15 P–Q4ch	K–Q4⁴
7 B–N5ch	N–Q2	16 QxNPch	R–B3⁵
8 Q–K2	QxNP?¹	17 P–B4ch	KxBP⁶
SEE DIAGRAM		18 Q–N3ch	KxP
9 Q–Q3!!	QxRch²	19 B–K3ch	....

White wins the Queen

¹ 8 . . . P–QR3 is good here. The Pawn capture is exploited by White in a startling manner.

² Black must go through with his plans.

³ 14 . . . K–N4; 15 P–Q4ch also loses quickly for Black.

⁴ If 15 . . . PxP; 16 B–B4ch wins Black's Queen; or if 15 . . . K–K5; 16 QxKP is mate.

⁵ Forced, if 16 . . . K–Q3; 17 QxQ, while after 16 . . . K–B5; 17 Q–N3 is mate.

⁶ If 17 . . . K–Q3 or 17 . . . KxQP, a Bishop check wins the Queen.

Black to Play. *White has won two Pawns and now regains a sacrificed piece, but the loss of time proves fatal.*

WHITE	BLACK	WHITE	BLACK
1 P–K4	P–QB4	9 Q–K3	B–Q3
2 N–KB3	N–KB3	10 NxP?[4]	BxN
3 N–B3	P–Q4	11 P–B4	....
4 PxP	NxP	SEE DIAGRAM	
5 B–B4	N–N3	11	O–O
6 Q–K2[1]	NxB	12 PxB	N–Q5!
7 QxN	N–B3!?[2]	13 Q–Q3[5]	B–B4
8 QxP[3]	P–K4	14 N–K4	Q–R5ch[6]

Black wins a piece

[1] Much better than 6 B–N5ch, B–Q2; 7 BxBch, QxB, and Black develops quickly.

[2] An interesting Pawn sacrifice; the alternative 7 . . . P–K3; 8 P–Q4, PxP; 9 NxP gives White's pieces too much scope.

[3] Safer is 8 O–O, P–K3; 9 P–Q4, PxP; 10 QN–N5.

[4] White should play 10 P–QR3 to guard against 10 . . . N–N5, a troublesome move to meet.

[5] If 10 K–Q1, B–N5ch; 11 N–K2, BxNch; 12 K–K1, NxPch, and White's Queen falls.

[6] Black continues with 15 . . . QxN, winning a piece.

White to Play. Black h a s opened up the game prematurely. Now White refutes his opponent's tactics by a clever series of exchanges ending in a Knight fork.

WHITE	BLACK	WHITE	BLACK
1 P-K4	P-QB4	9 B-QN5	Q-Q3[1]
2 N-KB3	P-Q3	10 PxP	NxP
3 P-Q4	PxP	SEE DIAGRAM	
4 NxP	N-KB3	11 N(Q4)xN	PxN[2]
5 P-KB3	N-B3	12 QxN!	QxQ[3]
6 P-QB4	P-K3	13 NxQ	PxB[4]
7 N-B3	P-Q4?	14 N-B7ch	K-Q1
8 BPxP	PxP	15 NxR	....

White has won the exchange

[1] Black's premature attempt to free his game, by advancing the Queen Pawn, is about to cause him far more trouble than one would suspect in this apparently safe position.

[2] If 11 ... NxN; 12 QxQ, BxQ; 13 PxN, PxN; 14 BxPch wins Black's Rook.

[3] On 12 ... PxB; 13 QxR wins.

[4] Unfortunately, the annoying Knight cannot be removed.

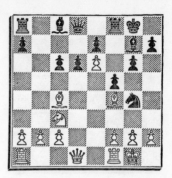

White to Play. Black h a s just castled, giving White the opportunity to play a winning combination based on a discovered check.

WHITE	BLACK	WHITE	BLACK
1 P–K4	P–QB4	9 P–K6	P–KB4[2]
2 N–KB3	P–Q3	10 O–O	B–KN2[3]
3 P–Q4	PxP	11 B–B4	O–O?[4]
4 NxP	N–KB3		SEE DIAGRAM
5 N–QB3	P–KN3	12 BxP!	QxB
6 B–QB4	N–B3	13 QxQ	PxQ
7 NxN!	PxN	14 P–K7ch	P–Q4[5]
8 P–K5	N–N5[1]	15 PxR(Q)ch	....

White has won the exchange

[1] If 8 . . . PxP; 9 BxPch, KxB; 10 QxQ wins.

[2] If 9 . . . BxP; 10 BxB, PxB; 11 QxN wins a piece.

[3] Black avoids the trap: 10 . . . P–Q4; 11 NxP, PxN; 12 B–N5ch, B–Q2; 13 BxBch and he must give up his Queen.

[4] Black should play instead 11 . . . N–K4.

[5] Too late, Black sees that 14 . . . R–B2 would not be answered by 15 BxRch, KxB, but by the simple 15 P–K8 (Q)ch.

White to Play. *Black has made a routine reply to an unusual move. Now White demonstrates how dangerous this can be.*

WHITE	BLACK	WHITE	BLACK
1 P–K4	P–QB4	9 B–N5ch	K–B1[3]
2 N–KB3	P–Q3	10 O–O	BxP[4]
3 P–Q4	PxP	11 B–R6ch	K–N1[5]
4 NxP	N–KB3	12 NxN	QxN
5 N–QB3	P–KN3	13 N–B5![6]	Q–B4ch
6 P–B4	B–N2?[1]	14 B–K3[7]	Q–B2
7 P–K5	PxP	15 N–R6ch	K–B1
8 PxP	N–Q4[2]	16 RxP	....

SEE DIAGRAM

Black has been checkmated

[1] A routine response, overlooking White's threats. 6 . . . N–B3; 7 NxN, PxN; 8 P–K5, N–Q2 is a satisfactory line.

[2] If 8 . . . N–N5; 9 B–N5ch, K–B1 (if 9 . . . B–Q2 or 9 . . . N–Q2; 10 QxN wins); 10 N–K6ch wins Black's Queen.

[3] If 9 . . . B–Q2 or 9 . . . N–Q2; 10 NxN wins a piece; if 9 . . . N–B3; 10 KNxN wins for White.

[4] If 10 . . . NxN; 11 N–K6ch mates quickly.

[5] Black cannot afford 11 . . . B–N2; 12 BxBch, KxB; 13 NxN, QxN; 14 N–B5ch winning the Queen.

[6] Threatening 14 QxQ, as well as 14 NxP mate.

[7] Now the threats are 15 BxQ and 15 Q–Q8 mate.

Black to Play. *White has developed slowly and wasted time by Pawn-snatching in the opening. Now he pays the penalty.*

WHITE	BLACK	WHITE	BLACK
1 P–K4	P–QB4	9 NxP?[2]	N–Q5[3]
2 N–QB3	N–QB3	10 NxNch?[4]	....
3 P–KN3	P–K3	SEE DIAGRAM	
4 B–N2	N–B3	10	QxN
5 KN–K2	P–Q4	11 P–KB3[5]	QxP!
6 PxP	PxP[1]	12 BxQ	NxBch
7 P–Q4	B–N5	13 K–B1	B–KR6
8 PxP	BxP		

White has been checkmated

[1] White's rather slow development has allowed Black to obtain a fine free position.

[2] Black's development is too far advanced for White to be able to make this capture, without running into trouble.

[3] Threatening to win White's pinned Knight.

[4] Loses quickly. The best chance was 10 QN–B3, although in that event 10 ... B–B6 is strong.

[5] This attempt to avoid the loss of a piece is refuted by a mating attack. If 11 B–B1 (to protect the Knight), N–B6 is mate.

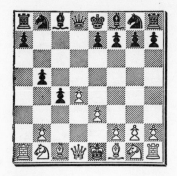

White to Play. *White wins a piece in one move, by seizing the weakened long diagonal.*

WHITE	BLACK	WHITE	BLACK
1 P–Q4	P–Q4	5 PxP	PxP?[3]
2 P–QB4	PxP		SEE DIAGRAM
3 P–K3	P–QN4?[1]	6 Q–B3[4]	....
4 P–QR4	P–QB3[2]		

White wins a piece

[1] These attempts to hold the gambit Pawn are generally best avoided, as too much time is lost in the process.

[2] If 4 . . . PxP; 5 QxPch, B–Q2; 6 QxBP, with tremendous positional advantage for White. If 4 . . . B–Q2; 5 PxP, BxP; 6 P–QN3, Q–Q4; 7 PxP, BxP; 8 Q–R4ch, and White wins the Bishop.

[3] Black means to hold on to the gambit Pawn at all cost. The result is the immediate loss of a piece.

[4] In order to avoid the loss of a Rook, Black must play 6 . . . N–QB3. After 7 QxNch, B–Q2, White with a piece for a Pawn has an easy win. Simple as this trap is, it is an important one for the beginner who worries about recovering the gambit Pawn.

White to Play. *White has played a combination to win the exchange. Having sacrificed a Knight he can now win Black's Queen Rook. But the idea is unsound and will cost White his Queen.*

WHITE	BLACK	WHITE	BLACK
1 P–Q4	P–Q4	7 N–K5?[2]	P–K3!
2 P–QB4	PxP	8 NxKBP[3]	KxN
3 N–KB3	P–QB3[1]	9 Q–B3ch	N–B3
4 P–K3	P–QN4		SEE DIAGRAM
5 P–QR4	Q–N3	10 QxR	B–N5ch
6 PxP	PxP	11 K–Q1	N–B3[4]

Black wins the Queen

[1] An important move in the theory of this opening. If Black can support and keep his Pawn, then 3 N–KB3 is refuted, and White must instead play 3 P–K3, to get back his Pawn.

[2] Once considered a winning move for White, but now found wanting. Correct is 7 P–QN3! (with winning chances if Black hangs on to his extra Pawn), PxP; 8 QxP, P–N5 (if 8 ... P–QR3; 9 BxPch, or if 8 ... B–Q2; 9 N–K5, P–K3; 10 NxB followed by 11 BxP); 9 Q–Q5, B–N2; 10 B–N5ch, B–B3; 11 N–K5!, QxB; 12 QxPch, K–Q1; 13 QxBch, and White has a decisive advantage.

[3] If 8 Q–B3, threatening 9 QxR as well as 9 QxPch, then 8 ... Q–N2 parries both threats.

[4] Black continues with 12 ... R–Q1 and 13 ... B–N2 winning the Queen.

White to Play. *Black seems to have a great many defenders of his extra Pawn. White breaks down all the defenses, and ends up with a decisive gain of material.*

WHITE	BLACK	WHITE	BLACK
1 P–Q4	P–Q4	7 PxP	PxP
2 P–QB4	PxP	8 P–QN3	PxP[3]
3 N–KB3	N–KB3	9 RxB!	NxR
4 P–K3	P–QN4	10 BxPch	N–Q2
5 P–QR4	P–B3[1]	11 BxNch[4]	QxB
6 N–K5	B–R3[2]	12 NxQ	....

SEE DIAGRAM

White has won the Queen for a Rook

[1] 5 . . . P–QR3 is no defense, for after 6 PxP, Black cannot retake. Best would be 5 . . . P–N5, returning the Pawn at once, with a playable game.

[2] The way in which this move is refuted is highly instructive.

[3] If 8 . . . Q–Q4; 9 PxP, PxP; 10 RxB, NxR; 11 Q–R4ch followed by 12 QxN wins for White.

[4] A mistake would be 11 BxN, Q–R4ch followed by 12 . . . QxB.

White to Play. Black has delayed one move in recapturing a Pawn—and falls into a trap. When he does take the Pawn, it costs him a Rook.

WHITE	BLACK	WHITE	BLACK
1 P–Q4	P–Q4	9 PxP	Q–B2?[1]
2 P–QB4	PxP	SEE DIAGRAM	
3 N–KB3	N–KB3	10 N–Q4!	BxP[2]
4 P–K3	P–K3	11 NxN	QxN
5 BxP	P–B4	12 B–B3	N–Q4[3]
6 N–B3	P–QR3	13 NxN	PxN
7 O–O	P–QN4	14 BxP	....
8 B–K2	N–B3		

White wins a Rook

[1] So far Black has developed satisfactorily, but the text is a mistake. He should be content with the simple 9 . . . BxP.
[2] If 10 . . . NxN; 11 PxN, and Black loses a Pawn without any compensation for it, but that was preferable to "regaining" the Pawn—and losing much more!
[3] Blocks the action of White's Bishop—but only for a moment.

White to Play. *White punishes Black's Pawn-snatching by a capturing check, which drives Black's King away, leaving the Queen unprotected.*

WHITE	BLACK	WHITE	BLACK
1 P–Q4	P–Q4	5 BxP	PxP?[1]
2 P–QB4	PxP		SEE DIAGRAM
3 N–KB3	P–QB4	6 BxPch[2]	KxB
4 P–K3	PxP	7 QxQ[3]	....

White has won the Queen

[1] 5 . . . P–K3 transposes to the usual line of play, with a good game.

[2] White takes advantage of the fact that Black's King is "overworked." The King has the double duty of guarding the Queen, as well as his Bishop's Pawn.

[3] This trap continues to claim many victims.

Black to Play. *White has just advanced his King Pawn —a plausible but premature move. Now Black can win the Queen Pawn.*

WHITE	BLACK	WHITE	BLACK
1 P–Q4	P–Q4	7 O–O	B–Q3
2 P–QB4	PxP	8 B–K2[2]	O–O
3 N–KB3	B–N5	9 P–K4?[3]	....
4 P–K3	P–K3		SEE DIAGRAM
5 BxP	N–KB3	9	BxN
6 N–B3	N–B3[1]	10 BxB	NxQP[4]

Black has won a Pawn

[1] Black is playing for an early . . . P–K4, possible here because of the unusual development of his Queen Bishop to N5.
[2] To free himself from the annoying pin of his King Knight.
[3] White's idea is to release his Queen Bishop, and develop it at N5 or K3, meanwhile establishing a strong Pawn center.
[4] Black wins an important Pawn for if 11 QxN, BxPch; 12 KxB, QxQ.

Black to Play. White has brought his Queen into play too soon. Now Black makes use of all his minor pieces to drive the Queen to a square where a Pawn can get in the final blow.

WHITE	BLACK	WHITE	BLACK
1 P–Q4	P–Q4	9 P–Q5?[2]	....
2 P–QB4	PxP	SEE DIAGRAM	
3 N–QB3	P–K3	9	B–KN5
4 P–K3	N–KB3	10 Q–N3	P–K5
5 BxP	P–QR3	11 Q–R4	N–K4[3]
6 Q–B3?[1]	N–B3!	12 B–N3	N–N3
7 KN–K2	B–Q3	13 Q–N5	P–R3
8 B–Q2	P–K4		

Black wins the Queen

[1] Early Queen development is not good. 6 N–B3 (controlling K5) is the natural course.

[2] Better, in such positions as this, where the Queen is likely to be harassed by enemy pieces, is some move which will lead to exchanges. In this case, 9 N–K4 was called for.

[3] By attacking the Bishop, Black gains time to bring another piece into action against the Queen.

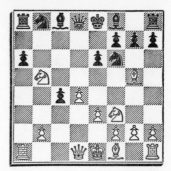

Black to Play. *White has played the opening badly. Now Black can win at least a Pawn.*

WHITE	BLACK	WHITE	BLACK
1 P–Q4	P–Q4		SEE DIAGRAM
2 P–QB4	P–K3	9	Q–N3!
3 N–QB3	N–KB3	10 N–R3?[4]	Q–R4ch
4 N–B3	P–QR3	11 K–K2[5]	N–K5!
5 B–N5[1]	PxP[2]	12 B–B4	BxN
6 P–K3	P–N4	13 RxB[6]	QxR!
7 P–QR4	P–B3	14 PxQ	N–B6ch
8 PxP?[3]	BPxP	15 K–K1	NxQ
9 NxP?	....		

Black has won the exchange

[1] Best is 5 PxP, PxP; 6 B–KN5, B–K2; 7 P–K3, QN–Q2; 8 Q–B2, O–O; 9 B–Q3, and White has an excellent game.

[2] Now Black decides to take the gambit Pawn, and hold on to it!

[3] This effort to win back the Pawn loses. White should instead play for attack by 8 N–K5, 9 P–B4, 10 B–K2 and 11 O–O.

[4] Loses quickly. Relatively better is 10 N–B3, QxNP; 11 Q–B1, B–R6! 12 P–K4, QxQch; 13 BxQ, B–N5; 14 B–Q2, BxN; 15 BxB, NxP; 16 BxP, NxB; 17 QR–B1, B–N2! 18 RxN, N–Q2, and Black's extra Pawn wins.

[5] If 11 Q–Q2, B–N5 wins the Queen, or if 11 N–Q2, QxB wins a piece.

[6] If 13 PxB, N–B6ch wins the Queen.

Black to Play. *Black astonishes his opponent — who thinks he has won a Pawn — by sacrificing his Queen, and then getting it back with one of White's Knights as interest!*

WHITE	BLACK	WHITE	BLACK
1 P–Q4	P–Q4	SEE DIAGRAM	
2 P–QB4	P–K3	6	NxN!
3 N–QB3	N–KB3	7 BxQ	B–N5ch
4 B–N5	QN–Q2	8 Q–Q2[2]	BxQch
5 PxP	PxP	9 KxB	KxB[3]
6 NxP?[1]	....		

Black has won a piece

[1] White carelessly snatches a Pawn before completing his development. Instead he should have played either 6 P–K3, or 6 N–B3.

[2] White must give back the Queen.

[3] A trap of such frequent occurrence that it has been seen even in master tournaments!

Black to Play. *Black bases his plan of attack on the fact that White's Queen is somewhat awkwardly placed.*

WHITE	BLACK	WHITE	BLACK
1 P–Q4	P–Q4	8 Q–N3?[2]	....
2 P–QB4	P–K3	SEE DIAGRAM	
3 N–QB3	N–KB3	8	N–K5![3]
4 B–N5	QN–Q2	9 BxN	PxB
5 N–B3	B–N5	10 N–K5[4]	P–B3
6 P–K3	P–B4	11 NxN	BxN
7 B–Q3[1]	Q–R4	12 B–R4[5]	B–R5![6]

Black wins the Queen

[1] Better is 7 BPxP, KPxP; 8 B–Q3.

[2] In this variation, which is related to the Cambridge Springs line, White must play with great care. Here he would be better off with 8 O–O, BxN; 9 PxB, QxBP; 10 R–B1 with attacking chances.

[3] With a triple attack on the pinned Knight.

[4] If 10 N–Q2, PxP; 11 PxP, BxN; 12 PxB, QxB, and Black wins a piece.

[5] Saves the Bishop, but—

[6] suddenly White's Queen has no move! If 13 QxBch, QxQ, and the pinned Knight cannot recapture.

Black to Play. *W h i t e ' s Queen Bishop is unprotected, and an easy target of attack. Black can capitalize on this positional weakness and win a piece.*

WHITE	BLACK	WHITE	BLACK
1 P–Q4	P–Q4	8 Q–B2	O–O
2 P–QB4	P–K3	9 B–Q3?[2]	....
3 N–QB3	N–KB3	SEE DIAGRAM	
4 B–N5	QN–Q2	9	PxP[3]
5 P–K3	P–B3	10 BxN	BPxB![4]
6 N–B3	Q–R4[1]	11 QxP	NxB
7 N–Q2	B–N5		

Black has won a piece

[1] This (Cambridge Springs) variation is one of the trickiest lines of play in this opening.

[2] Beware of playing this move against the Cambridge Springs Defense. Black's indirect attack on White's Queen Bishop often comes to fruition after B–Q3. The proper move instead, is 9 B–K2.

[3] Attacking one Bishop with the Pawn and the other Bishop with the Queen.

[4] The threat against White's Queen gives Black time to win the other Bishop.

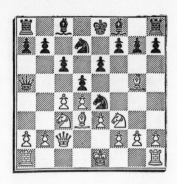

Black to Play. *This situation differs from the previous trap in that White's Bishop at N5 is protected. An exchange will bring about the desired position, where Black can win a piece by double attack.*

WHITE	BLACK	WHITE	BLACK
1 P–Q4	P–Q4	7 B–Q3[1]	N–K5!
2 P–QB4	P–K3	8 Q–B2?[2]	....
3 N–QB3	N–KB3	SEE DIAGRAM	
4 B–N5	QN–Q2	8	NxB
5 P–K3	P–B3	9 NxN	PxP[3]
6 N–B3	Q–R4		

Black wins a piece

[1] The safe way is 7 N–Q2, B–N5; 8 Q–B2, O–O; 9 B–K2.

[2] Natural enough, but it loses a piece instantly. 8 BxN is better, for after 8 . . . PxB; 9 N–K5!, NxN; 10 PxN, White's King Pawn is temporarily immune because of the mating threat at Q8.

[3] Two of White's pieces are threatened simultaneously, and one of them must be lost.

Black to Play. *White's last move was a very plausible one, as B4 is usually a good spot for a Bishop. This time it loses, as Black can win the Queen in two moves.*

WHITE	BLACK	WHITE	BLACK
1 P–Q4	P–Q4	10 QPxP	N–K5
2 P–QB4	P–K3	11 KNxN	PxN
3 N–QB3	N–KB3	12 O–O	BxN
4 B–N5	QN–Q2	13 PxB	NxP
5 P–K3	P–B3	14 QxP[1]	P–B3
6 N–B3	Q–R4	15 B–B4?[2]	....
7 N–Q2	B–N5		SEE DIAGRAM
8 Q–B2	O–O	15	B–B4!
9 B–K2	P–K4!	16 Q–Q4[3]	QR–Q1[4]

Black wins the Queen

[1] This is playable, but it has to be followed up carefully.
[2] 15 B–R4 is correct, after which Black can either recover his Pawn at once with 15 . . . QxBP, or play 15 . . . B–K3.
[3] If 16 QxB, N–B6ch; 17 BxN, QxQ wins.
[4] Capturing the Queen in the very middle of the board!

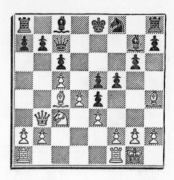

White to Play. *Black's attempt to counter-attack, by means of his Pawns, has weakened him on the important diagonals. White's pieces seize the strategic points, and in four moves the game is over.*

WHITE	BLACK	WHITE	BLACK
1 P–Q4	P–Q4	11 O–O	P–KN3[2]
2 P–QB4	P–K3	12 P–B5	B–N2
3 N–QB3	N–KB3	13 Q–N3	N–B1
4 B–N5	QN–Q2	14 B–B4	Q–B2
5 P–K3	P–B3		SEE DIAGRAM
6 N–B3	Q–R4	15 P–Q5!	P–KR3[3]
7 N–Q2	N–K5	16 P–Q6	Q–Q2
8 KNxN	PxN	17 B–K7	N–K3
9 B–R4	P–K4	18 N–N5![4]	....
10 B–K2	P–KB4?[1]		

White wins the Queen

[1] This weakens Black's position. 10 . . . B–N5 is better.

[2] Black is in trouble. 11 . . . B–Q3 is answered by 12 P–B5; or if 11 . . . B–N5; 12 P–B5!, BxN; 13 Q–N3, N–B1; 14 PxB, with considerable advantage.

[3] If 15 . . . PxP; 16 N–N5!, QxP; 17 BxP with the decisive threats of 18 B–B7ch, or 18 QR–B1.

[4] Black has no defense to the threat of 19 BxN, QxB; 20 N–B7ch, winning the Queen. If 18 . . . NxP; 19 B–B7 mate. If 18 . . . K–B2; 19 N–B7 wins, and finally if 18 . . . PxN; 19 BxP wins.

Black to Play. *The attack against White's exposed Bishop at R4 is the starting point of Black's combination, the ultimate aim of which is the winning of White's Queen.*

WHITE	BLACK	WHITE	BLACK
1 P–Q4	P–Q4	13 PxB	O–O
2 P–QB4	P–K3	14 B–QB4	P–KR3
3 N–QB3	N–KB3	15 B–R4?[3]	....
4 N–B3	QN–Q2		SEE DIAGRAM
5 B–N5	P–B3	15	NxKP!
6 P–K3	Q–R4	16 PxN[4]	Q–B4!
7 PxP	NxP	17 BxB	QxKPch
8 Q–N3	B–N5	18 K–Q1[5]	Q–Q6ch
9 R–B1	P–K4!?	19 K–K1	Q–K5ch!
10 NxP[1]	QNxN	20 K–Q2	QR–Q1ch
11 PxN	B–K3	21 BxR	RxBch[6]
12 P–QR3	BxNch[2]		

Black wins easily

[1] Not 10 PxP, N–B4 and 11 . . . N–R5. Best is 10 B–QB4.

[2] The clearest line is 12 . . . NxN; 13 QxB, QxQ; 14 PxQ, N–R7 followed by 15 . . . NxP with a fine ending.

[3] 15 B–B4 should be played.

[4] Or 16 BxB, NxPch followed by 17 . . . NxB, with a winning position.

[5] If 18 K–B1, PxBch wins.

[6] After 22 B–Q5, RxBch; 23 QxR, QxQch, the rest is easy.

Black to Play. *Black begins with a pin, then intensifies the pressure. White's efforts to free himself result in the loss of a Knight.*

WHITE	BLACK	WHITE	BLACK
1 P–Q4	P–Q4	9 B–Q3[2]	....
2 P–QB4	P–K3	SEE DIAGRAM	
3 N–QB3	N–KB3	9	B–N5[3]
4 B–N5	QN–Q2	10 QR–B1	N–K5[4]
5 P–K3	B–K2	11 BxN	PxB
6 N–B3	O–O	12 N–K5[5]	N–N3[6]
7 Q–B2	P–B3	13 B–R4	P–B3
8 P–QN3?[1]	Q–R4!	14 N–N4[7]	P–R4[8]

Black wins a piece

[1] Weakening the position of his Queen Knight, so that Black can employ the Cambridge Springs motif with good effect.
[2] 9 BxN would be better, but Black's pressure would still have been considerable.
[3] Now White's troubles really begin.
[4] Forcing White's reply.
[5] If 12 QxP, BxNch wins a piece.
[6] Now Black threatens 13 . . . P–B3.
[7] White seems to have avoided the loss of a piece.
[8] But this wins the piece after all.

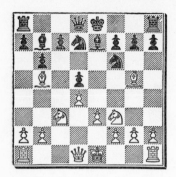

White to Play. Black *has fallen into one of the most subtle and beautiful traps ever seen on a chessboard! Fittingly enough it includes a Queen sacrifice.*

WHITE	BLACK	WHITE	BLACK
1 P–Q4	P–Q4	11 NxB	Q–K1
2 P–QB4	P–K3	12 NxBch	QxN
3 N–QB3	N–KB3	13 NxP	Q–K5[4]
4 B–N5	QN–Q2	14 NxNch	PxN
5 P–K3	B–K2	15 B–R6	QxNP
6 N–B3	P–QN3	16 Q–B3!!	QxQ[5]
7 PxP	PxP	17 R–N1ch	K–R1
8 B–N5!	B–N2[1]	18 B–N7ch	K–N1
SEE DIAGRAM		19 BxPch	Q–N5
9 N–K5[2]	O–O	20 RxQ	....
10 B–B6	BxB[3]		

Black has been checkmated

[1] The order of Black's moves is wrong. Before developing his Queen Bishop, Black should castle. In the present position, White is able to exploit the pin on Black's Queen Knight.

[2] Threatening to win a piece with 10 BxN, BxB; 11 BxNch.

[3] If 10 . . . R–N1; 11 BxB; RxB; 12 N–B6, and White continues in the same way as the text.

[4] Hoping to regain the lost Pawn.

[5] 16 . . . Q–N3 costs the exchange to begin with, and holds out no real hope.

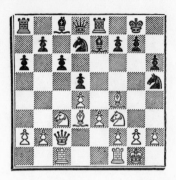

White to Play. *Black is in a trap which has caught players even of master strength. Can you see how White wins at least a Pawn, in one move?*

WHITE	BLACK	WHITE	BLACK
1 P–Q4	P–Q4	9 PxP[2]	KPxP
2 P–QB4	P–K3	10 B–Q3	R–K1
3 N–QB3	N–KB3	11 O–O	P–R3
4 B–N5	QN–Q2	12 B–KB4	N–R4?[3]
5 P–K3	B–K2	SEE DIAGRAM	
6 N–B3	O–O	13 NxP!	PxN?[4]
7 R–B1	P–B3	14 B–B7	....
8 Q–B2	P–QR3[1]		

White wins the Queen

[1] The defense adopted here by Black avoids the Pawn weaknesses which result from . . . P–QN3.

[2] This is usually a good exchange to make in situations such as this, where Black intends 9 . . . PxP; 10 BxP, P–QN4; 11 B–Q3, B–N2, and an eventual . . . P–B4.

[3] Black would like to remove one of the hostile Bishops. A natural desire, but it forms the basis of White's trap.

[4] The lesser evil is 13 . . . NxB; 14 NxN, and White has won a valuable Pawn.

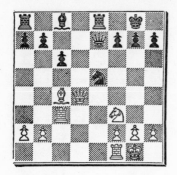

White to Play. *Black has just made the mistake of capturing a Pawn with his Knight, not realizing that this will cost him at least a piece.*

WHITE	BLACK	WHITE	BLACK
1 P–Q4	P–Q4	11 O–O	NxN
2 P–QB4	P–K3	12 RxN	P–K4[1]
3 N–QB3	N–KB3	13 P–K4	PxP
4 B–N5	QN–Q2	14 QxP	R–K1
5 P–K3	B–K2	15 P–K5	NxP?[2]
6 N–B3	O–O		SEE DIAGRAM
7 R–B1	P–B3	16 NxN	QxN[3]
8 B–Q3	PxP	17 R–K3	QxQ[4]
9 BxP	N–Q4	18 RxR	....
10 BxB	QxB		

Black has been checkmated

[1] Freeing his position.

[2] Black snaps at the offer, noticing only that the Pawn is attacked three times, and only defended twice. Black should play instead 15 . . . N–B1, followed by 16 . . . B–K3 and 17 . . . KR–Q1.

[3] Actually, Black cannot afford to recapture. Now he must lose his Queen or be mated.

[4] Loses instantaneously; but any other move loses at least the Queen.

White to Play. Black has weakened his white squares by his incomplete fianchetto. White's Bishop forces its way in to QN7, and wins the exchange.

WHITE	BLACK	WHITE	BLACK
1 P–Q4	P–Q4	9 Q–B2	QN–Q2[2]
2 P–QB4	P–K3		SEE DIAGRAM
3 N–QB3	N–KB3	10 N–K5[3]	B–K3[4]
4 B–N5	B–K2	11 N–B6	Q–K1
5 P–K3	O–O	12 B–QR6[5]	N–N1[6]
6 N–B3	P–QN3	13 NxBch	QxN
7 PxP	PxP	14 B–N7	....
8 B–Q3	B–KN5?[1]		

White wins the exchange

[1] Quite out of place after 6 . . . P–QN3.

[2] Now there is probably no good move available.

[3] Threatening to win a Pawn by 11 NxB, NxN; 12 BxPch, or by 11 NxN, NxN; 12 BxB, QxB; 13 NxP.

[4] If 10 . . . NxN; 11 PxN, N–K5; 12 BxB, QxB; 13 NxP, QxP; 14 BxN, and White wins a piece.

[5] In order to win the exchange by 13 B–N7.

[6] So that after 13 B–N7, NxN; 14 BxR, QxB, and the joke is on White.

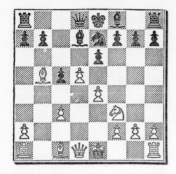

White to Play. *White beats down all resistance with a few powerful strokes, making good use of his advanced Queen Pawn.*

WHITE	BLACK	WHITE	BLACK
1 P-Q4	P-Q4	9 B-N5ch	B-Q2
2 P-QB4	P-K3	SEE DIAGRAM	
3 N-QB3	N-KB3	10 BxBch	QxB[3]
4 N-B3	P-B4	11 N-K5!	Q-N4[4]
5 BPxP	NxP	12 PxP!	PxP[5]
6 P-K4	NxN	13 QR-N1!	R-Q1[6]
7 PxN	N-B3[1]	14 QxRch	KxQ
8 P-Q5!	N-K2?[2]	15 RxQ	....

White has won a Rook

[1] The proper plan here is simplification by 7 ... PxP; 8 PxP, B-N5ch; 9 B-Q2, BxBch etc.

[2] Better is 8 ... PxP; 9 PxP, N-K2.

[3] If 10 ... KxB; 11 N-K5ch, K-K1; 12 Q-R4ch, and Black must give up a piece.

[4] If 11 ... Q-B1 (on 11 ... Q-B2; 12 P-Q6 wins); 12 Q-R4ch, K-Q1; 13 NxPch, K-B2; 14 B-B4ch, forces mate.

[5] Not 12 ... R-Q1; 13 PxP mate!

[6] The Queen cannot go to a square where the threat of mate by 14 Q-Q7 can be prevented.

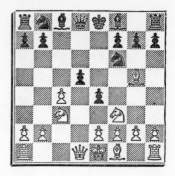

White to Play. *White can win a Pawn at once, and if Black carries out his threat of taking off the Knight, then White by a series of exchanges wins a Rook for his missing Knight.*

WHITE	BLACK	WHITE	BLACK
1 P–Q4	P–Q4		SEE DIAGRAM	
2 P–QB4	P–K3	8 NxQP!	PxN
3 N–QB3	N–KB3	9 NxNch	PxN[2]
4 N–B3	P–B4	10 QxQch	KxQ
5 B–N5	BPxP	11 BxPch	K–K1
6 KNxP	P–K4	12 BxR	....
7 N–B3	P–K5?[1]		

White has won the exchange

[1] Tempting, but it leads to quick loss. Correct is 7 . . . P–Q5; 8 N–Q5, B–K2!

[2] If 9 . . . K–K2; 10 N–Q5ch wins the Queen (interposition being impossible in the case of a double check). Or if 9 . . . QxN; 10 BxQ, B–N5ch, and White does not obligingly play 11 Q–Q2 (as he must do sometimes in somewhat similar positions) but simply interposes by 11 B–B3.

Black to Play. *Black is in check, and of the three possible moves to get out of check, two lose. But the third way wins! What is the move that wins?*

WHITE	BLACK	WHITE	BLACK
1 P–Q4	P–Q4	8 NxP?[1]	PxN!
2 P–QB4	P–K3	9 NxNch	....
3 N–QB3	N–KB3		SEE DIAGRAM
4 N–B3	P–B4	9	QxN![2]
5 B–N5	BPxP	10 BxQ	B–N5ch
6 KNxP	P–K4	11 Q–Q2[3]	BxQch
7 N(Q4)–N5	P–QR3	12 KxB	PxB

Black has won a piece

[1] White confuses this trap with the previous one. He should play instead either 8 N–R3, or if he likes complications, 8 Q–R4, B–Q2; 9 P–K4, PxBP; 10 BxP, PxN; 11 BxPch, KxB; 12 QxR, B–B3; 13 O–O, is an interesting line.

[2] If 9 ... K–K2; 10 N–Q5ch wins the Queen. Or if 9 ... PxN (which White probably expected) then 10 QxQch, KxQ; 11 BxPch, followed by 12 BxR wins for White.

[3] Unfortunately, White's Bishop at B6 cannot interpose, as his path is obstructed by Black's King Pawn.

White to Play. White does not even try to keep his two Bishops. He makes good use of the Knights instead, to enmesh Black's King in a mating net.

WHITE	BLACK	WHITE	BLACK
1 P–Q4	P–Q4		SEE DIAGRAM
2 P–QB4	P–K3	10 BxN	PxB
3 N–QB3	N–KB3	11 NxQP	Q–Q1[4]
4 N–B3	QN–Q2	12 N–B7ch	K–K2[5]
5 PxP	PxP	13 QxPch	K–Q3
6 Q–N3	P–B3	14 B–B4ch	N–K4[6]
7 P–K4!?	PxP?[1]	15 BxNch	K–B3
8 B–QB4	Q–K2[2]	16 Q–B4ch	K–Q2
9 N–KN5	N–Q4[3]	17 Q–K6	....

Black has been checkmated

[1] Correct is 7 . . . NxP! 8 NxN, Q–K2 with a plus for Black.
[2] 8 . . . PxN would be fatal: 9 BxPch, K–K2; 10 Q–K6 mate.
[3] Black's King Bishop Pawn cannot be given any further protection.
[4] If 11 . . . Q–Q3; 12 N–B7ch, K–K2 (if 12 . . . QxN; 13 QxPch, K–Q1; 14 N–K6 mate) ; 13 QxPch, K–Q1; 14 N(N5)-K6ch, QxN; 15 NxQ mate.
[5] If 12 . . . QxN, White mates in two moves.
[6] If 14 . . . K–B3; 15 Q–Q5ch, K–N3; 16 Q–N5 mate.

Black to Play. *White is threatening to win the exchange. If you were Black, what move would you play that would turn a seeming loss into a win?*

WHITE	BLACK	WHITE	BLACK
1 P–Q4	P–Q4		SEE DIAGRAM
2 P–QB4	P–K3	6	QxN!
3 N–QB3	N–KB3	7 BxQ	B–N5ch
4 B–B4	P–B4	8 Q–Q2[2]	BxQch
5 N–N5?[1]	BPxP	9 KxB	PxP[3]
6 N–B7ch	....		

Black has won two Pawns

[1] Threatening to win a Rook by 6 N–B7ch—but Black pays no attention! Better for White would have been 5 P–K3, or 5 N–B3.

[2] Unfortunately for White, there is no choice.

[3] The winning idea in this trap—a Queen sacrifice followed by a check regaining the Queen—is one that occurs often in this opening.

Black to Play. *White's Bishop has lost so much time in the opening, that Black can now, with one good move, force White's resignation!*

WHITE	BLACK	WHITE	BLACK
1 P–Q4	P–Q4	5 BxN?[2]	PxN!
2 P–QB4	P–K3	6 B–K5[3]	....
3 N–QB3	P–QB4	SEE DIAGRAM	
4 B–B4[1]	BPxP	6	BPxP[4]

Black wins a Rook

[1] A strong line for White is 4 BPxP, KPxP; 5 N–B3, N–QB3; 6 P–KN3, N–B3; 7 B–N2, B–K2; 8 O–O, O–O; 9 B–N5, B–K3; 10 PxP, BxP; 11 R–B1.

[2] On principle, an active piece should not be exchanged for an inactive one. In this case the Bishop is already in play, while the Knight has not yet been developed.

[3] 6 B–B4 is better, but not good enough to hold the game.

[4] White is helpless against the double threat of 7 ... PxR(Q), and 7 ... B–N5ch, winning White's Queen. Notice the curious fact that in this trap Black won without moving a piece!

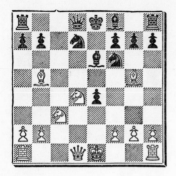

White to Play. White shows, in a few moves, how weak a pinned piece is, no matter how well protected it may appear to be. He hammers away at Black's Queen Knight, which is now protected four times!

WHITE	BLACK	WHITE	BLACK
1 P–Q4	P–Q4	8 B–N5ch	QN–Q2
2 P–QB4	P–K3	9 KNxP	PxP
3 N–QB3	P–QB4		SEE DIAGRAM
4 BPxP	KPxP	10 NxB	PxN
5 N–B3	N–KB3?[1]	11 BxN	PxB[3]
6 B–N5	B–K3	12 Q–R5ch	K–K2
7 P–K4![2]	BPxP	13 R–Q1[4]	....

White wins

[1] The proper move is 5 . . . N–QB3, after which 6 P–KN3, N–B3; 7 B–N2, B–K2; 8 O–O, O–O leads to the "normal" position in the Tarrasch Defense.

[2] Opening up the position in a highly advantageous manner.

[3] If 11 . . . QxB; 12 QxN mate.

[4] Black must give up Knight and Queen to avoid being mated.

White to Play. Black has just captured White's unprotected Queen Pawn with his Knight. This capture will now cost him a piece.

WHITE	BLACK	WHITE	BLACK
1 P–Q4	P–Q4	7 B–N2	B–N5
2 P–QB4	P–K3	8 N–K5	NxP?[1]
3 N–QB3	P–QB4	SEE DIAGRAM	
4 BPxP	KPxP	9 NxB	NxN
5 N–B3	N–QB3	10 P–K3[2]	Q–B3[3]
6 P–KN3!	N–B3	11 O–O![4]	....

White wins a Knight

[1] Loses on the spot! Black should play 8 . . . PxP; 9 NxB, PxN; 10 NxNch, QxN etc.

[2] Attacking one Knight with the Pawn, and discovering an attack on the other, with the Queen.

[3] Hoping for either 11 PxN, QxP mate, or 11 QxKN, N–B7ch.

[4] Simple and strong! White's King is safe from any counterattack, and Black must give up one of his Knights.

White to Play. Black *has won two Pawns, and seems about to win the exchange. Yet White, with one clever move, can either win a piece or force checkmate.*

WHITE	BLACK	WHITE	BLACK
1 P–Q4	P–Q4	9 N–K4	Q–Q4
2 P–QB4	P–K3	10 B–N2	QxKP[1]
3 N–QB3	P–QB4	11 B–B4	Q–R4
4 BPxP	KPxP	12 O–O	BxP?[2]
5 N–B3	N–QB3		SEE DIAGRAM
6 P–KN3	B–N5	13 R–K1!	BxQ[3]
7 N–K5	NxN	14 N–B6ch	K–Q1
8 PxN	P–Q5	15 R–K8	....

Black has been checkmated

[1] Black wins a Pawn, but White gains time to centralize his Knight, and post his Bishops on important diagonals.

[2] Apparently a winning move, but White has a beautiful reply.

[3] If 13 ... P–Q6; 14 QxP! either wins the Bishop or leads to the same finish as in the text. Or if 13 ... P–B4; 14 RxB, PxN; 15 RxPch and Black's Queen falls.

White to Play. Black has won a Pawn, but now White's pieces spring to life, and a sharp combination results in the win of a piece.

WHITE	BLACK	WHITE	BLACK
1 P–Q4	P–Q4	11 KPxP	PxP
2 P–QB4	P–K3	12 PxP	NxP[1]
3 N–KB3	P–QB4		SEE DIAGRAM
4 P–K3	N–QB3	13 NxN	QxN
5 N–B3	N–B3	14 N–Q5!	Q–B4[2]
6 B–Q3	B–K2	15 BxN	BxB[3]
7 O–O	O–O	16 Q–K4!	P–N3[4]
8 P–QN3	P–QN3	17 NxBch	K–N2
9 B–N2	B–N2	18 QxB	KxN
10 Q–K2	BPxP		

White has won a piece

[1] The capture of the attractive Pawn is fatal. 12 . . . R–B1 should be played.

[2] Black's only move to save his Queen and his King Bishop, as both are attacked.

[3] If 15 . . . PxN; 16 BxB wins a whole Rook, and if 15 . . . PxB; 16 Q–N4ch, K–R1; 17 NxB, QxN; 18 Q–R4! For if 18 . . . P–B4 to stop the mate, then 19 QxQ finishes Black.

[4] The only way to prevent being mated, but it costs a piece.

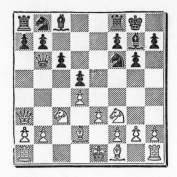

White to Play. B l a c k ' s Queen can move to only two squares. White makes use of this situation to force the win of the exchange.

WHITE	BLACK	WHITE	BLACK
1 P–Q4	P–Q4	8 Q–R3 !	P–K3
2 P–QB4	P–QB3	9 PxP	KPxP?[2]
3 N–KB3	N–B3		SEE DIAGRAM
4 P–K3	P–KN3	10 N–QR4	Q–Q1[3]
5 N–B3	B–N2	11 N–N6 !	PxN[4]
6 Q–N3	O–O	12 QxR	....
7 B–Q2	Q–N3[1]		

White has won the exchange

[1] Either 7 . . . P–K3, or 7 . . . QN–Q2 is better.

[2] Black recaptures with the King Pawn to free his Queen Bishop; but this leads to the loss of the exchange in a curious manner.

[3] If 10 . . . Q–B2, White still plays 11 N–N6! and wins in the same way as in the text.

[4] Forced, for if 11 . . . QxN; 12 B–R5 wins the Queen.

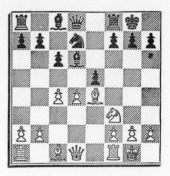

White to Play. Black's advance of his King Pawn was a natural attempt to free his cramped position. That the move was not timed properly is proved by White very quickly.

WHITE	BLACK	WHITE	BLACK
1 P–Q4	P–Q4	9 NxP	NxN
2 P–QB4	P–QB3	10 BxN	P–K4?[2]
3 N–KB3	N–B3		SEE DIAGRAM
4 P–K3	P–K3	11 PxP	NxP
5 N–B3	QN–Q2	12 NxN	BxN
6 B–Q3	B–Q3	13 BxPch![3]	KxB[4]
7 0–0	0–0	14 Q–R5ch	K–N1
8 P–K4	PxKP[1]	15 QxB	....

White has won a Pawn

[1] The right way is 8 . . . PxBP; 9 BxP, P–K4 with a playable game.

[2] Black should play instead either 10 . . . P–QB4, or 10 . . . N–B3.

[3] This is what Black overlooked. He may have expected 13 Q–R5, (which threatens mate as well as the Bishop) upon which he had 13 . . . P–KB4 as a resource.

[4] If 13 . . . K–R1; 14 Q–R5 with the threat of mate in two by 15 B–N6ch wins at once.

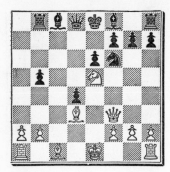

White to Play. *White can fork Queen and Rook with his Knight, but then Black could pin the Knight. Should White risk the pin, and play 14 N–B6?*

	WHITE	BLACK		WHITE	BLACK
1	P–Q4	P–Q4	12	NxN	PxN
2	P–QB4	P–QB3	13	Q–B3!	QR–N1[2]
3	N–KB3	N–B3		SEE DIAGRAM	
4	P–K3	P–K3	14	N–B6	B–N2
5	N–B3	QN–Q2	15	BxNP	Q–N3
6	B–Q3	PxP	16	P–QR4!	R–B1[3]
7	BxBP	P–QN4	17	N–R7ch	K–Q1[4]
8	B–Q3	P–QR3	18	NxR!	Q–R4ch
9	P–K4	P–B4[1]	19	B–Q2	QxB[5]
10	P–K5	PxP	20	PxQ	BxQ
11	NxNP	NxP	21	PxB	KxN

White has won the exchange

[1] If Black is to hold his own in the center, he must make this advance at once.

[2] If 13 . . . B–N5ch; 14 K–K2, QR–N1; 15 Q–N3! with a strong game for White. Or if 13 . . . Q–Q4; 14 QxQ, NxQ; 15 BxPch, K–K2; 16 N–B6ch, K–B3; 17 NxP, and White's two passed Pawns win easily.

[3] If 16 . . . R–R1; 17 NxPch, QxB; 18 NxQ, and White has a won ending.

[4] If 17 . . . QxB; 18 PxQ, BxQ; 19 NxR, and White wins.

[5] As good as there is.

White to Play. *White has developed his pieces, while Black was gathering Pawns. Now White's Queen comes powerfully into play.*

WHITE	BLACK	WHITE	BLACK
1 P–Q4	P–Q4	8 Q–B3	PxP[3]
2 P–QB4	P–QB3	9 QxB	N–Q3
3 N–KB3	N–B3	10 BxP!	P–K3[4]
4 N–B3	PxP	11 B–N5ch	K–K2[5]
5 P–QR4	B–B4	12 N–N6ch!	RPxN
6 N–K5	P–B4?[1]	13 N–Q5ch!	PxN
7 P–K4!	NxP[2]	14 Q–K5	....

SEE DIAGRAM

Black has been checkmated

[1] Either 6 . . . QN–Q2, or 6 . . . P–K3 is in order here.

[2] If 7 . . . PxP; 8 PxB, PxN; 9 QxQch, KxQ; 10 NxPch wins a Rook. Or if 7 . . . BxP; 8 NxB, NxN; 9 Q–B3, N–Q3 (forced); 10 BxP (threatening 11 QxPch, NxQ; 12 BxN mate), P–K3; 11 B–N5ch, K–K2 (a Knight interposition loses a piece at once); 12 PxP, NxB; 13 QxP mate.

[3] If 8 . . . N–Q3; 9 PxP wins a piece. Or if 8 . . . NxN; 9 QxB, P–B3; 10 BxP wins (10 . . . PxN permitting 11 B–B7 mate).

[4] If 10 . . . NxQ; 11 BxP mate, or if 10 . . . NxB; 11 QxP mate.

[5] If 11 . . . N–Q2; 12 BxNch, QxB; 13 Q B4, and wins.

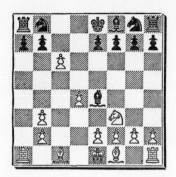

White to Play. How is White to win? If he plays 8 PxP, then the reply is 8 . . . BxP; or if he moves 8 P–B7, then Black's answer is simply 8 . . . N–QB3. In either case Black keeps his extra piece. And yet there is a win!

WHITE	BLACK	WHITE	BLACK
1 P–Q4	P–Q4	6 PxQ	BxN[3]
2 P–QB4	P–QB3	7 PxP!	B–K5?[4]
3 N–KB3	B–B4[1]		SEE DIAGRAM
4 Q–N3	Q–N3	8 RxP!![5]	RxR
5 PxP	QxQ[2]	9 P–B7[6]	....

And White wins

[1] A move which often leads to trouble for Black, as will be seen in this and the next trap.

[2] If 5 . . . PxP; 6 QxP wins a Pawn.

[3] If 6 . . . PxP; 7 N–B3, N–KB3; 8 N–QN5, N–R3; 9 RxN!, with advantage to White.

[4] Black has lost a Pawn, and should let it go at that; but he wants to hang on to the additional piece.

[5] The brilliant sacrifice that solves the problem.

[6] White's passed Pawn cannot be stopped from Queening.

White to Play. Here, para-doxically enough, it is Black's allegiance to the principles of sound development — not to move the same piece twice in the opening—that costs him the game.

WHITE	BLACK	WHITE	BLACK
1 P-Q4	P-Q4		SEE DIAGRAM	
2 P-QB4	P-QB3	9 PxN	NxP[3]
3 N-KB3	N-B3	10 Q-R4ch	K-K2[4]
4 P-K3	B-B4	11 Q-N4ch	K-Q2[5]
5 PxP	PxP	12 QxPch	Q-B2[6]
6 N-B3	P-K3	13 B-N5ch	K-Q1
7 N-K5	QN-Q2?[1]	14 QxRch	Q-B1[7]
8 P-KN4!	NxN[2]	15 QxP	....

White wins easily

[1] This is wrong, as is 7 . . . N-B3. The correct move is 7 . . . KN-Q2!, so that in the event of . . . NxN, the recapture PxN does not attack Black's King Knight.

[2] Best is 8 . . . B-N3, but after 9 P-KR4, P-KR4; 10 NxB, PxN, the weakness of Black's Pawn position is enough to lose.

[3] If 9 . . . BxP; 10 Q-R4ch, K-K2 (10 . . . Q-Q2; 11 B-N5 wins, or 10 . . . N-Q2; 11 QxB); 11 PxNch, PxP; 12 QxB wins.

[4] If 10 . . . Q-Q2; 11 B-N5 wins the Queen.

[5] If 11 . . . K-K1; 12 B-N5ch forces Black's Queen to inter-pose.

[6] Now if 12 . . . K-K1; 13 B-N5ch forces mate.

[7] On 14 . . . K-K2; 15 Q-K8 checkmates Black.

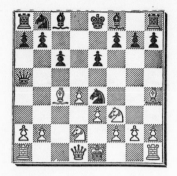

Black to Play. White is in an extremely subtle trap. He has just recaptured a Pawn with his King Bishop — apparently a good move, but it loses a piece.

WHITE	BLACK	WHITE	BLACK
1 P–Q4	P–Q4	7 B–R4?[1]	PxP!
2 P–QB4	P–K3	8 BxP?[2]	....
3 N–KB3	N–KB3	SEE DIAGRAM	
4 B–N5	P–B3	8	P–KN4!
5 P–K3	Q–R4ch	9 B–N3	P–N5!
6 QN–Q2	N–K5	10 N–K5[3]	B–N5[4]

Black wins a piece

[1] The right move is 7 B–B4, and White has a good game.

[2] White must instead reconcile himself to the loss of the Pawn, and play 8 Q–B2. The continuation might be 8 . . . NxN; 9 NxN, P–QN4; 10 B–K2, B–N5; 11 B–B3, B–N2; 12 P–QR3, BxNch; 13 QxB, QxQch; 14 KxQ, K–Q2! 15 P–QR4, K–B1, and Black keeps his Pawn. However, White with his two Bishops still has chances.

[3] If 10 B–Q3, NxB; 11 RPxN, PxN, and Black wins a piece.

[4] The pinned Knight cannot be defended any further.

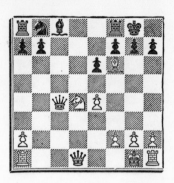

White to Play. White now forces the win by an elegant mating combination, with a stinging Queen sacrifice at the tail end of it.

WHITE	BLACK	WHITE	BLACK
1 P–Q4	P–Q4	12 K–N1[3]	O–O?[4]
2 P–QB4	P–K3		SEE DIAGRAM
3 N–KB3	N–KB3	13 Q–N4	P–KN3
4 B–N5	B–N5ch	14 Q–B4[5]	N–Q2
5 N–B3	PxP	15 P–K5	NxB
6 P–K4	P–B4	16 PxN	K–R1
7 BxP	PxP	17 R–QB1!	Q–Q4
8 NxP	Q–R4	18 Q–R6	R–KN1
9 BxN!	BxNch[1]	19 N–B3	Q–KR4
10 PxB	QxPch	20 N–N5!	QxQ
11 K–B1	QxBch?[2]	21 NxBP	....

Black has been checkmated

[1] Better is 9 ... PxB; 10 O–O, B–Q2; 11 R–B1, N–B3.

[2] Certainly it is hard to resist making this move—taking the Bishop with check!

[3] White now threatens 13 R–B1 as well as 13 BxP.

[4] Black's last chance was 12 ... N–Q2; 13 R–B1, Q–R3! (not 13 ... Q–N5; 14 BxP, KR–N1; 15 NxP, PxN; 16 Q–R5ch followed by 17 QxP) 14 BxP, KR–N1; 15 B–R6.

[5] Threatening 15 Q–R6.

Black to Play. *White's insistence on retaining his extra King Pawn is convincingly refuted by the able teamwork of Black's Knights.*

WHITE	BLACK	WHITE	BLACK
1 P–Q4	P–Q4	8 B–KB4?[2]	....
2 P–QB4	N–KB3		SEE DIAGRAM
3 PxP	NxP	8........	N–N5!
4 P–K4	N–KB3	9 B–K2[3]	QxQch
5 B–Q3	P–K4[1]	10 BxQ[4]	N–Q6ch
6 PxP	N–N5	11 K–B1	NxB
7 N–KB3	N–QB3		

Black has won a piece

[1] Of course not 5 . . . QxP; 6 B–N5ch, N–B3; 7 QxQ, and the pinned Knight is helpless to recapture.

[2] Bad, as both Bishops are now exposed (unprotected by Pawns) and easy objects of attack. Instead, White might have gone in for 8 B–KN5, B–K2; 9 BxB, QxB; 10 N–B3 with a good game.

[3] If 9 B–B2, Black still plays 9 . . . QxQch, winning as above.

[4] Or 10 KxQ, NxPch and White's King Rook falls.

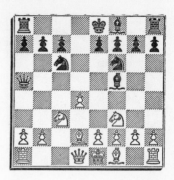

White to Play. *Black has placed his Queen in a dangerously exposed position. As a result, he must now give up a piece to avoid losing his Queen.*

WHITE	BLACK	WHITE	BLACK
1 P–Q4	P–Q4	6 B–Q2	N–B3?[3]
2 P–QB4	N–QB3	SEE DIAGRAM	
3 PxP	QxP	7 P–K4!	B–N3[4]
4 N–KB3	B–B4[1]	8 N–Q5![5]	....
5 N–B3	Q–R4[2]		

White wins the Queen

[1] 4 . . . P–K4 is more in the spirit of this defense. If then 5 PxP, QxQch; 6 KxQ, B–KN5; 7 B–B4, O–O–Och, and Black has a strong initiative with good prospects of regaining his Pawn as well.

[2] The Queen is exposed to dangers here. The retreat to Q1 was in order.

[3] A desperate position. The hope might have been 6 . . . B–N5, making room for the Queen to swing over to KR4.

[4] If 7 . . . BxP; 8 NxB, and Black cannot take back by 8 . . . NxN as his Queen is menaced by the Bishop.

[5] Notice how White's move 7 P–K4 created a support for the Knight at Q5.

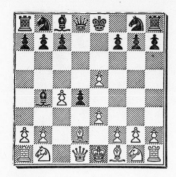

Black to Play. *A curious feature of this trap is the way Black can force a win by promoting a Pawn to a Knight at the seventh move of the game!*

WHITE	BLACK	WHITE	BLACK
1 P–Q4	P–Q4	5	PxP!
2 P–QB4	P–K4[1]	6 BxB[3]	PxPch
3 QPxP	P–Q5	7 K–K2	PxN(N)ch![4]
4 P–K3?[2]	B–N5ch	8 K–K1[5]	Q–R5ch
5 B–Q2	....	9 K–Q2	Q–B7ch

SEE DIAGRAM

Black has won a piece

[1] A tricky gambit favored by players who do not mind giving up a Pawn, in order to wrest the initiative from White.

[2] White should simply develop by 4 N–KB3.

[3] If 6 PxP, Q–R5ch; 7 P–N3, Q–K5; 8 N–KB3, QxPch with a superior game for Black. Or if 6 Q–R4ch, N–B3; 7 BxB, PxPch; 8 KxP, Q–R5ch with a winning attack. For example, if 9 P–N3, Q–Q5ch; 10 K–N2, QxPch and Black regains his piece.

[4] The whole point of the trap. The normally powerful 7 ... PxN(Q) would not do because of 8 QxQch, KxQ; 9 RxQ, and Black's advantage, if any, is minimal. And if 7 ... B–N5ch, then White escapes by 8 N–B3.

[5] If 8 RxN, B–N5ch wins White's Queen.

White to Play. Passive play and inferior defense by Black have led to this position in which White is able to force a win by an instructive King side attack.

WHITE	BLACK	WHITE	BLACK
1 P–Q4	P–Q4	11 PxP	BxP
2 N–KB3	N–KB3	12 B–KN5	B–K2
3 P–K3	P–K3	13 Q–K2[1]	Q–B2
4 B–Q3	B–K2	14 QR–Q1	R–Q1[2]
5 QN–Q2	O–O	15 N–K5	B–Q2?[3]
6 O–O	QN–Q2		SEE DIAGRAM
7 P–K4	PxP	16 BxPch	KxB[4]
8 NxP	NxN	17 BxN	BxB[5]
9 BxN	N–B3	18 Q–R5ch	K–N1
10 B–Q3	P–B4	19 QxPch	K–R2[6]

And White mates quickly

[1] Preventing the natural 13 . . . P–QN3, which would lose by 14 BxN, BxB; 15 Q–K4, and Black's Rook falls, as he must stop mate.

[2] 14 . . . B–Q2 is better.

[3] Now this move is a mistake. Better is 15 . . . P–KR3.

[4] If 16 . . . NxB; 17 BxB wins the exchange, as the Rook must remain to protect the Bishop.

[5] If 17 . . . PxB; 18 Q–R5ch, K–N2; 19 QxPch, K–R1 (or 19 . . . K–R3; 20 Q–N6 mate); 20 N–N6 mate.

[6] Black cannot prevent mate by 20 R–Q3 and 21 R–R3ch, etc.

White to Play.   *Black's inadequately defended King Bishop Pawn gives White the opportunity to win the game brilliantly.*

WHITE	BLACK	WHITE	BLACK
1 P–Q4	P–Q4	11 N–K5	B–N2?[3]
2 N–KB3	N–KB3	SEE DIAGRAM	
3 P–K3	P–K3	12 NxP!	KxN
4 B–Q3	QN–Q2	13 N–N5ch	K–N1[4]
5 QN–Q2	B–K2	14 QxPch	K–R1[5]
6 Q–K2	P–QR3?[1]	15 N–B7ch	K–N1
7 O–O	O–O	16 N–R6ch[6]	K–R1
8 P–K4	PxP	17 Q–N8ch!	R (or N) xQ
9 NxP	R–K1	18 N–B7	....
10 P–B3	P–QN4[2]		

Black has been checkmated

[1] 6 . . . P–B4 is better.
[2] Here Black should play 10 . . . P–B4.
[3] With this natural developing move Black falls into the trap. Relatively best was 11 . . . QNxN; 12 PxN, N–Q2.
[4] If 13 . . . K–B1; 14 NxKPch wins the Queen.
[5] If 14 . . . K–B1; 15 Q–B7 is mate.
[6] White disdains the mere winning of the Queen.

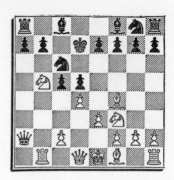

White to Play. *Having collected two Pawns, Black's Queen threatens to escape by checking. Can White prevent this and punish Black for his violation of opening principles?*

WHITE	BLACK	WHITE	BLACK
1 P–Q4	P–Q4		SEE DIAGRAM
2 N–KB3	P–QB4	8 B–B7![3]	N–N5[4]
3 B–B4	N–QB3	9 N–K5ch	K–K1[5]
4 P–K3	Q–N3	10 RxN![6]	PxR
5 N–B3	QxP?[1]	11 N–QB3!	PxN
6 N–QN5	K–Q2[2]	12 B–N5ch	B–Q2
7 QR–N1	QxRP	13 BxB	....

Black has been checkmated

[1] Such early Pawn-hunting expeditions with the Queen are always risky.

[2] To stop the threatened fork by 7 N–B7ch.

[3] Threatening to win the Queen by 9 N–B3, Q–R6; 10 R–N3.

[4] If 8 ... Q–R5; 9 N–B3 wins; or if 8 ... Q–R3; 9 R–R1, N–R4; 10 RxN, and White wins a piece.

[5] If 9 ... K–K3; 10 PxP, NxPch; 11 QxN, QxQ; 12 N–Q4ch, and White regains the Queen, leaving him a piece ahead.

[6] The first surprise move of a piquant mating combination.

White to Play. White's Bishops force the win of the exchange by pursuing Black's unfortunate Queen Rook with relentless efficiency.

WHITE	BLACK	WHITE	BLACK
1 P–Q4	P–Q4	8 P–KN4	B–N3
2 N–KB3	P–QB4	9 N–K5	R–B1?²
3 B–B4	N–QB3	SEE DIAGRAM	
4 P–K3	N–B3	10 NxN	PxN
5 N–B3	B–N5	11 B–QR6	R–R1
6 B–QN5	P–K3	12 B–N7	....
7 P–KR3	B–R4¹		

White wins the exchange

¹ The removal of the Queen Bishop from the protection of the Queen side is often dangerous. Black had two better alternatives: 7 . . . BxN; 8 QxB, P–QR3; 9 BxNch, PxB, or 7 . . . PxP; 8 PxP, B–R4; 9 P–KN4, B–N3; 10 N–K5, Q–N3; 11 P–QR4, B–N5 (stopping White from playing 12 P–R5 which would win a piece).

² An instinctive reply which loses the exchange. Black's best way of protecting his Queen Knight was probably by 9 . . . Q–B1.

Black to Play. *White has succeeded in holding on to his Pawn plus, at the cost of development. But now Black, with a Rook sacrifice, opens up the lines for his Queen to crash through with a mating attack.*

WHITE	BLACK	WHITE	BLACK
1 P–Q4	P–Q4	8 P–QB3[4]	....
2 B–B4	P–QB4		SEE DIAGRAM
3 BxN[1]	RxB	8	RxP!
4 PxP	P–K3	9 PxR[5]	Q–B8ch
5 Q–Q4?[2]	Q–B2	10 Q–Q1	BxPch
6 P–QN4[3]	P–QN3	11 N–Q2	BxN[6]
7 PxP	RxP		

White has been checkmated

[1] This cannot be good as a developed Bishop is exchanged for an undeveloped Knight, without any compensation.

[2] This attempt to keep the extra Pawn is bound to be repulsed with heavy losses.

[3] White continues consistently in a suicidal vein.

[4] All logical—and fatal!

[5] 9 Q–Q1 would hold out longer, but White's game would be ruined in a positional sense.

[6] White's stubbornness in holding on to the captured Pawn has been brilliantly refuted.

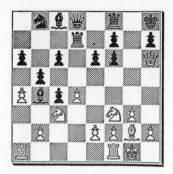

White to Play. Black has moved his King to make room for his Rook on the open file, but this move loses. White smashes Black's defenses with a brilliant combination.

WHITE	BLACK	WHITE	BLACK
1 P–Q4	N–KB3	10 B–N2	R–R2
2 P–QB4	P–K3	11 O–O	R–Q2
3 N–QB3	B–N5	12 Q–B1	O–O
4 Q–B2?	P–Q4	13 Q–R6	K–R1?[3]
5 B–N5?[1]	PxP	SEE DIAGRAM	
6 N–B3	P–N4	14 N–K4[4]	B–K2
7 P–QR4	P–B3	15 KN–N5	PxN
8 BxN	PxB[2]	16 N–B6!	BxN
9 P–KN3	P–QR3	17 B–K4	....

White mates next move

[1] This loses a Pawn for a doubtful attack, and is inferior to 5 PxP or 5 P–QR3. The popular way today is 5 PxP, QxP; 6 N–B3, P–B4; 7 B–Q2, BxN; 8 BxB, PxP; 9 NxP, P–K4; 10 N–B3, N–B3; 11 R–Q1, Q–B4; 12 P–K3, O–O.

[2] Alekhine suggested instead this interesting continuation: 8 ... QxB; 9 PxP, PxP; 10 Q–K4, Q–N3! 11 QxR, Q–B7, and Black has at least a draw.

[3] Black should first play 13 . . . BxN followed by 14 . . . K–R1.

[4] Threatening 15 NxP followed by 16 QxP mate, a threat which would force Black to give up his Queen.

Black to Play. *At first glance White's faulty fifth move has been justified, as he has regained his lost Pawn. But now Black by several sharp thrusts forces the win of material.*

WHITE	BLACK	WHITE	BLACK
1 P–Q4	N–KB3	8 PxP	NxP!
2 P–QB4	P–K3	9 BxP	....
3 N–QB3	B–N5	SEE DIAGRAM	
4 Q–B2	P–Q4	9	NxN
5 N–B3?[1]	PxP	10 PxN	BxN
6 P–K4	P–QN4	11 NPxB[3]	QxP![4]
7 P–QR4	B–N2![2]	12 B–Q2[5]	QxB[6]

Black has won a piece

[1] Best is either 5 PxP, QxP; 6 N–B3, or 5 P–QR3, BxNch; 6 QxB, N–K5; 7 Q–B2, P–QB4!

[2] Active play—better policy than attempting to hold the Pawn with 7 ... P–B3 etc.

[3] A Pawn is lost by 11 BPxB, but that was White's best chance.

[4] A pretty move! The Queen cannot, and the Bishop must not be taken! (If 12 PxB, QxR.) Black threatens 12 ... QxB, as well as 12 ... BxPch, and 13 ... BxR.

[5] Hoping to unpin the Bishop Pawn.

[6] White cannot capture the Bishop. His Pawn is now pinned on the file (13 PxB?, QxQ).

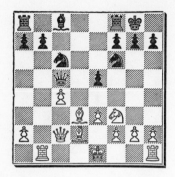

Black to Play. *The unfortunate line-up of three of his pieces on the diagonal QN1 to KR7 should have warned White of approaching catastrophe.*

WHITE	BLACK	WHITE	BLACK
1 P–Q4	N–KB3	11 PxP?[2]	QxBP
2 P–QB4	P–K3	12 QR–N1	P–K4
3 N–QB3	B–N5	13 B–Q3?[3]	....
4 Q–B2	P–Q4	SEE DIAGRAM	
5 PxP	QxP	13	P–K5!
6 P–K3	P–B4	14 BxP	NxB
7 B–Q2	BxN	15 QxN	B–B4[4]
8 PxB[1]	O–O	16 R–N5	QxR
9 N–B3	N–B3	17 PxQ	BxQ
10 P–B4	Q–Q3	18 PxN	BxP

Black has won the exchange

[1] This mode of capture gives Black the initiative in the center. 8 BxB is more promising.

[2] Much better is 11 B–B3.

[3] A superficial developing move, which is punished instantly. Better is 13 N–N5, P–KR3; 14 N–K4, NxN; 15 QxN, R–Q1, although Black still has a bit the better of it.

[4] Simultaneously attacking the Queen and Queen Rook on the same line.

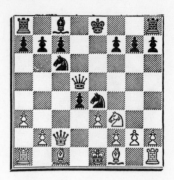

White to Play. *Black has failed to realize that his advanced Knight is in a precarious position. His unjustified effort to win a Pawn results in the loss of the Knight.*

WHITE	BLACK	WHITE	BLACK
1 P–Q4	N–KB3	8 P–K3	P–K4
2 P–QB4	P–K3	9 BPxP	QxP
3 N–QB3	B–N5	10 N–B3[1]	PxP?[2]
4 Q–B2	P–Q4		SEE DIAGRAM
5 P–QR3	BxNch	11 B–B4	Q–R4ch
6 QxB	N–K5	12 P–N4	Q–KB4[3]
7 Q–B2	N–QB3	13 B–Q3	....

White wins the Knight

[1] This sets a trap for the unwary player. More usual at this point is this line of play: 10 B–B4, Q–R4ch; 11 P–N4, NxNP; 12 QxN, N–B7ch; 13 K–K2!, Q–K8ch; 14 K–B3, NxR; 15 B–N2, B–K3; 16 P–Q5, O–O–O, with exciting complications, and chances for both sides.

[2] Best was 10 . . . N–B3, saving the Knight by running away.

[3] If 12 . . . NxNP; 13 QxNch wins at once.

Black to Play. *White has just captured a Bishop with his QRP — a blunder which loses the game. After Black's next move White will lose his Queen or be checkmated.*

WHITE	BLACK	WHITE	BLACK
1 P–Q4	N–KB3	9 P–K4	Q–B3
2 P–QB4	P–K3	10 O–O–O	P–QN3
3 N–QB3	B–N5	11 B–Q3	P–QR4
4 Q–N3	P–B4	12 P–QR3?[3]	P–R5![4]
5 PxP	N–B3	13 PxB?[5]	....
6 N–B3	N–K5		SEE DIAGRAM
7 B–Q2	NxQBP[1]	13	NxNP
8 Q–B2	O–O[2]	14 Q–N1	N–N6

White has been checkmated

[1] Another way for Black to equalize is 7 . . . NxB; 8 NxN, P–B4; 9 P–K3, BxP; 10 B–K2, O–O.

[2] More usual is 8 . . . P–B4 to prevent White from seizing the center with P–K4, but the text, an innovation of Kashdan's, has its points.

[3] A serious weakening move. White should play 12 K–N1.

[4] Black refuses to be frightened.

[5] There was still time for 13 K–N1.

White to Play. *Black should have been more suspicious of his opponent's generosity in allowing him to win a Pawn with his Queen. White now wins a piece in two moves by means of a Pawn fork.*

WHITE	BLACK	WHITE	BLACK
1 P–Q4	N–KB3	9 P–K4[1]	Q–B3
2 P–QB4	P–K3	10 O–O–O	BxN[2]
3 N–QB3	B–N5	11 BxB	Q–B5ch
4 Q–N3	P–B4	12 N–Q2[3]	QxBP?[4]
5 PxP	N–B3		SEE DIAGRAM
6 N–B3	N–K5	13 P–QN4!	N–R3
7 B–Q2	NxQBP	14 P–N5	....
8 Q–B2	O–O		

White wins a Knight

[1] Not as good as it looks, as the King Pawn is readily subject to attack. Better would be 9 P–QR3, BxN; 10 BxB, preventing the subsequently powerful . . . Q–B3.

[2] Black should continue his development with 10 . . . P–QN3, but he sees a chance to win a Pawn.

[3] To save the important King Pawn.

[4] Black, under the impression that he has forced the win of a Pawn, overlooks the fact that White might have permitted it!

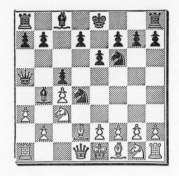

White to Play. *Black has set a trap, but falls into one himself! White does not hurry about taking the proffered Bishop, but instead "puts the question" to another piece.*

WHITE	BLACK	WHITE	BLACK
1 P–Q4	N–KB3	6 B–Q2	N–B3
2 P–QB4	P–K3	7 Q–Q1![2]	NxP?[3]
3 N–QB3	B–N5		SEE DIAGRAM
4 Q–N3	P–B4	8 P–K3![4]	....
5 P–QR3	Q–R4[1]		

White wins a piece

[1] 5 . . . BxNch is simpler. The text move may lead to trouble,

[2] Leaving Black nothing better than 7 . . . BxN; 8 BxB, Q–Q1; 9 P–Q5!, after which White's game is very strong. Not liking the looks of this, Black sets a trap.

[3] So that if 8 PxB, QxR; 9 QxQ, N–B7ch, and Black regains the Queen, remaining the exchange ahead.

[4] But this is the anti-trap! White wins a piece by force: if 8 . . . BxN; 9 BxB, Q–B2; 10 PxN, and White has an easy win.

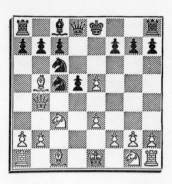

Black to Play. *White has won a Bishop with his Queen, taking advantage of the pin on Black's Queen Knight. But Black can break the pin and win White's Queen.*

WHITE	BLACK	WHITE	BLACK
1 P–Q4	N–KB3	7 PxP	N–K5
2 P–QB4	P–K3	8 B–N5	NxQBP
3 N–QB3	B–N5	9 QxB?[2]	....
4 Q–N3	N–B3		SEE DIAGRAM
5 P–K3	P–Q4	9	N–Q6ch![3]
6 P–B5[1]	P–K4	10 BxN[4]	NxQ

Black has won the Queen

[1] Gives Black the initiative by allowing the following advance. Better was the simple 6 N–B3.

[2] White thinks this is safe, as the Knight which attacks the Queen, is pinned. He should play instead 9 Q–B2, although Black would still have much the better game.

[3] The Knight fork attacks both King and Queen.

[4] Forced, but the capture releases the pin on the other Knight.

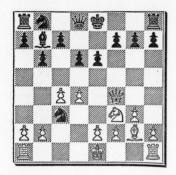

White to Play. Black has not reckoned with the dangerous possibility of a sudden attack on the long diagonal.

WHITE	BLACK	WHITE	BLACK
1 P–Q4	N–KB3	9 Q–B4	NxN?²
2 P–QB4	P–K3	SEE DIAGRAM	
3 N–KB3	P–QN3	10 N–N5!³	P–KB3
4 P–KN3	B–N2	11 BxB	PxN
5 B–N2	B–N5ch	12 Q–K3	N–Q2
6 B–Q2	BxBch	13 QxPch	K–B1
7 QxB	P–Q3¹	14 BxR	QxB⁴
8 N–B3	N–K5	15 P–B3⁵	....

White wins a Knight

¹ This, in combination with Black's next move, is not best. Better would be 7 . . . O–O; 8 N–B3, N–K5; 9 Q–B2, P–KB4.

² Black has nothing better than 9 . . . Q–B3.

³ Threatening 11 QxP mate, as well as 11 BxB followed by 12 BxR. This idea appears frequently in the Queen's Indian Defense.

⁴ Attacking White's King Rook. White's natural reply, 15 O–O, would allow Black to win by 15 . . . Q–K5! If then 16 QxN, NxP is mate, or if 16 QxQ, NxQ, and Black has won two pieces for a Rook.

⁵ The attack on White's Rook has been warded off, and Black must lose one of his Knights.

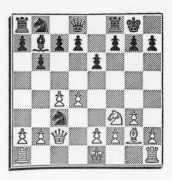

White to Play. *Nine out of ten players would without hesitation play 10 QxN—and overlook the surprise move by which White can win. What is the surprise move?*

WHITE	BLACK	WHITE	BLACK
1 P–Q4	N–KB3	8 N–B3	N–K5
2 P–QB4	P–K3	9 Q–B2	NxN?[2]
3 N–KB3	P–QN3		SEE DIAGRAM
4 P–KN3	B–N2	10 N–N5![3]	N–K5
5 B–N2	B–N5ch	11 BxN	BxB
6 B–Q2	BxBch	12 QxB[4]	QxN
7 QxB[1]	O–O	13 QxR	....

White has won the exchange

[1] Stronger than 7 QNxB, as the Knight belongs on B3. Although the Queen may be chased from this square by Black's Knight, the loss of time incurred is negligible.

[2] Black must play 9 . . . P–KB4 to avoid the trap. The continuation might be 10 N–K5!, P–Q4; 11 PxP, PxP; 12 O–O, N–Q2; 13 P–B4, QN–B3; 14 QR–B1, and White still has the edge.

[3] With the double threat of 11 QxP mate, as well as 11 BxB followed by 12 BxR.

[4] Still threatening mate.

White to Play. *Black is unaware of the danger to which his King Bishop is exposed. White closes the exit gate, and his threats of winning the Bishop force Black to yield the exchange.*

WHITE	BLACK	WHITE	BLACK
1 P–Q4	N–KB3	8 B–B4	P–Q4?[2]
2 P–QB4	P–K3		SEE DIAGRAM
3 N–KB3	P–QN3	9 P–B5![3]	PxP
4 P–KN3	B–N2	10 P–QR3	B–R4
5 B–N2	B–N5ch	11 PxP	P–B3[4]
6 B–Q2	Q–K2	12 B–Q6	....
7 O–O	O–O?[1]		

White wins the exchange

[1] In view of the resulting difficulties, 7 . . . BxB is clearly indicated.

[2] 8 . . . B–Q3 leaves Black with a backward development, but avoids loss of material.

[3] Cutting off the Bishop, and intending to win it with 10 P–QR3, B–R4; 11 P–QN4.

[4] Makes room for the Bishop's flight, but now White has a new, and unanswerable thrust.

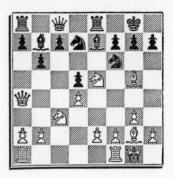

White to Play. *Black's weak handling of the opening has allowed his opponent to obtain a powerful bind on the position. White's next move wins the exchange.*

WHITE	BLACK	WHITE	BLACK
1 P–Q4	N–KB3	8 N–K5	O–O
2 P–QB4	P–K3	9 PxP	PxP
3 N–KB3	P–QN3	10 B–N5	QN–Q2?[2]
4 P–KN3	B–N2	11 Q–R4[3]	R–K1
5 B–N2	Q–B1		SEE DIAGRAM
6 O–O	P–Q4[1]	12 B–R3![4]	....
7 N–B3	B–K2		

White wins the exchange

[1] Generally speaking, Black is better off in this opening by advancing the Queen Pawn one square. The text blocks the action of the Queen Bishop, and allows White to post his King Knight strongly at K5. A good line for Black is 6 . . . P–B4; 7 P–N3, PxP; 8 B–N2, B–K2; 9 NxP, BxB; 10 KxB, P–Q4; 11 PxP, NxP.

[2] 10 . . . P–KR3 might enable Black to hold on a bit longer.

[3] Threatening to win a piece by 12 NxN, QxN; 13 QxQ, NxQ; 14 BxB.

[4] This move would also have won, had Black played 11 . . . P–B3. White's threat is 13 B(N5)xN, BxB; 14 BxN. If 12 . . . Q–Q1; 13 NxN, NxN; 14 BxN wins the exchange; or if 12 . . . R–Q1; 13 NxN, RxN; 14 BxN wins for White.

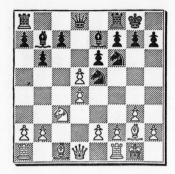

White to Play. Black again comes to grief on the long diagonal, when White uncovers an attack on the unprotected Queen Bishop.

WHITE	BLACK	WHITE	BLACK
1 P–Q4	N–KB3	9 PxP	NxN?[2]
2 P–QB4	P–K3		SEE DIAGRAM
3 N–KB3	P–QN3	10 P–Q6!	BxB[3]
4 P–KN3	B–N2	11 PxB	QxKP
5 B–N2	B–K2	12 PxN!	BxR[4]
6 N–B3	O–O	13 PxN	QxP
7 O–O	P–Q4[1]	14 QxB[5]	....
8 N–K5	QN–Q2		

White has won two pieces for a Rook

[1] Black can get an even game with 7 . . . N–K5; 8 Q–B2, NxN; 9 QxN, B–K5; 10 R–Q1, P–Q3; 11 N–K1, BxB; 12 NxB, N–Q2.

[2] Black should play 9 . . . NxP, with a fair game.

[3] If Black captures the Queen Pawn instead, there follows 11 BxB, R–N1; 12 PxN, and White wins. However, 10 . . . N–B3! saves Black.

[4] If Black's Knight moves, then 13 KxB wins a piece.

[5] Again and again we see how careful Black must be in this opening to guard against tactical surprises, based on threats to his unprotected Queen Bishop.

White to Play. *The long diagonal seems to be wellbarricaded here; yet White finds a clever way to break through and force the win of a Pawn.*

WHITE	BLACK	WHITE	BLACK
1 P–Q4	N–KB3	9 P–K4	QN–Q2[1]
2 P–QB4	P–K3		SEE DIAGRAM
3 N–KB3	P–QN3	10 NxQBP!	BxN
4 P–KN3	B–N2	11 KPxP	PxP[2]
5 B–N2	B–K2	12 PxP	B–N2
6 N–B3	O–O	13 P–Q6!	BxB[3]
7 O–O	P–Q4	14 PxB	QxP
8 N–K5	P–B3	15 KxB[4]	....

White has won a Pawn

[1] This leads to trouble. Black might try 9 ... PxBP; 10 NxP(B4), B–R3; 11 P–N3, P–QN4; 12 N–K5, P–N5; 13 N–K2, BxN; 14 QxB, QxP; 15 B–N2, and Black has an extra Pawn as compensation for White's attacking prospects. The position is so harmless in appearance, that Black can hardly be criticized for his last move; White's winning idea is rather subtle.

[2] If 11 ... B–N2; 12 P–Q6 leads to the same finish as the text.

[3] If 13 ... BxP; 14 BxB wins a Pawn for White.

[4] White with a Pawn more, and a Passed Pawn at that, has an easy win.

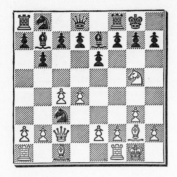

Black to Play. *Here we see a trap in reverse, on the long diagonal. The trap is set to catch Black, but it is White who is caught.*

WHITE	BLACK	WHITE	BLACK
1 P–Q4	N–KB3	8 Q–B2	NxN
2 P–QB4	P–K3	9 N–N5?[1]	....
3 N–KB3	P–QN3		SEE DIAGRAM
4 P–KN3	B–N2	9	NxPch![2]
5 B–N2	B–K2	10 K–R1[3]	BxBch
6 O–O	O–O	11 KxB	BxN
7 N–B3	N–K5		

Black has won a piece

[1] White thinks he has the same threats as in Trap 260: 10 QxP mate, and 10 BxB followed by 11 BxR. He is quickly disillusioned! He should play instead either 9 PxN, or 9 QxN.

[2] The useful check that turns a seeming loss for Black into a win.

[3] If 10 QxN, BxB; 11 KxB, BxN, and Black wins a piece.

White to Play. Once again the unmasking of the long diagonal is the basic motif. Black has exposed his Knight to attack and must lose material.

WHITE	BLACK	WHITE	BLACK
1 P–Q4	N–KB3	SEE DIAGRAM	
2 P–QB4	P–K3	8 KN–Q2!	N–Q3[2]
3 N–KB3	P–QN3	9 P–B5!	BxB[3]
4 P–KN3	B–N2	10 PxN	BxR[4]
5 B–N2	B–K2	11 PxB	QxP
6 O–O	O–O	12 NxB	....
7 Q–B2	N–K5?[1]		

White has won two pieces for a Rook

[1] This is the right move when White plays 7 N–B3; but after 7 Q–B2, Black should reply 7 ... B–K5.

[2] An attempt to prevent the loss of material, but it fails. However, if 8 ... NxN; 9 BxB, NxR; 10 BxR, and Black's Knight is imprisoned. Or if 8 ... P–KB4; 9 NxN, PxN; 10 BxP, BxB; 11 QxB, and White wins a Pawn.

[3] The Knight dare not move, as it must protect the Bishop.

[4] If 10 ... BxP; 11 KxB, with a piece ahead for White.

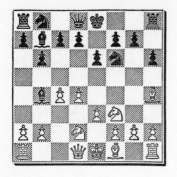

Black to Play. *White now loses a piece by force. In the main variation Black's King Knight Pawn makes a spectacular journey to the seventh rank and forks two pieces.*

WHITE	BLACK	WHITE	BLACK
1 P–Q4	N–KB3	7 QN–Q2?[3]	....
2 P–QB4	P–K3		SEE DIAGRAM
3 N–KB3	P–QN3	7	P–KN4!
4 B–N5[1]	B–N2	8 B–N3	P–N5!
5 P–K3	P–KR3	9 P–QR3[4]	PxN
6 B–R4[2]	B–N5ch	10 PxB	PxP[5]

Black wins a piece

[1] Not as strong as it looks. The logical continuation is 4 P–KN3. This trap shows why Black's Queen side fianchetto is best countered with a King side fianchetto.

[2] Not fatal, but it gives White an uncomfortable game. 6 BxN instead is preferable.

[3] White can best avoid the loss of a piece with 7 KN–Q2, although Black still has the initiative.

[4] If 9 N–K5, Black replies 9 . . . N–K5 winning the pinned Knight.

[5] The Pawn fork wins a piece.

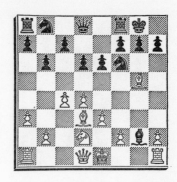

White to Play. *Black has shown poor judgment in accepting the offer of the King Knight's Pawn. White now demonstrates the power exerted by a Rook, when it controls an open file.*

WHITE	BLACK	WHITE	BLACK
1 P–Q4	N–KB3	9 B–Q3!	BxP?[1]
2 P–QB4	P–K3	SEE DIAGRAM	
3 N–KB3	P–QN3	10 KR–N1	B–N2
4 B–N5	B–N2	11 B–R6[2]	N–K1[3]
5 QN–Q2	B–N5	12 RxPch!	NxR[4]
6 P–QR3	BxNch	13 Q–N4	Q–B3[5]
7 NxB	O–O	14 B–N5	....
8 P–K3	P–Q3		

White wins the Queen

[1] Opening the King Knight file for the sake of winning a Pawn is risky play. Black should play instead 9 . . . QN–Q2.

[2] Threatening 12 BxP followed by a ruinous discovered check.

[3] The lesser evil would have been 11 . . . P–N3, giving up the exchange, but Black thought he could protect his Knight Pawn by the text move.

[4] After 12 . . . K–R1, there is a quick mate with 13 RxPch, K–N1; 14 Q–N4ch etc.

[5] Stops White's threat of 14 QxN mate, but loses the Queen.

White to Play. *White ex-changes several pieces, then gets a grip on Black's Knight by means of a pin and forces the win of material.*

WHITE	BLACK	WHITE	BLACK
1 P–Q4	N–KB3	12 B–B5	N–K5?[2]
2 P–QB4	P–K3		SEE DIAGRAM
3 N–KB3	P–QN3	13 BxB	QxB
4 N–B3	B–N2	14 NxN	PxN
5 B–N5	B–N5	15 QxBP!	PxN[3]
6 Q–B2	P–KR3	16 QxB	PxP[4]
7 B–R4	O–O	17 KR–B1	KR–Q1
8 P–K3	P–Q4[1]	18 R–B7	QR–N1
9 PxP	PxP	19 Q–B6	Q–B3
10 B–Q3	QN–Q2	20 BxN	....
11 O–O	B–K2		

White has won a piece

[1] 8 . . . P–Q3 would be more in the spirit of the opening.

[2] This attempt to extricate himself forcibly from his cramped position, lands Black in a snare which his opponent has pre-pared for him. Black should have played 12 . . . P–B3 fol-lowed by 13 . . . N–K1.

[3] Refusing the Knight is no better. Thus if 15 . . . B–B1; 16 N–K5, R–Q1; 17 N–B6 followed by 18 QxRch.

[4] If 16 . . . Q–N4; 17 QxBP, and White has won two Pawns.

White to Play. It is not easy to see at first glance that White can win a piece. He does so by forcing one of Black's Bishops into an unprotected position, and then a double attack does the trick.

WHITE	BLACK	WHITE	BLACK
1 P-Q4	N-KB3	9 P-K4	P-Q4
2 N-KB3	P-QN3	10 P-K5	N-KN5[2]
3 P-K3	B-N2	11 B-N5	P-QR3?[3]
4 B-Q3	P-K3		SEE DIAGRAM
5 QN-Q2	P-B4	12 BxNch!	BxB
6 P-B3	N-B3	13 P-N4	B-K2
7 O-O	B-K2	14 N-Q4[4]	NxKP[5]
8 PxP	BxP[1]	15 P-KB4	....

White wins a piece

[1] 8 . . . PxP is better.

[2] The attack on White's King Pawn is tempting.

[3] This too looks good, as the Bishop's retreat 12 B-R4 would cost the King Pawn after 12 . . . P-QN4, while 12 BxNch gives Black the advantage of the two Bishops.

[4] Simultaneously opening fire on two Black pieces.

[5] Temporary relief.

Black to Play. *White has not castled, and his King Bishop is unprotected. Black takes advantage of these weaknesses to combine an attack on the Bishop with a mating threat.*

WHITE	BLACK	WHITE	BLACK
1 P–Q4	N–KB3	8 NxP?[2]	....
2 N–KB3	P–QN3	SEE DIAGRAM	
3 P–B4	B–N2	8	N(Q2)xN
4 N–B3	P–Q4	9 PxN[3]	NxN
5 PxP	NxP	10 QxQch[4]	RxQ
6 P–KN3	N–Q2	11 PxN[5]	BxB
7 B–N2	P–K4![1]		

Black has won a piece

[1] A brilliant offer of a Pawn which White cannot take safely with either Knight or Pawn.

[2] White should spurn the Pawn, and castle instead. The following trap shows what happens when White captures with his Pawn.

[3] If 9 NxN, BxN; 10 BxB (10 PxN, BxB wins a piece for Black) QxB, and Black wins a piece. White cannot continue with 11 PxN, as 11 ... QxRch; 12 K–Q2, R–Q1ch is murder.

[4] If 10 BxB, QxQ mates White.

[5] If 11 BxB, R–Q8 mate.

Black to Play. *White intends to give up his Queen for two pieces and the prospect of winning a third piece, or even Black's Queen. Looks good, but Black has some winning ideas of his own!*

WHITE	BLACK	WHITE	BLACK
1 P–Q4	N–KB3	8 PxP?[1]	NxP
2 N–KB3	P–QN3	9 Q–R4ch?[2]	....
3 P–B4	B–N2	SEE DIAGRAM	
4 N–B3	P–Q4	9	B–B3
5 PxP	NxP	10 N(KB3)xN	BxQ
6 P–KN3	N–Q2	11 BxN[3]	B–N5![4]
7 B–N2	P–K4!	12 BxPch[5]	K–B1[6]

And Black wins

[1] The previous trap shows how Black wins after 8 NxP.

[2] Better is 9 Q–N3, N(Q4)xN; 10 NxN (threatening 11 QxP mate), B–Q4 (not 10 . . . Q–Q8ch; 11 QxQ, NxQ; 12 BxB, QR–N1; 13 B–B6ch); 11 BxB, QxB; 12 QxQ (not 12 QxN, QxRch, and certainly not 12 O–O, NxP mate), NxQ, and the positions are equal.

[3] With all sorts of threats: one is 12 BxPch, K–K2; 13 B–N5ch, winning the Queen; another is 12 NxP, and Black's Queen, both Rooks, and his Queen Bishop are threatened!

[4] Threat: 12 . . . QxB!

[5] If 12 BxR, Q–Q8 mate.

[6] White's threats have disappeared, leaving Black with a winning advantage in material.

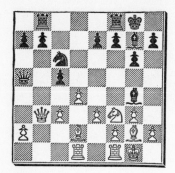

Black to Play. *An exchange of Pawns clears the way for Black's Queen to swing over to the King side, and there exert the pressure needed to threaten White's Knight.*

WHITE	BLACK	WHITE	BLACK
1 P–Q4	N–KB3	9 PxN	N–B3
2 P–QB4	P–KN3	10 P–K3	Q–R4
3 N–QB3	P–Q4	11 Q–N3	R–N1
4 N–B3	B–N2	12 B–Q2[1]	B–N5![2]
5 PxP	NxN4	13 QR–Q1?[3]	....
6 P–KN3	O–O		SEE DIAGRAM
7 B–N2	P–QB4	13	PxP
8 O–O	NxN	14 BPxP	Q–R4![4]

Black wins the exchange

[1] Not the best, as White soon runs into trouble. 12 B–QR3 is simpler and more effective.

[2] Threatening 13 . . . BxN; 14 BxB, PxP; 15 KPxP, NxP!, and Black wins a Pawn.

[3] 13 Q–N2 is better. The move played is intended to protect the Bishop, and thus prevent the possibility pointed out in the previous note, but now White's Knight will be the object of the pin!

[4] Black threatens to win the Knight. If White moves the Knight, Black wins the exchange. Or if 15 P–K4, NxP; 16 NxN, BxR; 17 RxB (or 17 QxB, QxQ etc.), BxN, winning the exchange and a Pawn.

Black to Play. White has thoughtlessly captured an unprotected Pawn. Black demonstrates that it was an error by winning a piece.

WHITE	BLACK	WHITE	BLACK
1 P–Q4	N–KB3	6 NxP?[1]	......
2 P–QB4	P–KN3	SEE DIAGRAM	
3 N–QB3	P–Q4	6	NxB![2]
4 N–B3	B–N2	7 NxN	P–K3
5 B–N5	N–K5		

Black wins one of the Knights

[1] White captures the Pawn, as he sees that Black's King Pawn is pinned, and cannot harm him. Instead of this capture which loses, a good continuation for White is 6 PxP, NxB; 7 NxN, P–K3; 8 N–B3, PxP; 9 P–K3, O–O; 10 B–K2, P–QB3; 11 O–O, as Lasker played against Botvinnik at Nottingham in 1936.

[2] Gets rid of White's trump—the pinning piece!

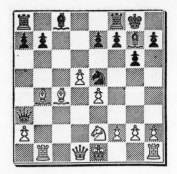

Black to Play. It is far from easy to see that White's successful attempt to win the Queen leads to loss of the game for him! Black's next move is reminiscent of the famed Lewitzky-Marshall brilliancy!

WHITE	BLACK	WHITE	BLACK
1 P-Q4	N-KB3	10 PxP	Q-R4ch
2 P-QB4	P-KN3	11 B-Q2	Q-R6
3 N-QB3	P-Q4	12 QR-N1[2]	O-O
4 PxP	NxP	13 P-Q5[3]	N-K4!
5 P-K4	NxN	14 B-N4?[4]	....
6 PxN	P-QB4[1]		SEE DIAGRAM
7 B-QB4	B-N2	14	Q-B6!!
8 N-K2	N-B3	15 PxQ[5]	NxPch
9 B-K3	PxP	16 K-B1	B-R6

White has been checkmated

[1] Black strikes vigorously at the hostile center.

[2] In order to answer 12 ... NxP with 13 B-N4 winning the Queen.

[3] Apparently decisive, for if the attacked Knight moves, then 14 B-N4 wins the Queen.

[4] Wins the Queen, but ...

[5] Other moves permit Black to play either 15 ... QxNP or 15 ... QxKP, gaining material and keeping the initiative, with a win in sight.

White to Play. *Hoping to simplify by exchanges, Black has just played his Knight to K5. But White can now force the win of a Pawn by a neat finesse.*

WHITE	BLACK	WHITE	BLACK
1 P–Q4	N–KB3	7 B–Q2	N–K5?[1]
2 P–QB4	P–KN3	SEE DIAGRAM	
3 N–QB3	P–Q4	8 PxP!	NxN[2]
4 P–K3	B–N2	9 PxP![3]	QNxP[4]
5 Q–N3	P–B3	10 BxN	....
6 N–B3	O–O		

White has won a Pawn

[1] In this somewhat cramped position, Black makes a plausible attempt to free himself. 7 . . . P–N3, or 7 . . . P–K3 should instead be played.

[2] If 8 . . . PxP; 9 QxQP wins a Pawn.

[3] The point! White comes out a Pawn ahead, no matter what his opponent replies.

[4] If 9 . . . N–K5; 10 PxP, BxNP; 11 QxB regains the piece with a plus of two Pawns.

Black to Play. *Black convincingly shows up the flaws in his opponent's development. Black "sacrifices" a Knight, and quickly gets in return a Bishop and two Pawns.*

WHITE	BLACK	WHITE	BLACK
1 P-Q4	N-KB3	9 B-K3	N-Q2[2]
2 P-QB4	P-KN3	10 N-K2?[3]	....
3 N-QB3	B-N2	SEE DIAGRAM	
4 P-K4	P-Q3	10	KN-K4![4]
5 N-B3	O-O	11 PxN	NxP
6 B-Q3[1]	B-N5	12 Q-N3	NxBch
7 P-KR3	BxN	13 K-Q2	NxNP[5]
8 QxB	N-B3		

Black has won two Pawns

[1] Not a good square for the King Bishop in this opening. Better is 6 B-K2.

[2] Black has already seized the initiative.

[3] 10 P-Q5 must be played, despite the fact that it opens the long diagonal for Black's King Bishop.

[4] Either Knight can go to K4, forking Queen and Bishop, with the same result.

[5] Two masters have fallen into this trap, and the late World Champion Dr. Alekhine overlooked it in his annotations.

Black to Play. White has ignored the unprotected state of his Queen Bishop, and this gives Black the opportunity of demonstrating the power of the pin as a tactical weapon.

WHITE	BLACK	WHITE	BLACK
1 P–Q4	N–KB3	8 PxP	PxP
2 N–KB3	P–KN3	9 NxP?[2]	....
3 P–K3	B–N2	SEE DIAGRAM	
4 B–Q3	P–Q3	9........	N–N5![3]
5 P–QN3	O–O	10 QxN[4]	NxN
6 B–N2	QN–Q2[1]	11 Q–K2[5]	N–B6ch!
7 O–O	P–K4	12 QxN	BxB

Black wins the exchange

[1] White's conservative play is not calculated to create difficulties for Black.

[2] Trying to win a Pawn, as it is not clear how Black is to regain it. If instead 9 BxP, NxB; 10 NxN, N–N5; 11 NxN (if 11 P–KB4, NxKP wins the exchange), BxR; and now if 12 P–QB3 (to lock in the Bishop) then 12 ... BxN; 13 QxB, QxB wins for Black.

[3] White's pinned Knight is suddenly attacked by three pieces.

[4] If 10 P–KB4, NxKP wins the exchange.

[5] The Queen must move, as it is threatened by two of Black's pieces.

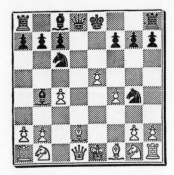

Black to Play. *White has made too many Pawn moves. As a result, Black has superior development and splendid attacking possibilities for his Knights.*

WHITE	BLACK	WHITE	BLACK
1 P–Q4	N–KB3	8 B–Q2	....
2 P–QB4	P–K4	*SEE DIAGRAM*	
3 PxP	N–N5	8	N–K6![3]
4 P–B4?[1]	P–Q3	9 Q–N3[4]	N–Q5![5]
5 P–K4	N–QB3	10 Q–Q3[6]	B–KB4
6 PxP[2]	BxP	11 QxN(K3)	N–B7ch
7 P–K5?	B–N5ch		

Black wins the Queen

[1] A good line for White is 4 P–K4, NxKP; 5 P–B4, KN–B3; 6 N–KB3, B–B4; 7 N–B3, P–Q3; 8 P–QR3.

[2] Gets rid of the doubled Pawn, but at the cost of assisting Black's development.

[3] Black takes advantage of the pin to post a Knight on enemy terrain.

[4] 9 Q–B1 is somewhat better, but White's position would remain bad.

[5] Now 10 QxB, or 10 QxN would be answered by 10 . . . N–B7ch winning White's Queen.

[6] Or 10 Q–R4ch, B–Q2, and White's Queen falls.

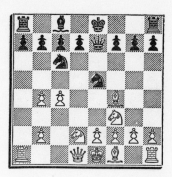

Black to Play. White is taught a lesson: beware of snapping so readily at expensive bait! Gift horses—on the chessboard at least—must be looked in the mouth!

WHITE	BLACK	WHITE	BLACK
1 P–Q4	N–KB3	6 N–B3	Q–K2
2 P–QB4	P–K4	7 P–QR3	KNxKP
3 PxP	N–N5	8 PxB?[1]	....
4 B–B4	B–N5ch		SEE DIAGRAM
5 N–Q2	N–QB3	8	N–Q6[2]

White has been checkmated

[1] White can get a good game by 8 NxN, NxN; 9 P–K3, BxNch; 10 QxB, O–O; 11 B–K2, etc. Or he can play 8 P–K3, BxNch; 9 QxB, P–Q3; 10 B–K2.

[2] This trap, absurdly simple as it may seem to be, has occurred several times in serious play—most recently, in a Pennsylvania State Championship game.

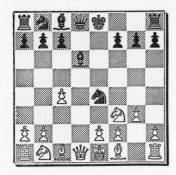

Black to Play. *It is difficult to realize that Black in this simple position, has a forced win. White's failure to make a simple developing move provided the opportunity.*

WHITE	BLACK	WHITE	BLACK
1 P–Q4	N–KB3	6 P–KN3?[3]	....
2 P–QB4	P–K4		SEE DIAGRAM
3 PxP	N–K5[1]	6	NxBP![4]
4 N–KB3[2]	P–Q3	7 KxN	BxPch!
5 PxP	BxP	8 PxB[5]	QxQ

Black has won the Queen

[1] A tricky move, favored by such bold spirits as Tartakover.

[2] White gets an excellent game by 4 N–Q2, N–B4; 5 KN–B3, N–B3; 6 P–KN3, Q–K2; 7 B–N2, P–KN3; 8 N–QN1!, the purpose of this retreat being to develop the Knight at B3 (now that it no longer serves a useful purpose at Q2) from where it can first dominate, then post itself on the strong point Q5.

[3] White should play 6 QN–Q2, not only to get another piece into play quickly, but also to force Black's Knight to declare its intentions.

[4] Attacking Queen and Rook. If White does not capture he must lose at least the exchange.

[5] Unfortunately, White's King cannot get back to K1 to protect the Queen.

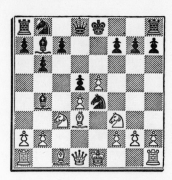

White to Play. *White refutes Black's pin by a paralyzing counter-pin, which nets White two pieces.*

WHITE	BLACK	WHITE	BLACK
1 P–Q4	N–KB3	SEE DIAGRAM	
2 P–QB4	P–K3	9 Q–R4ch	N–B3
3 N–QB3	P–QN3[1]	10 B–QN5	BxNch
4 P–K4	B–N2	11 PxB	Q–Q2[3]
5 B–Q3	P–Q4	12 P–K6![4]	PxP
6 BPxP	PxP	13 N–K5	NxQBP
7 P–K5	N–K5	14 Q–B2	Q–Q3
8 N–B3	B–N5?[2]	15 QxN[5]	....

White wins two pieces

[1] Best is 3 . . . B–N5 to exert pressure on the Knight, and thereby prevent 4 P–K4.

[2] 8 . . . B–K2 is much better, although White's game is still superior.

[3] If 11 . . . NxQBP; 12 BxNch, K–B1 (or 12 . . . BxB; 13 QxBch followed by 14 QxN wins two pieces for White); 13 Q–N4ch, and White wins two pieces.

[4] Making room for the Knight—another attacker of the pinned piece.

[5] Black cannot save his remaining Knight.

White to Play. *White wins with a magnificent sacrifice! He gives up his Queen to break down the barrier surrounding Black's King, gets the King into the open, then forces checkmate quickly.*

WHITE	BLACK	WHITE	BLACK
1 P–Q4	N–KB3	10 B–R3ch	K–N1[3]
2 P–QB4	P–K3	11 R–N3	BxP
3 N–QB3	P–QN3	SEE DIAGRAM	
4 P–K4	B–N5	12 QxPch!	KxQ
5 P–K5	N–K5	13 R–N3ch	K–R3[4]
6 Q–N4	NxN	14 B–B1ch	K–R4
7 PxN	BxPch?[1]	15 B–K2ch	K–R5
8 K–Q1	K–B1[2]	16 R–R3	....
9 R–N1	N–B3		

Black has been checkmated

[1] There was nothing better than 7 . . . B–KB1.

[2] If 8 . . . BxR; 9 QxP, R–B1; 10 B–N5, P–B3; 11 BxP, RxB; 12 PxR, P–Q4 (White threatened 13 Q–N8 mate) ; 13 P–B7ch, K–Q2; 14 P–B8 (Q)ch, and White wins. Or if 8 . . . O–O; 9 B–R6, P–N3; 10 R–B1, and White wins the exchange.

[3] Forced, as 10 . . . N–K2 or 10 . . . P–Q3 is refuted by 11 Q–B3 attacking two pieces.

[4] If 13 . . . Q–N4; 14 RxQch, K–R3; 15 B–B1, B–R3; 16 R–N8ch, K–R4; 17 B–K2ch, K–R5; 18 P–N3 mate.

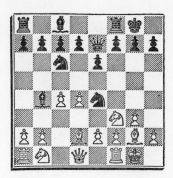

White to Play. *White bases his plan to win a piece on the fact that Black's Bishop can be locked out and then surrounded by Pawns.*

WHITE	BLACK	WHITE	BLACK
1 P–Q4	N–KB3	7 O–O	N–K5?[1]
2 P–QB4	P–K3		SEE DIAGRAM
3 N–KB3	B–N5ch	8 B–K3![2]	Q–K1[3]
4 B–Q2	Q–K2	9 Q–B2	P–B4
5 P–KN3	O–O	10 P–B5!	B–R4
6 B–N2	N–B3	11 P–QR3[4]	....

White wins a piece

[1] 7 . . . BxB is natural and correct.

[2] Secures the Bishop from exchange, and leaves Black's Bishop stranded. White's threat now is 9 P–QR3, B–R4 (if 9 . . . B–Q3; 10 P–B5); 10 P–QN4, B–N3; 11 P–B5.

[3] To make room for the Bishop's return—he hopes. If 8 . . . P–QN3; 9 P–B5, PxP; 10 P–QR3, PxP (or 10 . . . B–R4; 11 PxP wins); 11 NxP, NxN; 12 QBxN, and White wins one of the two threatened pieces.

[4] Black cannot prevent 12 P–QN4, winning the Bishop.

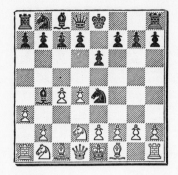

Black to Play. *White has wasted only one move, but that is enough to give Black time to bring his Queen into play with terrific effect.*

WHITE	BLACK	WHITE	BLACK
1 P–Q4	N–KB3	5	Q–B3![4]
2 P–QB4	P–K3	6 P–B3[5]	Q–R5ch
3 N–KB3	N–K5[1]	7 P–N3	NxP
4 KN–Q2![2]	B–N5	8 R–N1[6]	N–K5ch
5 P–QR3?[3]	....	9 R–N3	NxR[7]
	SEE DIAGRAM		

Black has won a Rook

[1] A tricky move, but not to be recommended, because it neglects Black's development.

[2] In order to play P–B3 at the first opportunity.

[3] White wants to compel Black to exchange Bishops, or if 5 . . . B–R4, to win a piece by 6 P–QN4, NxN; 7 QxN, B–N3; 8 P–B5. He should have played instead 5 Q–B2, P–Q4; 6 N–B3, P–KB4; 7 N(Q2)xN, BPxN; 8 B–B4.

[4] Threatens 6 . . . QxP mate.

[5] If 6 Q–B2, QxPch wins a Pawn and maintains the attack.

[6] If 8 PxN, QxP is mate.

[7] Black has a winning attack, besides the extra Rook. A continuation might be: 10 Q–N3 (to give the King room), N–B4ch; 11 K–Q1, QxQP; 12 PxB; N–K6ch; 13 K–K1, Q–R5 mate.

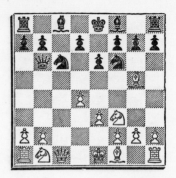

Black to Play. *Black forces White into a pin, then adds pressure. After driving away a defender of the pinned piece, and applying more pressure, Black makes further resistance impossible.*

WHITE	BLACK	WHITE	BLACK
1 P–Q4	N–KB3	7	Q–R4ch
2 N–KB3	P–K3	8 QN–Q2[4]	N–K5
3 B–N5	P–B4	9 B–KB4	P–KN4
4 P–B3[1]	PxP	10 B–N3	P–N5
5 PxP	Q–N3	11 N–K5	QNxN
6 Q–B1[2]	N–B3	12 BxN	B–N5
7 P–K3?[3]	....	13 Q–Q1[5]	BxNch
SEE DIAGRAM		14 K–K2	Q–N4

White has been checkmated

[1] 4 P–K3 is more accurate, avoiding the ensuing difficulties.
[2] The simplest was 6 BxN, for if 6 . . . QxNP; 7 BxP, BxB; 8 QN–Q2, and Black cannot capture the Queen Pawn, as after 8 . . . BxP; 9 QR–N1, Q–B6; 10 R–B1, Q–N7; 11 RxBch wins a piece.
[3] Fatal; White should have interpolated 7 BxN.
[4] If 8 Q–Q2, B–N5; 9 N–B3, N–K5, and the attack on White's Queen, Queen Knight, and Queen Bishop wins at once. White could fight on longer with 8 K–K2, but loss is inevitable.
[5] The alternative 13 BxR, BxNch winning the Queen, is of course hopeless for White.

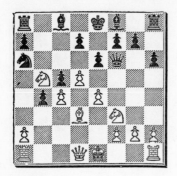

White to Play. *White forces Black's Queen to lose still more time, and then he opens up the position. His minor pieces get to work and quickly put an end to the opposing King's career.*

WHITE	BLACK	WHITE	BLACK
1 P–Q4	N–KB3		SEE DIAGRAM
2 N–KB3	P–K3	11 P–K5!	Q–Q1[4]
3 P–B4	P–B4	12 PxP	QPxP[5]
4 P–Q5	P–QN4	13 B–K4!	QxQch
5 B–N5![1]	P–KR3	14 RxQ	QR–N1
6 BxN	QxB	15 B–B6ch	K–K2
7 N–B3	P–N5	16 NxP	P–N4
8 N–QN5	N–R3	17 B–N5!	B–KN2
9 P–K4	QxP?[2]	18 N–B6ch	K–B1
10 B–Q3	Q–B3[3]	19 R–Q8	....

Black has been checkmated

[1] If 5 PxKP, KBPxP; 6 PxP, P–Q4; 7 P–K3, B–Q3; 8 N–B3, O–O; 9 B–K2, B–N2, and Black's tremendous centralization is worth much more than a Pawn.

[2] Black should play 9 . . . P–K4.

[3] Black gets his Queen back into the game, but it is too late.

[4] If 11 . . . Q–B5; 12 P–N3, Q–N5; 13 P–KR3, Q–R4; 14 P–N4, and White wins the Queen.

[5] If 12 . . . BPxP; 13 B–N6ch, K–K2; 14 Q–Q6 mate.

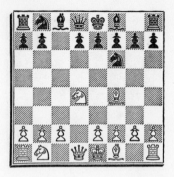

Black to Play. *White's thoughtless play has exposed him to a murderous combination of a Pawn fork followed by a Queen fork.*

WHITE	BLACK	WHITE	BLACK
1 P–Q4	N–KB3		SEE DIAGRAM
2 N–KB3	P–B4	4	P–K4![3]
3 B–B4?[1]	PxP	5 BxP	Q–R4ch
4 NxP?[2]	....	6 N–B3	QxB

Black has won a piece

[1] 3 P–Q5 instead cramps Black's game considerably, as it prevents his Queen Knight from occupying its best square, B3.

[2] Loses at once. 4 QxP was better, although Black gains time after 4 ... N–B3, when White's Queen must retreat.

[3] Hits at both pieces, forcing White to capture the Pawn.

Black to Play. *Again neglected development carries a severe penalty. After only four moves, White must either lose his Queen or be checkmated!*

WHITE	BLACK	WHITE	BLACK
1 P–Q4	N–KB3	4 P–KR3?[2]	....
2 N–Q2	P–K4[1]	SEE DIAGRAM	
3 PxP	N–N5	4	N–K6![3]

Black wins the Queen

[1] This rarely seen gambit is a relative of the Budapest Defense.

[2] Plausible, but fatal. These instinctive moves (chasing an enemy piece away) must be guarded against. White should have gone about his business of development with 5 KN–B3.

[3] Attacking and winning the Queen, for if 5 PxN, Q–R5ch; 6 P–N3, QxP is mate. This delightful brevity occurred in a tourney for the championship of Paris in 1924, between Messrs. Gibaud and Lazard, and is the shortest tournament game ever played.

White to Play. Black has played the opening weakly— to punish him White selects from his armory of tactical weapons a device known as "the pin followed by a Knight fork."

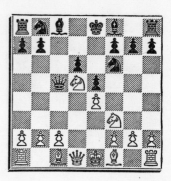

WHITE	BLACK	WHITE	BLACK
1 P–Q4	P–QB4	6 N–Q5[4]	N–KB3?[5]
2 PxP[1]	Q–R4ch[2]		SEE DIAGRAM
3 N–B3	QxBP	7 P–QN4!	Q–B3
4 P–K4	P–K4?[3]	8 B–QN5!	QxB
5 N–B3	P–Q3	9 N–B7ch	....

White wins the Queen

[1] More usual is 2 P–Q5, to keep up the pressure. With White's Pawn at Q5, Black's Queen Knight will find it difficult to develop normally.

[2] 2 . . . P–K3 is correct, and Black would be playing (with colors reversed) a sort of Queen's Gambit Accepted. The early development of the Queen leads to trouble.

[3] This, which permits White's Knight full control of Q5, cannot be good.

[4] Involving a threat which Black overlooks.

[5] One of the rare times when this move is not good.

White to Play. *Black has set a clever trap; but White counters with an astonishing refutation! Instead of taking his opponent's Queen, he sacrifices both of his Rooks!*

WHITE	BLACK	WHITE	BLACK
1 P–Q4	P–KB4	12 K–B2	QxR
2 P–K4	PxP	13 BxP	P–Q3[3]
3 N–QB3	N–KB3	14 BxP	N–B3
4 B–KN5	P–KN3	15 B–N5	B–Q2
5 P–B3	PxP	16 BxN	PxB
6 NxP	B–N2	17 Q–K2ch	K–B2[4]
7 B–Q3	P–B4	18 N–N5ch	K–N1
8 P–Q5	Q–N3	19 N–K7ch	K–B1
9 Q–Q2	QxP[1]	20 N–B5ch	K–N1
10 QR–N1	NxP?![2]	21 Q–B4ch	B–K3
SEE DIAGRAM		22 QxB	....
11 NxN!	QxRch		

Black has been checkmated

[1] Wrong policy, as usual; but this time Black has an ingenious plan in mind.

[2] So that if 11 RxQ, BxN, and after winning White's Queen, which is pinned, Black will be three Pawns to the good.

[3] Black is helpless. If 13 ... K–B2; 14 Q–B4ch, K–N1; 15 B–B4, or if 13 ... N–R3; 14 B–Q6, and White wins easily.

[4] If 17 ... K–Q1; 18 B–B7ch, K–B1; 19 Q–R6 mate.

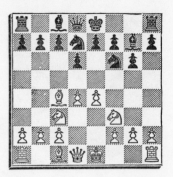

White to Play. *Black's King Knight could have been developed at B3 as far back as Black's first move. Now its "development" is punished by a clever Pawn push, which wins at least a piece.*

WHITE	BLACK	WHITE	BLACK
1 P–Q4	P–KN3	6 P–K5!	PxP[2]
2 P–K4	B–N2	7 PxP	N–KN1[3]
3 N–KB3	P–Q3	8 BxPch![4]	KxB[5]
4 N–B3	N–Q2	9 N–N5ch	K–K1[6]
5 B–QB4	KN–B3?[1]	10 N–K6	....

SEE DIAGRAM

White wins the Queen

[1] Premature—and too late! 5 . . . P–K4 should be played, and if 6 N–KN5, N–R3. 5 . . . P–QB4 is another possibility.

[2] If 6 . . . N–N5; 7 N–KN5, N–R3 (the Knight was attacked) ; 8 BxPch, NxB (or 8 . . . K–B1; 9 N–K6ch winning the Queen) ; 9 N–K6 wins the Queen.

[3] If 7 . . . N–R4; 8 P–KN4 wins the Knight.

[4] This shows up the flaw in Black's method of opening.

[5] If 8 . . . K–B1; 9 BxN, RxB; 10 P–K6 wins the pinned Knight.

[6] If 9 . . . K–B1; 10 N–K6ch wins the Queen.

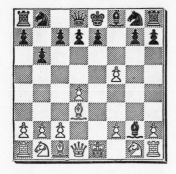

White to Play. Black innocently imagines that he will win a Rook. Actually, he has exposed his King, and succumbs to a mating attack.

WHITE	BLACK	WHITE	BLACK
1 P–Q4	P–QN3[1]	5 Q–R5ch	P–N3
2 P–K4	B–N2	6 PxP	N–KB3
3 B–Q3	P–KB4?[2]	7 PxPch!	NxQ
4 PxP[3]	BxP?	8 B–N6[4]	....

SEE DIAGRAM

Black has been checkmated

[1] Not good because it allows White to build up a strong Pawn center. Better is 1 . . . P–Q4, or 1 . . . N–KB3.

[2] Setting a trap for White. Black hopes to win a Rook after 4 PxP, BxP. Black should have played 3 . . . P–K3, or 3 . . . P–KN3.

[3] White "falls" into the trap.

[4] A 300-year-old trap which still catches them to-day over the board, and—believe it or not—in correspondence play!

Black to Play. B l a c k ' s pieces enjoy so much mobility, and White's so little, that it takes but a few moves to pin White to death.

WHITE	BLACK	WHITE	BLACK
1 P–QB4	P–K4	9 Q–Q3	P–Q4!
2 N–QB3	N–KB3	10 P–N3	....
3 N–B3	N–B3		SEE DIAGRAM
4 P–Q4	PxP	10	P–Q5![4]
5 NxP	B–N5	11 QxQP	R–Q1
6 NxN[1]	NPxN	12 BxPch	K–B1
7 P–KN3?[2]	Q–K2[3]	13 B–Q5[5]	RxB!
8 B–N2	B–R3!	14 PxR	QxP

White has been checkmated

[1] Frees Black's game unduly. 6 B–N5 is stronger.

[2] This is probably the losing move. The correct development would be 7 Q–N3, B–B4; 8 P–K3, O–O; 9 B–K2, R–K1; 10 O–O etc.

[3] Threatening to win a Pawn with 8 . . . Q–K5. Black has already seized the initiative.

[4] A powerful stroke.

[5] If 13 Q–K3, QxQ; 14 BxQ, BxNch wins.

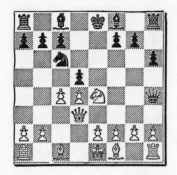

White to Play. *Black offers a Pawn to open up lines of attack for his pieces. White should refuse the offer, and instead return the extra Pawn.*

WHITE	BLACK	WHITE	BLACK
1 P–QB4	P–K4	8 Q–Q3	P–Q4 !
2 N–QB3	N–KB3	SEE DIAGRAM	
3 N–B3	N–B3	9 PxP?[3]	N–N5 !
4 P–Q4	P–K5	10 Q–N1[4]	B–KB4[5]
5 N–KN5[1]	P–KR3 !	11 N–Q6ch	PxN !
6 KNxKP[2]	NxN	12 QxB	P–KN3
7 NxN	Q–R5	13 Q–N1	R–B1[6]

Black wins the exchange

[1] 5 N–Q2 is a good alternative.

[2] Best, though not obvious, is 6 P–Q5, PxN; 7 PxN, B–B4.

[3] White should give back the Pawn by 9 N–B3, PxP; 10 QxP, QxQP.

[4] The only square from which he can protect his Knight, and guard the threat of . . . N–B7ch. If instead 10 Q–N5ch, P–B3; 11 PxP, PxP wins for Black.

[5] Forcing White's reply, as the Knight can no longer be protected.

[6] Black continues with 14 . . . N–B7, and wins the exchange.

White to Play. White can win a piece by playing 10 BxNch. What is wrong with this idea?

WHITE	BLACK	WHITE	BLACK
1 P–QB4	P–K4	9 NxNch	QxN!
2 N–QB3	N–QB3	SEE DIAGRAM	
3 P–KN3	N–B3	10 BxNch?	PxB
4 B–N2	B–N5	11 QxRch[2]	K–Q2
5 P–K3	P–Q3	12 QxR	Q–B6[3]
6 KN–K2	B–N5	13 K–Q1[4]	QxNch
7 Q–N3	QR–N1[1]	14 K–B2	QxBPch
8 N–Q5	B–QB4	15 K–N1	Q–Q6

White has been checkmated

[1] White threatened to win a piece with 8 BxNch.
[2] It is hard to resist winning a Rook or two.
[3] The reason for the two Rook offer—Black has his opponent in a mating net.
[4] If 13 K–B1, QxNch; 14 K–N1, B–KR6 followed by mate. Or if 13 O–O, B–KR6 forces mate.

Black to Play. *Black should retreat his Knight to K2. If he moves it to Q5 he will lose a piece.*

WHITE	BLACK	WHITE	BLACK
1 P–QB4	P–K4	6 PxN	....
2 N–QB3	N–QB3		SEE DIAGRAM
3 P–KN3	N–B3	6	N–Q5?[1]
4 B–N2	B–N5	7 P–K3	N–B4[2]
5 N–Q5	NxN	8 Q–N4[3]	....

White wins a piece

[1] Believe it or not, but this move was played in a game conducted by correspondence! Which shows that a great deal of time devoted to thinking does not necessarily produce good moves. The exposed position of Black's Bishop and Knight indicates that disaster will follow quickly.

[2] If 7 ... N–N4; 8 Q–R4 wins a piece by a Queen fork.

[3] Winning a piece by a Queen fork after all!

Black to Play. *Black must move his Bishop to avoid White's threat of winning a piece by 7 NxB. Does it matter to what square he moves it?*

WHITE	BLACK	WHITE	BLACK
1 P–QB4	P–K4		SEE DIAGRAM
2 N–QB3	N–KB3	6	B–QB4?[3]
3 N–B3	N–B3	7 P–Q4!	B–N3
4 P–K3	B–N5[1]	8 NxNch	QxN
5 N–Q5	P–Q3?[2]	9 P–Q5	....
6 Q–R4	....		

White wins the Knight

[1] 4 . . . P–Q4 is simple and good. The move made also has merit, but it has to be followed up with care.

[2] 5 . . . P–K5! is the move, avoiding the embarrassing attack which now follows.

[3] Loses a piece. No better is 6 . . . NxN; 7 PxN, and the pinned Knight falls; or if 6 . . . P–QR4; 7 NxB and both of the Bishop's protectors are pinned and helpless. Best is 6 . . . B–R4! which saves the piece.

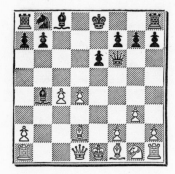

Black to Play. *Black can capture White's Queen Pawn, and after 11 BxB win the exchange by checking. Can he afford this loss of time in order to win material?*

WHITE	BLACK	WHITE	BLACK
1 P–QB4	N–KB3		SEE DIAGRAM
2 N–QB3	P–K3	10	QxP?
3 P–K4	P–B4	11 BxB	Q–K5ch
4 P–KN3[1]	P–Q4	12 B–K2	QxR
5 P–K5	P–Q5	13 Q–Q6	N–B3[2]
6 PxN	PxN	14 B–KB3!	QxNch
7 NPxP	QxP	15 K–K2	N–Q5ch[3]
8 P–Q4	PxP	16 QxN[4]	QxRP
9 PxP	B–N5ch	17 Q–Q6	....
10 B–Q2	....		

White forces checkmate

[1] 4 P–K5 does not have much sting: Black plays 4 . . . N–N1 followed by . . . P–Q3, . . . N–QB3 etc.

[2] If 13 . . . QxNch; 14 K–Q2 and White mates, or wins the Queen.

[3] If 15 . . . QxR; 16 BxNch, PxB; 17 Q–K7 mate.

[4] Now White's Rook is guarded.

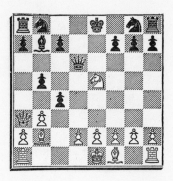

Black to Play. *Black can now win a piece by a subtle move, basing his plan on the fact that White's Queen Bishop has the double duty of guarding the Queen and the Knight.*

WHITE	BLACK	WHITE	BLACK
1 N–KB3	P–Q4	6 QxB[2]	B–N2
2 P–B4	PxP	7 P–QN3?[3]	Q–Q3
3 N–R3	P–K4	8 B–N2?[4]	....
4 NxKP	BxN		SEE DIAGRAM
5 Q–R4ch[1]	P–N4	8	P–B6![5]

Black wins a piece

[1] Not 5 PxB, Q–Q5 attacking Rook and Knight simultaneously.
[2] White must avoid this trap; 6 QxPch, P–B3; 7 NxP (B6), NxN; 8 QxNch, B–Q2; 9 Q–K4ch, B–K2, and Black has won a piece.
[3] Better is 7 P–K3, Q–Q3; 8 QxQ, PxQ; 9 N–B3, N–QB3; 10 P–QN3, P–Q4; 11 PxP, QPxP; 12 P–QR4, and White has an excellent game.
[4] Instead of this, White should exchange Queens.
[5] If 9 BxP, QxQ, or if 9 PxP, QxN, and finally if 9 QxQ, PxQ and two of White's pieces are attacked.